The Princeton Review

Cracking the

PSAT*

NMSQT

2010 Edition

Jeff Rubenstein and Adam Robinson

PrincetonReview.com

Random House, Inc. New York

The Princeton Review, Inc.
2315 Broadway
New York, NY 10024
E-mail: editorialsupport@review.com

*PSAT/NMSQT is a registered trademark of the College Board.

ISBN 978-0-375-42928-6
ISSN 1549-6120

Editor: Heather Brady
Production Editor: Meave Shelton
Production Coordinator: Kim Howie

Printed in the United States of America.

10 9 8 7 6 5 4 3 2 1

2010 Edition

John Katzman, Chairman, Founder
Michael J. Perik, President, CEO
Stephen Richards, COO, CFO
Rob Franek, VP Test Prep Books, Publisher

Editorial
Seamus Mullarkey, Editorial Director
Laura Braswell, Senior Editor
Rebecca Lessem, Senior Editor
Selena Coppock, Editor
Heather Brady, Editor

Production Services
Scott Harris, Executive Director, Production Services
Kim Howie, Senior Graphic Designer

Production Editorial
Meave Shelton, Production Editor
Emma Parker, Production Editor

Research & Development
Ed Carroll, Agent for National Content Directors
Liz Rutzel, Project Editor

Random House Publishing Team
Tom Russell, Publisher
Nicole Benhabib, Publishing Manager
Ellen L. Reed, Production Manager
Alison Stoltzfus, Associate Managing Editor
Elham Shabahat, Publishing Assistant

Acknowledgments

Thanks to Lauren Akamine for her thorough review. Thanks also to Heather Brady, Meave Shelton, and Kim Howie and the staff and students of The Princeton Review.

Special thanks to Adam Robinson, who conceived of and perfected the Joe Bloggs approach to standardized tests, and many other techniques in this book.

PRACTICE TEST 2 ANSWERS

Section 1	Section 2	Section 3	Section 4	Section 5	
1. B	1. A	25. B	21. E	1. D	31. A
2. E	2. B	26. E	22. E	2. C	32. E
3. B	3. E	27. A	23. E	3. B	33. C
4. D	4. C	28. B	24. A	4. A	34. A
5. E	5. B	29. C	25. C	5. B	35. C
6. E	6. E	30. A	26. A	6. D	36. D
7. C	7. D	31. C	27. B	7. E	37. D
8. B	8. E	32. E	28. B	8. C	38. D
9. E	9. B	33. E	29. 139	9. C	39. B
10. B	10. A	34. C	30. 1 or 2	10. E	
11. A	11. D	35. E	31. $\frac{4}{3}$ or 1.33	11. D	
12. B	12. B	36. C	32. 90	12. C	
13. B	13. B	37. E	33. 6563	13. A	
14. D	14. C	38. A	34. 105	14. D	
15. C	15. D	39. B	35. 9	15. B	
16. C	16. B	40. A	36. 8	16. C	
17. A	17. C	41. B	37. $\frac{16}{5}$ or 3.2	17. C	
18. C	18. D	42. E		18. C	
19. B	19. D	43. A	38. $\frac{2}{9}$ or .222	19. B	
20. A	20. C	44. C		20. E	
21. D		45. D		21. E	
22. E		46. C		22. A	
23. B		47. A		23. D	
24. A		48. B		24. D	
				25. B	
				26. B	
				27. B	
				28. E	
				29. A	
				30. B	

You will find a detailed explanation for each question beginning on page 358.

NO TEST MATERIAL ON THIS PAGE.

Contents

...So Much More Online!

More Practice...

- Free SAT online demonstration with a full-length practice SAT and interactive lessons
  - Daily vocabulary "Word du Jour" with definition and sample sentences

More Good Stuff...

- Chat with other students in our discussion forum
- Tips for a strong essay
- PSAT at-a-glance outline
- Articles on SAT techniques to get you ready for the next step
- E-mail tips for the SAT

...then College!

- Detailed profiles for hundreds of colleges help you find the school that is right for you
- Dozens of Top 10 ranking lists including Quality of Professors, Worst Campus Food, Most Beautiful Campus, Party Schools, Diverse Student Population, and tons more
- Useful information about the admissions process
- Helpful information about financial aid and scholarships
- Cool videos give you a student's-eye-view of many colleges
- Counselor-O-Matic combines your academic and extracurricular history with your school preferences to find the perfect college for you

princetonreview.com/cracking

Look For These Icons Throughout The Book

 Go Online   More Great Books

Part I
Orientation

Chapter 1
What Is
the PSAT/NMSQT?

The PSAT/NMSQT—from now on, we'll just call it the PSAT—is a standardized test given primarily to high school juniors to give them a "preliminary" idea of how well they'll score on the SAT. The test is also used to determine which students are eligible for National Merit recognition (as well as scholarships). This chapter will give you a general overview of the test and how it is used, along with the basics to start your preparation.

How Do You Pronounce PSAT/NMSQT, Anyway?

Ah, yes—first thing's first. Well, to be honest, we're not really sure. You can pronounce it *pee-sat-nim-squit* if you want. But we think it's easier just to call it the PSAT.

When Is the PSAT Given?

Keep on Schedule
You'll take the PSAT in the fall of your junior year. Plan to take the SAT in either the spring of your junior year or the fall of your senior year.

The PSAT is officially administered twice each year, on one Saturday and one Wednesday in October. Your school will announce the exact dates at the beginning of the school year, or you can find out on the Web: The Princeton Review at **PrincetonReview.com**, or the College Board at **www.collegeboard.com**.

How Do I Sign Up for the PSAT?

You don't have to do anything to sign up for the PSAT; your school will do all the work for you. Test registration fees can vary from school to school, so be sure to check with your guidance counselor if you have questions about how much the PSAT will cost you.

What About Students with Special Needs?

If you have a diagnosed learning difference, you will probably qualify for special accommodations on the PSAT. However, it's important that you get the process started early. The first step is to speak to your school counselor who handles learning differences. Only he or she can file the appropriate paperwork. You'll also need to gather some information (documentation of your condition) from a licensed practitioner and some other information from your school. Then your school counselor will file the application for you.

Happily, you need to apply for accommodations only once; with that single application you'll qualify for accommodations on the PSAT, SAT, SAT Subject Tests, and AP tests. The one exception to this rule is that if you change schools, you'll need to have a counselor at the new school refile your paperwork.

Does the PSAT Play a Role in College Admissions?

No. The PSAT plays no role in college admissions. It's really just a practice test for the SAT.

The one exception is for that very small group of students, about 4 percent of all students nationwide, whose PSAT scores qualify them for National Merit recognition. (We'll tell you more than you ever wanted to know about that in the next section.) Recognition as a commended scholar, semifinalist, or finalist for National Merit is a fairly impressive addition to your college admissions portfolio, and is something that you should certainly pursue if you're seriously in contention for it.

What Happens to the Score Report from the PSAT?

Only you, your high school, and the National Merit Scholarship Corporation (who cosponsor the PSAT) will receive copies of your score reports. They won't be sent to colleges.

And What Will Be on It?

The Math sections of the PSAT test only basic arithmetic, algebra, and geometry. The Critical Reading sections test your vocabulary and your ability to answer questions about a passage you've just read. The Writing Skills section, oddly enough, has nothing to do with writing. It tests your ability to recognize a narrow range of errors in English grammar and several points of style. In this book, we'll review the math, vocabulary, and grammar you'll need…and there really isn't much!

So if the PSAT is a test of basic math, vocab, and a few grammar rules, why isn't it just like tests in school? Glad you asked! It's because the test-makers know how Mr. Jones tests you in Math, so when they want to trick you, they do the opposite. If you approach the tricky questions the "school way" you'll take much longer than you should or get totally stuck, but if you know the shortcuts you can be done in seconds, sometimes, or at least know that you're getting the question right. Think about it. When you want to do well on Mr. Jones's math test what do you do? You practice math the way you know he'll test it later. So when it's the PSAT folks giving you the test, practice the way you know they'll test it. The good news is that the test writers don't like to work too hard. They're still using most of the same old tricks they've used since the test was first given, and we've helped generations of students overcome them. In this book, we're going to show you how to avoid the traps and maximize your score.

Who Writes the PSAT, Anyway?

The PSAT is written and administered by Educational Testing Service (ETS), under contract by the College Board. You might think that the people at ETS are educators, or professors of education, or teachers. They're not. The people who work for ETS are average folks who just happen to make a living writing tests. In fact, they write hundreds of tests, for all kinds of organizations. They're a group of "testers-for-hire" who will write a test for anyone who asks.

The folks at ETS aren't really paid to educate; they're paid to write and administer tests. And even though you'll be paying them to take the PSAT, you're not their customer. The people really being served by ETS are the colleges, who get the information they want at no cost. This means that you should take everything that ETS says with a grain of salt and realize that its testing "advice" isn't always the best advice. (Getting testing advice from ETS is a bit like getting first-date advice from your parents.)

Every test reflects the interests of the people who write it. If you know who writes the test, you will know a lot more about what kinds of answers will be considered "correct" answers on that test.

SO THEN WHAT IS THE PRINCETON REVIEW?

Shortcuts
The Princeton Review's techniques are the closest thing there is to a shortcut to the PSAT. However, there is no shortcut to learning these techniques.

The Princeton Review is the nation's leading test-preparation company. In just a few years, we became the nation's leader in SAT preparation, primarily because our techniques work. We offer courses and private tutoring for all of the major standardized tests, and we publish a series of books to help in your search for the right school. If you'd like more information about our programs or books, give us a call at 800-2-Review, or find us on the Web at **PrincetonReview.com**.

HOW TO USE THIS BOOK

This book is divided into two main parts. The first part of the book (Chapters 1–11 and the subsequent Drill Answers) contains both general testing strategies and question-specific problem-solving instruction. The back of the book contains two practice PSATs. The study guide that follows will give you a plan of attack for these things and the rest of the book. There is no single plan that will fit everyone, so be prepared to adapt the plan that appears below to your own needs.

The first practice test will give you an idea of your strengths and weaknesses, both of which can be a source of improvement. If you're already good at something, additional practice can make you great at it; if you're not so good at something, what you should do about it depends on how important it is. If the subject is one that comes up on the test often, you'll want to spend a lot of time on it; if it only comes up once in a while, you'll want to spend very little time working on it and remember that it's something you should put off until you've done easier things or skip entirely.

How do you know what's important? We'll tell you throughout the book when techniques like Plugging In come up, but you can also get an idea from the layout of the book and the structure diagrams on page 34. If you're not so great at Critical Reading or Sentence Completions, you're going to need to work on these things because they represent a lot of questions. If you're not so hot at functions, you can tell that these aren't as important as Plugging In or Math Basics, because they appear in the Advanced section.

A Note about Vocabulary

Vocabulary is an important part of most standardized tests and success in life itself, though in most other ways standardized tests are nothing like real life. This book will give you a lot of techniques and shortcuts that you can use on the PSAT and later when you take the SAT, but while there are useful tools for learning vocab, there are no shortcuts that will magically implant words into your brain, not yet anyway. Important vocab for the PSAT (The Hit Parade in this book) is pretty much the same as it is for the SAT, so if you keep studying it from now until the SAT (and beyond) the task will be far less painful and you'll probably be very pleasantly surprised by how much your reading score improves.

Time Management

To manage your PSAT preparation, make use of the study guide on the following pages. This guide will break down the daunting task of PSAT prep into bite-sized pieces we call sessions. We have mapped out tasks for each session to be sure you get the most out of this book. Sessions will generally take between an hour or two, unless you're taking a practice test. The tests will be the first and last sessions, so you should be sure to plan to have about two and a half hours for these sessions. Most other sessions will last between an hour and two hours, so plan to take a short break in the middle, and if it looks like the session is going to exceed two hours feel free to stop and pick up where you left off on the next day.

When You Take a Practice Test

You'll see when to take practice tests in the session outlines below. Here are some guidelines for taking these tests.

- Time yourself strictly. Use a timer, watch, or stopwatch that will ring, and do not allow yourself to go over time for any section. If you try to do so at the real test, your scores will probably be canceled.
- Take a practice test in one sitting, allowing yourself breaks of no more than two minutes between sections. You need to build up your endurance for the real test, and you also need an accurate picture of how you will do.

- Always take a practice test using an answer sheet with bubbles to fill in, just as you will for the real test. For the practice tests in the book, use the attached answer sheets. You need to be comfortable transferring answers to the separate sheet because you will be skipping around a bit.
- Each bubble you choose should be filled in thoroughly, and no other marks should be made in the answer area.
- As you fill in the bubble for a question, check to be sure you are on the correct number on the answer sheet. If you fill in the wrong bubble on the answer sheet, it won't matter if you've worked out the problem correctly in the test booklet. All that matters to the machine scoring the test is the No. 2 pencil mark.

Managing the Math Sections

After you've taken the practice test, you'll have three scores: math, reading, and writing. There's a lot of math in this book, so you'll need to use your math score to figure out which exact subjects you need the most help in and where your study time will be best spent. The guide that appears below is geared toward someone whose math score is in the middle range, from about the mid 50s to the low 60s, so if your score is lower or higher than this, you'll need to make some adjustments.

If your score is lower than the range mentioned above, your plan should be to spend the three math sessions working only on Chapters 7 and 8 and doing little or nothing in Chapter 9, unless you've got extra time and have thoroughly mastered the two prior chapters, including additional online practice and drills.

If your score is higher than average, you should plan to spend very little time working through Chapter 7, unless you've missed some easy questions on the math sections and don't know why. You'll want to spend most of your time working on Chapters 8 and 9, so skim Chapter 7 for anything that looks unfamiliar and work through those portions then move on to Chapter 8 and work on the math techniques. Working on additional drills on the topics covered in Chapters 8 and 9 will fill out the three sessions devoted to math.

Session-by-Session Study Guide

Session Zero You're involved in this session right now. Finish reading the first two chapters so you'll know what the test is about, why it is important for you to take, and what to expect from the rest of the book. This step probably won't take you long, so if you've got a couple of hours to devote to a session and you've finished these chapters, you can go on to Session One and take the first practice test.

Session One Take Practice Test 1 (in the back of this book) and score it. You'll use this result to get an idea of how many questions you should attempt on each section and the parts of the math sections you should concentrate on.

Session Two Work through Chapters 3 and 4 of the general introduction. Work through Chapter 5, the Sentence Completions, and Week 1 of the Hit Parade. You may want to make flashcards for the Hit Parade vocabulary words.

Session Three Work through the Math Basics in Chapter 7 and the corresponding drills.

Session Four Work through the Writing Skills in Chapter 10 and associated drills. Study Week 2 of the Hit Parade.

Session Five Work through the Critical Reading section in Chapter 6 and associated drills. Study Week 3 of the Hit Parade.

Session Six Work through Math Techniques, Chapter 8. Techniques like Plugging In are central to doing well on the math sections, so it's not like you can practice them too much. If you've already finished Chapter 8 in Session 3, start Chapter 9 if there's time. Study Week 4 of the Hit Parade.

Session Seven Work through the Advanced Math Principles in Chapter 9. Study Week 5 of the Hit Parade.

Session Eight Take Practice Test 2. Use the techniques you've been practicing throughout the book. Score your test and go through the explanations, focusing on where you may have missed the opportunity to use a technique and your decisions about whether you should have attempted a question or not, given your pacing goals and Personal Order of Difficulty.

Some of the terminology in the study guide may be unfamiliar to you now, but don't worry, you'll get to know it soon. Also, you'll want to refer back to this study guide at each session to keep yourself on track.

One important note: In this book, any sample question you see will have a question number that indicates where it would appear on the PSAT. That's why you may see a question 4 followed by a question 14—the question number indicates the PSAT question level instead of its order in the chapter. The discussion on pages 32–35 provides more information about question numbers and order of difficulty.

HOW IS THE PSAT STRUCTURED AND SCORED?

The PSAT has five sections, which are always given in the same order.

Section	Number of Questions	Time
Critical Reading	24	25 minutes
Math	20	25 minutes
Critical Reading	24	25 minutes
Math	18	25 minutes
Writing Skills	39	30 minutes

You'll receive three scores for the PSAT: a Critical Reading score, a Math score, and a Writing Skills score. Each of these scores will be reported on a scale of 20 to 80, where 20 is the lowest score and 80 is the highest score. Your scores will be mailed to your high school principal. He or she will distribute them to you about six to eight weeks after you take the test. If you are homeschooled, your score report will be mailed directly to your house.

HOW DOES THE SAT DIFFER FROM THE PSAT?

The SAT differs significantly from the PSAT in structure, though the questions on the two tests are similar. The SAT has 10 sections for a total of 3 hours and 45 minutes of testing. One of those sections doesn't count toward your score; it's called the Experimental section and its only purpose is to try out questions to see whether they can be used in later tests. The PSAT has no Experimental section.

Here's a breakdown of how the tests differ:

	SAT	PSAT
Structure	10 sections	5 sections
Length	3 hours 45 minutes	2 hours 10 minutes
Purpose	College admissions	NMSQT (see Chapter 2)
Scoring	2400	Selection index out of 240

Here's how an SAT might look, compared to the PSAT. (Remember, though, that the sections on the SAT can appear in a different order.)

SAT		
Section	Number of Questions	Time
Writing	1 essay	25 minutes
Critical Reading	24 multiple-choice	25 minutes
Math	20 multiple-choice	25 minutes
Writing	35 multiple-choice	25 minutes
Critical Reading	24 multiple-choice	25 minutes
Math	18 multiple-choice	25 minutes
Experimental	?? multiple-choice	25 minutes
Math	16 multiple-choice	20 minutes
Critical Reading	19 multiple-choice	20 minutes
Writing	14 multiple-choice	10 minutes

You'll notice that the PSAT is much shorter than the SAT and the SAT includes an essay. However, the multiple-choice question types are the same.

What Does the PSAT Score Mean for My SAT Score?

Very little. Like the SAT, the PSAT gives you a Math score, a Writing score, and a Critical Reading score, using a 20-to-80 scale that is easy to convert to the SAT's familiar 200-to-800 scale. It seems as if you should be able to just add a zero to the end of each score to find out what your future SAT scores will be: a 65 on the PSAT Math section, say, would be a 650 on the SAT Math. Pretty easy, right?

Maybe a little too easy. Think about it like this: World-class sprinters can complete a 100-yard dash in under ten seconds. Going at the same speed, an athlete should be able to run a mile in under three minutes. But has anyone ever run a mile that quickly? Not even close! No one can run at top speed for such a long distance because fatigue sets in. Now consider that the PSAT has five sections and lasts for just over two hours, while the SAT has ten sections and flirts with the four-hour mark. Isn't fatigue likely to be a factor there as well? Many students are disappointed to find that their SAT scores don't match up with their PSAT scores because it's so much harder to stay sharp for four hours than it is to stay sharp for two. Throw in the fact that the SAT has an essay and some slightly more advanced math, while the PSAT doesn't, and you can see that the two tests are actually quite different for the test taker.

How Much Should I Prepare for the PSAT?

Study

If you were getting ready to take a biology test, you'd study biology. If you were preparing for a basketball game, you'd practice basketball. So, if you're preparing for the PSAT (and eventually the SAT), study the PSAT. ETS can't test everything (in fact, they test very little), so concentrate on learning what they *do* test.

If you're in that very small group of students who are in contention for National Merit recognition, it may be worth your while to put in a good deal of time preparing for this test. After all, if you can raise your scores from 71 or 72 to 74 or 76 on one or more of the sections on the PSAT, this may well put you in a better position for National Merit. Otherwise, you should prepare enough so that you feel more in control of the test and have a better testing experience. (Nothing feels quite as awful as being dragged through a testing experience feeling like you don't know what you're being tested on or what to expect—except perhaps dental surgery.) The other reason to prepare for the PSAT is that it will give you some testing skills that will help you begin to prepare for the tests that actually count, namely the SAT and SAT Subject Tests.

The bottom line is: The best reason to prepare for the PSAT is that it will help you get an early start on your preparation for the SAT.

Chapter 2
All About National Merit Scholarships

The NMSQT part of the name PSAT/NMSQT stands for National Merit Scholarship Qualifying Test. That means that the PSAT serves as the test that will establish whether or not you are eligible for National Merit recognition. This chapter will help you figure out what that may mean for you.

How Do I Qualify for National Merit?

To qualify for any National Merit recognition, you must:

- be a U.S. citizen or permanent resident who intends to become a U.S. citizen
- be enrolled full-time in high school
- take the PSAT in the third year of high school (for four-year programs). Slightly different rules apply if you're in a three-year program or other course of study.
- be fully endorsed and recommended for a Merit scholarship by your high school principal
- have a record of strong academic performance throughout high school
- complete the National Merit Scholarship Corporation (NMSC) Scholarship Application
- obtain high scores on the SAT, which you'll take later in the year

The Index

How does your PSAT score qualify you for National Merit? The people at National Merit use a selection index, which is the sum of your Math, Critical Reading, and Writing Skills scores. For instance, if your PSAT scores were 60 Math, 50 Critical Reading, and 60 Writing Skills, your index would be 170.

Math + Critical Reading + Writing Skills = National Merit Index

$$60 \quad + \quad 50 \quad + \quad 60 \quad = \quad 170$$

The Awards and the Process

In the fall of their senior year, about 50,000 students will receive one of two letters from NMSC: either a Letter of Commendation or a letter stating that they have qualified as semifinalists for National Merit.

Commended Students   Roughly two-thirds of these students (about 34,000 total students each year) will receive a Letter of Commendation by virtue of their high scores on the test. This looks great on your college application, so if you have a reasonable chance of getting one, it's definitely worth your time to prepare for the PSAT. Make no mistake, though, these letters are not easy to get. They are awarded to students who score between the 95th and the mid-99th percentiles—that means to the top 4–5 percent in the country.

If you receive this honorable mention from NMSC, you should be extremely proud of yourself. Even though you won't continue in the process for National Merit scholarships, this commendation does make you eligible for special scholarships sponsored by certain companies and organizations, which vary in their amounts and eligibility requirements.

Semifinalists   The other third of these students—those 16,000 students who score in the upper 99th percentile in their states—will be notified that they are National Merit semifinalists. If you qualify, you'll get a letter announcing your status as a semifinalist, along with information about the requirements for qualification as a finalist. These include maintaining high grades, performing well on your SAT, and getting an endorsement from your principal.

Becoming a National Merit semifinalist is quite impressive, and if you manage it, you should certainly mention it on your college applications.

What does "scoring in the upper 99th percentile in the state" mean? It means that you're essentially competing against the other people in your state for those semifinalist positions. Since some states have higher average scores than others, this means that if you're in states like New York, New Jersey, Maryland, Connecticut, or Massachusetts, you need a higher score to qualify than if you live in other states. However, the majority of the indices are in the range of 200–215. (This means approximate scores of 70 Critical Reading, 70 Math, 70 Writing Skills.)

Many students want to know exactly what score they need. Sadly, National Merit is notoriously tight-lipped about these numbers. They release them only on rare occasions and generally don't like to announce them. However, it's not hard to get some pretty reliable unofficial data on what it takes to be a semifinalist. Below you'll find the most up-to-date qualifying scores for the class of 2008 National Merit semifinalists:

Alabama	209	Missouri	211
Alaska	213	Montana	207
Arizona	211	Nebraska	207
Arkansas	201	Nevada	208
California	218	New Hampshire	215
Colorado	213	New Jersey	221
Connecticut	217	New Mexico	208
D.C.	223	New York	219
Delaware	219	North Carolina	214
Florida	212	North Dakota	202
Georgia	214	Ohio	211
Hawaii	213	Oklahoma	207
Idaho	204	Oregon	213
Illinois	213	Pennsylvania	214
Indiana	213	Rhode Island	212
Iowa	209	South Carolina	210
Kansas	212	South Dakota	203
Kentucky	208	Tennessee	213
Louisiana	206	Texas	215
Maine	211	Utah	202
Maryland	221	Vermont	216
Massachusetts	223	Virginia	217
Michigan	209	Washington	215
Minnesota	213	West Virginia	200
Mississippi	202	Wisconsin	208
		Wyoming	200

Note, however, that while these numbers are probably roughly the same from year to year, they do change somewhat. These should be used only to give you a rough idea of the range of scores for National Merit recognition.

Finalists   The majority of semifinalists (more than 90 percent) go on to qualify as finalists. Students who meet all of the eligibility requirements will be notified in February of their senior year that they have qualified as finalists. This means that they are now eligible for scholarship money, though it doesn't necessarily mean that they'll get any. In fact, only about half of National Merit finalists actually win scholarships. What determines whether a student gets money or not? There is a final screening process, based on criteria that NMSC doesn't release to the public, to determine who actually gets these scholarships. There are about 8,000 total scholarships awarded, which fall into three groups: National Merit $2,500 scholarships, scholarships sponsored by businesses, and scholarships sponsored by colleges. These scholarships are based on various criteria, and the awards are of varying amounts.

Though the amounts of money are never huge, every little bit helps, and the award itself looks great in your portfolio. So if you think you are in contention for National Merit recognition, study hard. If not, don't sweat it too much, but prepare for the PSAT anyway because it is good practice for the SAT.

But I'm Not a Junior in High School Yet...

If you are not yet a junior, and you're interested in National Merit, you will have to take the test again your junior year in order to qualify.

A certain number of schools give the PSAT to students in their sophomore year—and sometimes even earlier. These schools hope that earlier exposure to these tests will help their students perform better in later years. If you're not yet in your junior year, the PSAT won't count for National Merit scholarship purposes, so it's really just a trial run for you. It's still a good idea to go into the test prepared in order to feel and test your best. After all, there's nothing more unpleasant than an unpleasant testing experience, except maybe having a tooth drilled or watching the sad downward spiral of certain pop stars.

What If I'm in a Three-Year or Other Nonstandard Course of Study?

If you're going to spend only three years in secondary school, you have two options for when to take the PSAT for National Merit purposes: You can take it either in your next-to-last year or in your last year of secondary school. However, our advice is this: If you're in any program other than a usual four-year high school, be sure to talk to your guidance counselor. He or she will consult with NMSC and help ensure that you take the PSAT at the right time. This is important, because not taking the PSAT at the right time can disqualify you for National Merit recognition.

What If I Miss the PSAT Administration My Junior Year?

If you aren't concerned about National Merit scholarships, there's no reason to do anything in particular—except, perhaps, to obtain a few PSAT booklets to practice on, just to see what fun you missed.

However, if you want to be eligible for National Merit recognition, then swift action on your part is required. If an emergency arises that prevents you from taking the PSAT, you should write to the National Merit Scholarship Corporation *immediately* to request alternate testing dates. If your request is received soon enough, they should be able to accommodate you. (NMSC says that this kind of request must absolutely be received by March 1 following the missed PSAT administration.) You'll also need a signature from a school official.

For More Information

If you have any questions or problems, the best person to consult is your school guidance counselor, who can help make sure you're on the right track. If you need further help, contact your local Princeton Review office at 800-2-REVIEW or **PrincetonReview.com**. Or, you can contact National Merit directly:

National Merit Scholarship Corporation
1560 Sherman Avenue, Suite 200
Evanston, IL 60201–4897
(847) 866–5100
www.nationalmerit.org

Chapter 3
General Strategies

In this chapter, we'll discuss some strategies that apply to the PSAT as a whole. Keep these in mind throughout the entire test, and you'll improve your score.

PROCESS OF ELIMINATION

You don't have to know how to solve a problem in order to get the correct answer (or to at least be able to make a good guess). If you can cross off four, or three, or even just two *wrong* answers, you'll be a whole lot closer to finding the *right* one. This technique, called Process of Elimination (which we'll call POE from now on), will be your new best friend. Aggressively using POE will get you points on the PSAT.

1. What is the capital of Malawi?

If you were to see this problem on the PSAT (don't worry, you won't), you'd probably be stuck—not to mention a little upset. But problems on the PSAT usually have answer choices, like the following:

1. What is the capital of Malawi?
    (A) Washington
    (B) Paris
    (C) Tokyo
    (D) London
    (E) Lilongwe

Not so bad anymore, is it? By knowing which choices must be wrong, you can often figure out what the answer is—even without knowing *why* it's the correct answer.

Since four of the five choices on any given question are wrong, it's much easier to identify at least some of these and get rid of them. Sometimes, you can even get all the way to the right answer just by using POE, so use POE whenever you can.

—————————————○—————————————

5. Although the piranha, a species of carnivorous fish, is
                          A
    native to the waters of the Amazon, they can be seen in
        B   C
    aquariums throughout the world. No error
        D   E

Here's How to Crack It

Here's a sample Writing Skills question. Often the correct answer on a Writing Skills question will jump out at you as you read the question; in some cases, however, it won't. This means we should use POE. Let's look at each part in turn. "A species of" is okay, so (A) can't be the answer. "Native to" is the correct idiom, so (B) can also be crossed off. We might have a question about (C): Should the word here be "they" or "it"? If we're unsure, we can leave (C) alone for the moment.

How about (D)? "Throughout the world" is okay, so (D) can be eliminated. So now we're down to either (C) or (E). (The answer is (C) because "the piranha" is singular and "they" is plural.)

What's most important is the technique you used, not whether you got the right answer above. You had a one-in-two shot on this problem. Those are fantastic odds, and you should take a guess. In cases where you're not sure of the answer (and this may happen often), immediately think POE. Better guesses mean more points on the PSAT!

Try to answer this question using POE before reading the explanation below.

Be Test-Smart
Many students with good grades get below-average scores because they refuse to guess.

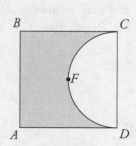

18. If *ABCD* is a square with sides 8, and arc *CFD* is a semicircle, what is the area of the shaded region?

(A) $16 - 8\pi$
(B) $16 - 16\pi$
(C) $64 - 8\pi$
(D) $64 - 16\pi$
(E) 64

Here's How to Crack It

Even before we try to solve this problem, let's use POE. We know that the value of π is a little more than 3. If we replace π with 3 in the answers above, what do you notice? Choices (A) and (B) are negative numbers. They can't be right. If we get no further on this problem, we can guess from among (C), (D), and (E), which is a guess that we should take. But what else do we know about the figure? They've told us that the length of the side is 8, so the area is 64, which rules out choice (E), because the shaded area is obviously smaller than the whole square. Already we're down to two, but we seem to be on a roll, so why stop now? Look at the shaded area. Is it more than or less than half? Sure, it's more than half, which is 32. Applying the same trick as we did with choices (A) and (B), we get that choice (C) is about 64 minus 24, or 40, so that works, and choice (D) is around 64 minus 48, which is 12, so that's out, leaving only (C).

Okay, we won't be able to get all the way to the right answer using just POE all of the time. But the question above was a hard question, so if we'd run out of other questions that we knew we could get right and this was what we had left, it would certainly be worth taking a run at with POE on our side.

We know this isn't how you're taught to solve problems and take tests in school. In fact, your geometry teacher would probably have a fit if you were to do most of your work in class like this. That's because in school, what matters is *how* you get a problem right. But this isn't school. It's the PSAT. The only thing that matters on the PSAT is whether you have the correct bubble filled in. How you get that answer right is completely up to you. So don't treat the PSAT like a test in school. Do whatever you need to do (legally!) to get the right answer, and use strategies suited to getting the best score on this test.

POE is a technique that can be used on every multiple-choice problem on the PSAT. By getting rid of answers that you know are wrong, you can improve your chances of guessing correctly and may be able to find the right answer to a question you don't know how to solve. Remember, it doesn't matter how you get to the right answer, as long as you get there.

POE AND GUESSING

So we've talked about POE, but what then? Should you guess if you've gotten rid of one answer? Two? Three? It depends. Technically, if you can eliminate even one answer it is to your benefit to guess, but if you can only get rid of one choice on a particular question, is that really the question you should be working on right then? Maybe. But only if you've got nothing left to attempt that you could work all the way through and get right.

If you get stuck on a question that's harder than you expected and you can eliminate one or more answers, do so quickly and move on. Before you get caught up in a question, though, you should consider whether or not there's something easier to do first, something you can get the whole point for instead of getting bogged down and then rolling the dice.

In the next chapter we'll talk about pacing, which is the number of questions you should attempt to reach your goal score. For now, suffice it to say that it's probably not all of them. If you find that there are enough questions you can do to reach your pacing goal without guessing, then go ahead and do those and keep working on questions you can answer until the time's up. If you run out of questions you can do before you reach your magic number, then you'll need to use POE and guess on a few more questions than you were pacing for.

How the PSAT Is Scored

To generate your final score, ETS first computes your raw score. You get one raw score point for every correct answer and lose one-quarter of a raw score point for every wrong answer on your bubble sheet. Blanks are not counted at all. This raw score is then converted to a scaled score on the 20–80 scale. You can find sample score-conversion tables in the back of this book.

	Raw Points
Correct answer:	+1
Blank:	0
Incorrect answer:	$-\dfrac{1}{4}$

So should you guess? Well, let's look at the scoring system and see how it applies to guessing. The PSAT is a five-option multiple-choice test. If you guess completely randomly on five questions you should—by random chance—get one of these five correct and four of them wrong. Since you'll get one point for the one correct answer and lose one-quarter of a point for each of the four wrong answers, your net raw score will be zero. Thus, random guessing should not help or hurt you on the PSAT. It simply counts for nothing.

So don't waste your time on random guessing. However, if you are working on a problem that you need to answer to meet your pacing goals and you can eliminate even one answer with POE, you should guess! The more answer choices you can eliminate, the better your odds for guessing correctly will be, and the more points will be added to your score.

We've talked a little about POE already, but we'll be talking throughout the book about the kinds of wrong answers you should be on the lookout for in different parts of the test, so keep an eye out for them.

USING YOUR BOOK

Write Now
Feel free to write all over
this book. You need to get
in the habit of making the
PSAT booklet your own.

At school, you generally aren't allowed to write in your textbooks. (In some cases, they'll even charge you for the book if you do.) But on the PSAT, the booklet is yours—so use it. Even though you will use your calculator for figuring, you should be working extensively in your test booklet, e.g., setting up your calculations, drawing and redrawing figures, and most important, physically crossing off answers—that helps you avoid getting lost as you work through POE.

Don't worry about anyone looking at your booklet and seeing your messy handwriting. Though the proctor will probably collect the booklets at the end of the test for security purposes, nobody will ever look at your booklet after the test.

MAKING THE MATH WORK EASIER

Ballparking

Here's one of those POE tools we promised you. Ballparking means *estimating and eliminating,* that is, using the conditions in the question to get an idea of what the answer should be, then eliminating answers that are too big or too small. If you're stuck or running out of time, you'll need a way to get rid of answers quickly so you can guess and move on. Ballparking is a great tool for quickly rejecting answers on math questions.

Have a look at the following:

5. If 12 cans of food can feed 8 dogs for one week, how many cans of food would be needed to feed 6 dogs for 2 weeks?

    (A)   9
    (B)   12
    (C)   18
    (D)   24
    (E)   48

Here's How to Crack It

Before you start to calculate, estimate. If 12 cans will feed eight dogs for one week, and we want to know how many cans we'd need for *two* weeks, the answer is probably larger than 12. So eliminate (A) and (B). But we're only feeding *six* dogs for two weeks, so the answer must be less than 24. Eliminate (D) and (E). Now the only answer left is (C).

If you're wondering whether it's realistic to expect to be able to Ballpark down to one answer on the test, the answer is: It depends. It's fairly common on easier problems, but in those cases you can often just solve it. So let's try it where it will be useful, on a hard question:

16. If the circle with center 0 has a radius of 3, and $AB = BC$, what is the area of triangle ABC ?

    (A) 9
    (B) 18
    (C) 9π
    (D) 18π
    (E) 27π

Here's How to Crack It

Since we know that the radius of the circle is 3, we're just a small step away from figuring out the area. The formula for the area of a circle is $A = \pi r^2$, so the area of the circle is 9π, or about 27. We can estimate that the area of the triangle is less than half the area of the circle, so (A) is the only possibility.

Look Carefully at What the Questions Are Asking For

The test writers know that students are rushed when taking the PSAT. The writers use that to their advantage when designing questions. One of the biggest mistakes students make on the PSAT is working too quickly and making careless mistakes. A common careless mistake is answering the wrong question. You need to know what they're asking for before you can choose the correct answer. Let's look at an example:

---

4. If $6(3p - 2q) = 18$, what is the value of $3p - 2q$?

    (A)   2
    (B)   3
    (C)   4
    (D)   6
    (E)   18

Here's How to Crack It

You might be tempted to multiply out $6(3p - 2q)$ on this problem, which gives you $18p - 12q$. That seems like a logical first step, right? Unfortunately, if you do this, you'll be doing this problem the hard way. Why? Look carefully at what the problem is asking you to solve for. The question doesn't ask for the value of p or q alone; it asks for the value of $3p - 2q$. What's the easiest way to figure that out? Simply divide both sides of the equation by 6, and you get $(3p - 2q) = 3$.

The moral: Always look at what the question is asking for. In math class, you're almost always asked to solve for x or y, but on the PSAT you may be asked to solve for $3x - y$, or $3p - 2q$, or some other strange expression. In these cases, there's usually an easier way to solve the problem than the way you might solve it in math class.

Taking Bite-Sized Pieces

Another common way that the question writers make life difficult for you is throwing a lot of information at you at once to try to confuse you. When this happens, stay calm and take the information in Bite-Sized Pieces. By breaking up a wordy problem, you can transform a long, difficult problem into a few shorter, easier ones. Sound good? Let's look at one together.

12. Lauren and Abbey are performing science experiments in which they each start off with a collection of 6 fruit flies. If Lauren's species of fruit flies triples its population every four days and Abbey's species of fruit flies doubles its population every three days, how many fruit flies will they have if they combine their collections at the end of 12 days?

(A) 96
(B) 162
(C) 192
(D) 258
(E) 324

Here's How to Crack It

Sure, this problem looks like it's going to be a pain, but let's see how difficult it really is when we work through it just a little bit at a time.

Lauren's species of fruit flies triples its population every four days.
She starts with 6.
After 4 days, she has 18.
After 8 days, she has 54.
After 12 days, she has 162.
So Lauren ends up with 162 fruit flies.

Now let's do the same with Abbey.
Abbey's species of fruit flies doubles its population every three days.
After 3 days, she has 12.
After 6 days, she has 24.
After 9 days, she has 48.
After 12 days, she has 96.
Abbey ends up with 96 fruit flies.

Now all we have to do is add Lauren's fruit flies to Abbey's fruit flies. 162 + 96 = 258, so the correct answer is (D). Watch out for the partial answers; 96 and 162 both appear in the list!

Summary

- POE—Process of Elimination—is your best friend on most of the problems on the test. It will help you stay focused on eliminating wrong answers instead of just jumping to pick one, and it will help you guess aggressively to maximize your score.

- Even though you're going to use your calculator for math, it pays to use your test booklet for figuring, POE, and basically anything you need to keep track of.

- If you're stuck on a math question or running out of time, use ballparking to get rid of one or more answers quickly, so you can guess and move on.

- Read the questions carefully to make sure you answer the right question, and take bite-sized pieces to work through each problem step by step. Both will help you avoid choosing trap and partial answers.

Chapter 4
Advanced Strategies

In this chapter, we'll discuss an overall PSAT game plan: figuring out how many problems you should do, which problems you should do, and how to avoid the answers that ETS plants to trap the average student, whom we'll call Joe Bloggs.

WHO IS JOE BLOGGS?

Joe Bloggs is the average test taker. He thinks what works in school will work just as well on the PSAT, so he goes for the obvious answers and uses a typical high-school approach regardless of whether a question is easy or difficult or somewhere in between. The problem with this approach is that ETS knows how things are taught and tested in school, so they can choose to trick him wherever they like, and they write the hard questions to do just that. If you've ever taken a standardized test you've probably noticed that some questions are harder than others. (In fact, most sections start out easy and get harder as you go along, as we'll see on the next page.)

When Joe is faced with an easy question he does fine. That's part of what it means to be easy. When he's faced with a medium question he does all right about half of the time and gets into trouble the other half of the time. When he's confronted with a hard question, he does the same things he would do if he were working on an easy question—but here there are tricks and traps all over the place; consequently, he gets nearly every hard question wrong.

So how can Joe help you do better on the test? If you were walking on a path in the woods behind a friend and your friend tripped on a root, would you trip over it too? Probably not, unless you were filming the latest version of *Dumberer and Dumberer*. Watch for the things that trip Joe up and avoid tripping over them yourself.

PACING

Most students think that you need to do every problem on the PSAT to get a good score. And most students *hurt* their score because they try to do *too many* problems.

Here's what Joe Bloggs does: Joe thinks that he has to finish every problem on the PSAT. In an attempt to do just this, he works as quickly as he can. This means that he rushes through the easy problems—the ones that he should get right—and makes some careless errors, which cost him valuable points. Then he gets to the medium problems. These take more time, are more convoluted, and have a few trap choices in them. Joe gets about half of these right. Then Joe gets to the hard questions. These are designed so Joe will get almost all of them wrong, yet Joe insists on spending lots of time on these problems—for no points at all. What kind of score does Joe get? He gets the average score of about 51.

As you can see, this probably isn't the best strategy. There are two reasons it doesn't make sense to try every problem on the test. First, it's very hard to finish every question while maintaining a high level of accuracy. During timed tests, people naturally rush—and then they make careless errors and lose points. Almost everyone is better off *slowing down*, using the time allotted to work on *fewer* problems, and answering more of those problems correctly. You'll get a higher score if you do only 75 percent of the problems on this test and answer them correctly than if you do all of the problems and answer about half correctly.

Second, not every question is of the same level of difficulty. In fact, most of the problems on this test are arranged in increasing order of difficulty: The earlier questions are easier, and they get gradually harder until the final questions, which are so difficult that only a small percentage of test takers answer them correctly. Hard questions are worth no more than easy questions, so why waste time working on them? Most testers are much better off skipping many of the hard questions and applying all their time to the easy and medium-level questions.

How Many Questions Should I Do?

Only do the number of problems you need for your target score. You're *much* better off doing fewer problems and increasing your accuracy than doing too many problems and getting only a few of them right.

So what should your target score be? Well, your target score should be higher than the score you got on your practice test (now would be a good time to take Practice Test 1 if you haven't already), but should still be reasonable and attainable. If you're currently scoring 50, trying to score a 65 right away will only hurt you, because you would have to rush to finish all the problems you need to do. Try to work your way up in reasonable stages. Pick a score range approximately 5 points higher than the range in which you're currently scoring. If you're currently scoring 50, aim for a 55; when you have reached 55, then you can aim for 60.

The Right Number of Questions for Your Target Score

The pacing charts that follow show you how many problems you need to do in order to get a certain score. You should use all of the time you're given to do only the number of problems indicated by the charts, and answer them as accurately as possible. (The numbers in the charts allow for a small margin of error.) Of course, if you find you have more time after having done this, go ahead and try a few more.

On the Math section, for instance, if you're aiming for a 55, you should just do 15 of the problems in Section 2. Which 15 problems? The 15 that *you* like the best. (More on this to come.) Many of the problems you should focus on will probably be among the first 15; but if you don't like problem number 11, skip it and do number 16 instead.

Math Target Score	Raw Points Needed	Questions to Do on Section 2	Questions to Do on Section 4
35	5	5	5
40	9	8	7
45	14	10	10
50	18	13	11
55	23	15	13
60	27	17	16
65	31	19	17
70	34	all	all
75	36	all	all
80	38	all	all

Below is the pacing chart for Critical Reading. If you're aiming for a 55, you want to do 17 questions on each section (for a total of 34 problems). Which 17? The ones that you like best. There's plenty of Critical Reading to choose from; maybe you like the shorter, paragraph-length passages better than the longer passages. Do you like simple line reference questions or the more general author tone questions?

Critical Reading Target Score	Raw Points Needed	Questions to Do on Section 1	Questions to Do on Section 3
35	7	6	6
40	11	8	8
45	16	11	11
50	21	13	13
55	27	17	17
60	32	19	19
65	38	22	22
70	42	all	all
75	45	all	all
80	47	all	all

Finally, here's the pacing chart for the Writing Skills section:

Writing Skills Target Score	Raw Points Needed	Questions to Do on Section 5
35	5	10
40	9	15
45	13	19
50	17	23
55	21	27
60	25	31
65	28	34
70	32	all
75	35	all
80	38	all

WHICH PROBLEMS SHOULD I DO?

As we mentioned on the previous page, you should do whichever problems are the easiest and quickest for *you*.

The Order of Difficulty

Most of the questions on the PSAT are arranged in increasing order of difficulty, as you can see on the charts below. The rest have no order of difficulty (OOD), which means it's up to you to choose the questions that are easiest for you to do.

You should notice in the chart that for sections that have an order of difficulty, approximately the first third of each section is easy, the next third is medium, and the last third is difficult. So you should always pay attention the question number you're working on in these sections, because it will give you important hints about how to approach the question. If it's an easy question, go ahead and use the techniques to answer it and don't second-guess yourself. If it's a medium question, be careful, use POE and the techniques, and watch for the occasional trick. If it's a difficult question, keep in mind that there's something in the question that caused it to be given that high number, a Joe Bloggs answer or two, or maybe it's worded in a tricky way or presents a great deal of information that will be easy to get tripped up in. On hard questions you need to be sure first of all that you should be working on that question at all, a subject that goes beyond order or difficulty and into the next topic, Personal Order of Difficulty.

Your Personal Order of Difficulty

The chart on the previous page shows questions that are considered "easy," "medium," and "hard" by the average test taker. The average number of people who get that question right determines whether a question is easy, medium, or hard by ETS standards.

But for any one test taker, who—for example—might like algebra better than geometry, a question that is usually considered "medium" might be easy. Or vice versa.

This means that you should always answer the questions on the PSAT according to your Personal Order of Difficulty, or POOD—that is, answer the ones that are easiest for you. If you're going to do 14 math questions on a section, you want to find the easiest 14. While it's a good bet that most of the first 14 math questions will be the easiest for you, if you find one or two questions in that group that you don't like, *skip them.* Then find a few other questions elsewhere in the section that look easier for you.

Joe Bloggs Answers

Let's revisit our friend Joe Bloggs and look at another way he can help us on the PSAT. Suppose for a moment that you could look at the page of the tester next to you (you can't). Also, suppose that you know for a fact that every one of your neighbor's answers on the test is wrong. If on problem 20, he marked (C) as his answer, what you do? Eliminate choice (C), right?

Even though you can't look at your neighbor's page, you can use this principle to get points on the test by looking for Joe Bloggs answers. When the folks at ETS write the PSAT, they write it in a very particular way. They write it so that Joe will get most of the easy problems correct, some of the medium problems correct, and none of the hard ones correct.

How do they do this? The test writers are very good at knowing what kinds of answer choices are attractive to the average person. (They've been doing it for more than 40 years.)

Joe Bloggs, the average tester, always picks the answer that first attracts him. Choices that first attract him on math problems have nice round numbers that can be easily derived from other numbers in the problem. Choices that attract him on verbal problems have familiar words that remind him of words in the question or passage.

Joe's Hunches
Should you always just eliminate any answer that seems to be correct? No! Remember what we said about Joe Bloggs:
1. His hunches are correct on easy questions.
2. His hunches are sometimes correct and sometimes incorrect on medium questions.
3. His hunches are always wrong on difficult questions.

On easy multiple-choice questions, pick the choice that Joe Bloggs would. On hard questions, be sure to eliminate the choices that Joe Bloggs would pick.

Question Type	Joe Bloggs Selects	How Joe Does
Easy	What seems right	Mostly right
Medium	What seems right	So-so
Hard	What seems right	All wrong!

What does this mean for you? When you're working on easy problems, pick the choice that seems right to you. When you're working on medium problems, be careful. If you got the answer too quickly, check your work. Medium problems should take more work than easy problems. If you're working on a hard problem, eliminate the choices that first seem attractive; they are almost always traps.

Remember, Joe Bloggs gets the easy problems right. *Only cross off Joe Bloggs answers on the hard problems.* How do you know how hard a question is? By its *question number.*

Take a look at the following example:

20. Michelle rode her bicycle from her house to school at an average speed of 8 miles per hour. Later that day, she rode from school back home along the same route at an average speed of 12 miles per hour. If the round trip took her 1 hour, how many miles long is the round trip?

    (A)   8

    (B) $9\frac{3}{5}$

    (C)   10

    (D) $11\frac{1}{5}$

    (E)   12

Here's How to Crack It

Which choice do you think seems attractive at first to Joe? When he sees the numbers 8 and 12 and the word "average," he will probably average 8 and 12 to get 10. Therefore, Joe will pick (C).

But now you know better. This problem is number 20, the hardest problem on the section. You know that Joe will get it wrong. So cross off choice (C).

If Joe doesn't pick (C), what else might he pick? He'll pick either (A) 8, or (E) 12, because those are the numbers that appear in the problem. Cross them off as well. Then guess from either (B) or (D). (The answer is (B), but we're not going to spend time on why right now.) If you can quickly cross off a few choices on a hard problem and make a good guess, you'll be in great shape.

Figuring out the right number of problems to do, how to pace yourself, and how to avoid the Joe Bloggs traps are keys to a good PSAT strategy. You're probably eager to get to the rest of the book, but make sure you've taken the time to understand this chapter before moving on. A solid overall approach is crucial to getting your best score on this test.

Summary

o   Remember to memorize your pacing goals so that you know exactly how many problems to do—you don't have to do every problem to get a great score.

o   The questions on most sections are arranged in Order of Difficulty from easier to harder, which may make it easier to find the problems that are easier for you to do.

o   Use your Joe Bloggs instincts on easy and hard problems (according to the test writers' OOD). For easy problems, Joe Bloggs answers tend to be right, while on hard problems, they are almost always wrong.

Part II
Cracking the PSAT/NMSQT

Chapter 5
Sentence
Completions

A Sentence Completion question will consist of a sample sentence in which one or two words have been replaced by blanks. Below the sentence, you'll find five answer choices, each of which consists of a word or words. This chapter will give you the techniques you need to approach Sentence Completions for maximum accuracy and minimum wasted time and stress.

Solving Sentence Completions relies on two things: First, your ability to figure out what kind of word should go in the blank, and second, your vocabulary. We will focus mostly on technique in this chapter. To work on vocabulary, turn to Chapter 11 for the Hit Parade—The Princeton Review's list of vocabulary words that show up most often on the PSAT.

THE INSTRUCTIONS

Of course, you don't want to take up valuable time during the test to read the directions, so let's learn them now. Here are the instructions for Sentence Completions as you will see them on the PSAT and SAT:

Each sentence below has one or two blanks, each blank indicating that something has been omitted. Beneath the sentence are five words or sets of words labeled A through E. Choose the word or set of words that, when inserted in the sentence, best fits the meaning of the sentence as a whole.

Example:

Medieval kingdoms did not become constitutional republics overnight; on the contrary, the change was -------.

(A) unpopular (B) unexpected (C) advantageous
(D) sufficient (E) gradual   Ⓐ Ⓑ Ⓒ Ⓓ ●

ETS's answer to this sample question is (E).

ORDER OF DIFFICULTY

Sentence Completion questions will appear on both Critical Reading sections of the PSAT. They will be questions 1–8 in Section 1 and questions 25–29 in Section 3. Their order of difficulty looks like this:

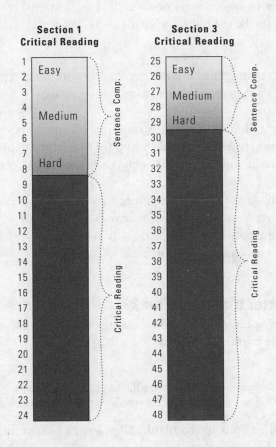

DON'T BE LIKE JOE

Before we talk about the best way to solve Sentence Completions, we should first discuss how *not* to solve them. How does Joe Bloggs, the average student, approach Sentence Completions? The natural way, which seems most intuitive to Joe, is to do the following: He tries to solve these questions by rereading the sentence five times, trying a different word in the blank each time, and hoping to find the one that "sounds right." That is, he does the following:

Joe tries choice (A):

> Medieval kingdoms did not become constitutional republics overnight; on the contrary, the change was *unpopular*.

Joe tries choice (B):

> Medieval kingdoms did not become constitutional republics overnight; on the contrary, the change was *unexpected*.

A Reminder
On easy questions, the answers that seem right to Joe really are right; on hard questions, the answers that seem right to Joe are wrong. In both cases, though, he spends way too much time on them.

Joe tries choice (C):

> Medieval kingdoms did not become constitutional republics overnight; on the contrary, the change was *advantageous*.

Joe tries choice (D):

> Medieval kingdoms did not become constitutional republics overnight; on the contrary, the change was *sufficient*.

Joe tries choice (E):

> Medieval kingdoms did not become constitutional republics overnight; on the contrary, the change was *gradual*.

Unfortunately, while this method is intuitive, it's not a very good strategy. Not only is it a waste of time (why would you want to read the sentence *five times*?), but it's often unreliable, since many of the choices sound pretty good.

What Joe doesn't know is that the correct answer on a Sentence Completion question is not correct because of how it *sounds*, but because of what it *means*. So the best way to solve Sentence Completions is to figure out what the word in the blank should mean. The question is, how?

You're Smarter than You Think

Try the following exercise: In the following sentence, what word do you think should go in the blank?

> 1. Susan was ------- when the formula, which had worked just yesterday, failed to produce the expected result.

What word did you put in the blank? "Perplexed" or "confused"? Something of this sort has to be the word in the blank.

How about this one:

> 2. Although she was never considered pretty as a child, Margaret grew up to be a ------- adult.

What word did you put in the blank? "Beautiful" or "pretty" or "lovely"? You can figure out what the word in the blank has to mean without looking at the answer choices.

Try it once more:

> **3.** Once a cheerful person, the years of fruitless struggle
> against government waste made him a very ------- man.

Even if you couldn't figure out the exact word that went in the blank, you probably figured out that it had to be a word meaning "unhappy" or "bitter." That will be good enough to get the right answer, or at least to make a very good guess at the right answer.

You see, you're smarter than you think. This is why you should always approach Sentence Completion questions by *speaking for yourself*. Don't look down at the answer choices; if you do, you'll be tempted to use the Joe Bloggs method of trying each word, one at a time, and hoping that one of them sounds right. In fact, you should always approach Sentence Completions the same way we just did: Read the sentence, and put your own word into the blank.

THE METHOD

As you've seen, it's entirely possible to figure out what kind of word goes in the blank just by reading the sentence carefully, and it's much faster than trying every answer choice. To make sure that you speak for yourself, you should actually place your hand over the answer choices so you're not tempted to read them until you've picked your own word for the blank.

Sentence Completion Rule #1
Cover the answer choices until you know what the answer should be.

So here's our method so far for solving Sentence Completions:

1. Cover the answer choices with your hand. This will ensure that you don't do what Joe does, which is to read the sentence five times, trying one of the answer choices each time.
2. Speak for yourself: Read the sentence, and write your own word in the blank.
3. Only after you've put your own word in the blank should you uncover the answer choices and pick the word that comes closest to the word that you came up with.

But how do you know what word to put in the blank? You never have to guess randomly; in fact, ETS always puts clues into the sentences to tell you what sort of word goes in the blank. By learning how to look for these clues, you can reliably figure out what sort of word has to go in the blank, every time.

Speak for Yourself, Part I: The Clue and Trigger Words

To help you speak for yourself, learn to look for the *clue* and *trigger words*.

The Clue

We just saw that you could figure out the meaning of the word in the blank without looking at the answer choices. How did you think you were able to know what word went in the blank? Without realizing it, you were using clues in the sentence. There are *always* clues in the sentence that tell you what the word in the blank is supposed to mean.

Let's look back at the first sample problem and see what kind of clues we can find in it.

> **1.** Susan was ------- when the formula, which had worked just yesterday, failed to produce the expected result.

How did you know that the word had to be something like "perplexed"? Because this sentence contains a clue: *the formula, which had worked just yesterday, failed to produce the expected result.* This clue tells us how Susan must feel: namely, that she felt "perplexed" or "puzzled." We're going to underline clues, so go ahead and underline the phrase from question 1, italicized above. Remember, it's your book, so write in it and write in your test booklet on test day.

How about in this sentence?

> **2.** The park was so ------- that children could play in it for hours without getting bored.

What kind of word would you put in this blank, and why? You probably chose a word like "interesting" or "varied." You probably knew this because the park is described as a place where *children could play for hours without getting bored.* This is the clue that tells us that the park must be a terribly interesting place to be.

The meaning of the word that goes in the blank isn't random—rather, there is always evidence somewhere else in the sentence that tells you what the word in the blank should mean. This evidence is called the clue. *Every sentence has some clue in it. Look for the clue, underline it, and it will help you determine the word that goes in the blank.*

Hold an Audition

If you were directing *Romeo and Juliet* you wouldn't audition everyone for every part, would you? For Juliet you'd only invite teenage girls to audition. With Sentence Completions you can follow a similar procedure; know what you're looking for ahead of time.

Why Every Sentence Needs a Clue

Every sentence on the PSAT must have some sort of clue in it, or else the question wouldn't have just one correct answer. In that case, the question wouldn't be a good one anymore, and ETS couldn't use it on the PSAT. Let's see why. Take a look at this problem:

1. John made some ------- comments about Marcus's
   artwork.

   (A) intelligent
   (B) critical
   (C) interesting
   (D) dry
   (E) appreciative

Can you see why this problem would never appear on the PSAT? Because any of the answers might work. There's not enough information in the sentence to make one choice better than any other. Without a clue, the question just won't work. Look at this example:

1. John made some ------- comments about Marcus's
   artwork, which John thought was fantastic.

   (A) intelligent
   (B) critical
   (C) interesting
   (D) dry
   (E) appreciative

In this case, the word that would best fit would be (E), because of the clue *which John thought was fantastic.* Note that if the clue changes, so does the meaning of the word in the blank.

1. John made some ------- comments about Marcus's
   artwork, which John thought was the worst he had ever
   seen.

   (A) intelligent
   (B) critical
   (C) interesting
   (D) dry
   (E) appreciative

In this case, the answer would be (B). By changing the clue, we changed the meaning of the word that should go in the blank.

Suppose you're having trouble identifying the clue, though. There are two questions you can ask yourself to help you find it.

- Who or what is the blank talking about?
- What does the sentence say about that thing?

Let's look at number 1 on page 46 again. Who or what is the sentence talking about? The formula. What does it say about the formula? *That it failed to produce the expected result,* so that's the clue.

It will work for number 2 as well. Who or what was that sentence talking about? The park. What does it say about the park? *That the children could play in it for hours without getting bored,* so that's the clue. Remember to underline it.

Trigger Words

One more important tool for figuring out the meaning of the word in the blank is *trigger words.* These are words in the sentence that tell you how the word in the blank relates to the clue. When you see a trigger word, circle it.

Trigger words are words we use every day. For instance, look at the following sentences:

I really like you, *and* _____
I really like you, *but* _____

You already know more or less how these sentences would end, don't you? The first sentence would continue with something positive that goes along with liking someone, such as:

I really like you, *and* I'd like to get to know you better.

In contrast, the second sentence would change direction and end with something not quite so nice, such as:

I really like you, *but* you're really not my type.

Now let's see how trigger words work in a sample sentence. Recall the second example:

2. *Although* she was never considered pretty as a child, Margaret grew up to be a ------- adult.

Same or Opposite?

The most common same-direction trigger words are *and, because, so, therefore, since,* and *in fact.*

The most common opposite-direction trigger words are *but, however, yet, although, though, in contrast, rather,* and *despite.* When you see these words, the word in the blank will usually mean the opposite of the clue.

Same-Direction Triggers	Opposite-Direction Triggers
and	but
because	however
so	yet
therefore	although/though
since	in contrast
in fact	rather

How did you know that the word in the blank had to be a word like "beautiful"? Because the word *although* told you that there was a change in direction or contrast in the sentence: She was *not pretty as a child*, but she *was* a pretty *adult*.

There are also trigger words that indicate that the word in the blank has the same meaning as the clue. For instance:

> 4. (Because) Susan could not stand Jim's boorish manners, she ------- to be near him at parties.

In this case, what sort of word goes in the blank? The trigger word *because* tells you that the word in the blank will have a similar meaning to the clue *could not stand Jim's boorish manners*. The word in the blank must therefore be something like "hated" or "despised."

Punctuation Triggers

In addition to the words to the right, there are a couple of punctuation triggers. Both colons (:) and semicolons (;) act as same-direction triggers and show us that what follows the colon or semicolon will be an explanation or further description of something that came before. Take a look at this sentence:

> 2. John's friend was rather ------- (:) He never spoke unless he was forced to.

In this case, we know that the word in the blank should be a word that means "unwilling to speak"—a word like "quiet" or "taciturn" would do nicely.

Time Triggers

One other, more subtle, kind of trigger, which acts as an opposite-direction trigger, is the time trigger. A time trigger draws a contrast between what used to be true and what is true today. Here's an example:

> 3. (Once) a cheerful person, the years of futile struggle against government waste made him a very ------- man.

In this case, we know that the word in the blank needs to be a word opposite to "cheerful"—perhaps a word like "gloomy" or "cynical." Why? We know that at one point in the past, this person was cheerful; however, since that time, something has changed. Therefore, the word in the blank should be something that contrasts with "cheerful."

When trying to find the right word for the blank, always look for the clue and trigger words. They will tell you what sort of word you need.

A Reminder
Circle the triggers!

Speak for Yourself—Part II

Here are a few Sentence Completion problems from which we've removed the answer choices. (The complete problems with answer choices follow.) Read the sentence, underline any clues, circle any triggers, then write your own word in the blank using the clues and triggers to guide you. Then use POE to eliminate choices that don't match yours.

1. Many feature films are criticized for their ------- content, even though television news is more often the medium that depicts violent events in excessive detail.

4. In a scathing message to his troops, General Patton insisted that he would ------- no further insubordination, no matter how brutal the ensuing engagements might become.

Now that you've identified the clues and triggers, let's crack these problems.

---

1. Many feature films are criticized for their ------- content, even though television news is more often the medium that depicts violent events in excessive detail.

   (A) discretionary
   (B) graphic
   (C) dramatic
   (D) artistic
   (E) honest

Here's How to Crack It

The clue in this sentence is *depicts violent events in excessive detail*. The word in the blank should mean something like "violent" or "violence in detail." You can often "recycle" the clue, that is, the word or words you fill in the blank don't have to be fancy, they just need to complete the meaning of the sentence. So feel free to recycle the word violent and use it as your own word.

Now let's use POE to get the answer. Does discretionary mean violent? Nope. Cross it off. (Oops, what if we don't know what discretionary means? Then we should keep it for the time being. If it's the only answer left then we'd pick it, but if we find a better match we'd pick that instead.) Does graphic mean violent? Seems pretty close, so keep it for now. Does dramatic mean violent? Nope. Cross it off. Does artistic mean violent? Definitely not. Finally, does honest mean violent? No. So, we're left with (B). Go ahead and pick it.

Okay, ready for the next one?

⎯⎯⎯⎯⎯○⎯⎯⎯⎯⎯

4. In a scathing message to his troops, General Patton insisted that he would ------- no further insubordination, no matter how brutal the ensuing engagements might become.

    (A) impede
    (B) brief
    (C) denote
    (D) brook
    (E) expose

Here's How to Crack It

The clues here are *insisted* and *no further insubordination, no matter how*.... Did you pick a word like "tolerate" or "stand for" in this case? That's exactly the meaning of the correct answer. The words in the answer choices are hard, but eliminate what you can, keep the words you don't know, and take a good guess. The answer is (D).

⎯⎯⎯⎯⎯○⎯⎯⎯⎯⎯

Two Blanks: Twice as Easy

Some of the Sentence Completion questions will have two blanks rather than just one. To solve these questions, do them one blank at a time. Pick one blank or the other, whichever seems easier to you, and figure out what word should go in the blank. (Hint: Often, but not always, the second blank is easier to figure out.) Then cross off all of the choices that don't work for that blank.

If more than one choice remains, then pick a word for the other blank, and see which of the remaining answer choices works best.

Have a look at these examples:

⎯⎯⎯⎯⎯○⎯⎯⎯⎯⎯

2. The scientific community was ------- when a living specimen of the coelacanth, which ichthyologists had feared was -------, was discovered by deep-sea fishermen.

    (A) perplexed . . common
    (B) overjoyed . . dangerous
    (C) unconcerned . . exterminated
    (D) astounded . . extinct
    (E) dismayed . . alive

Shoe Store
If you were shopping for shoes and one didn't fit, you wouldn't bother trying on the other one, would you? Half wrong is all wrong. If one answer doesn't fit, cross out the whole choice.

Here's How to Crack It

The clue for the second blank is that a *living specimen* was found, which the scientists *feared was*.... So the second blank must mean something like "dead." Only choices (C) and (D) are possible, so we can eliminate the others. Now look at the first blank. How did the scientists feel about the discovery? They were probably happy about it. Of (C) and (D), which choice works with the first blank? Choice (D).

Let's do another:

5. Chang realized that she had been ------- in her duties; had she been more -------, the disaster may well have been avoided.

   (A) unparalleled . . careful
   (B) irreproachable . . aware
   (C) derelict . . vigilant
   (D) arbitrary . . interested
   (E) neglectful . . insensible

Here's How to Crack It

The clue for the second blank is that the *disaster may well have been avoided,* so the second blank must be a word like "careful." This will allow us to eliminate (D) and (E). The word in the first blank must be a word like "neglectful," since Chang failed to do her duty. The only remaining choice that works for the first blank is (C).

Here's one more:

5. Although Jane's professors reproached her as a ------- during her first year in college, she became attentive and ------- once she found a major that interested her.

   (A) neophyte . . assiduous
   (B) sycophant . . critical
   (C) malingerer . . focused
   (D) beginner . . average
   (E) candidate . . distracted

Here's How to Crack It

Remember to cover the answers before reading the sentence! Although we know that the first blank is probably a bad thing (because Jane's professors *reproached* her), we don't have great clues. So let's move on to the second blank. The clue for the second blank is *attentive*, so we can recycle it and use attentive as our own word. Then we can eliminate (B), (D), and (E), because they don't mean anything close to *attentive*.

Now we have a better idea of what goes in the first blank. Because of the trigger *although,* the first blank means a person who is the opposite of *attentive.* Perhaps we would write down *slacker.* Our two remaining answer choices are (A) and (C). If you don't know what *neophyte* means, remember to leave it there—it could be correct. (C) does mean *slacker* though, so that's our best answer

---

Relationship Between the Blanks

Remember we said that all questions have clues? Well, in some tricky questions the clues may be pretty unclear or missing altogether because one blank is the clue for the other blank. In this case we'll have to do things a little bit differently, namely, use the relationship between the blanks to eliminate answers that don't have that some relationship. For example, take a look at the question that follows:

5. Because their new album is more ------- than previous ones, the band may alienate their fans who like ------- music.

If you tried to fill in the blanks with your own words, you might come up with something like *traditional* for the first blank and *experimental* for the second. But you could just as easily switch those words in the blanks and the sentence would still make sense, so we can't do this one blank at a time. The word that goes in the first blank is dependent on the word in the second blank, and vice versa. So the key is to focus on the *relationship between the blanks*—whether they're the same or different.

In this sentence, we're pretty clearly looking for words that are different. So we would eliminate any answer choices with words that were the same or that didn't have any relationship at all.

Let's try another one. Keep in mind that triggers can really help you because they tell you about the relationship between clues and blanks.

4. The author is reliably -------; every book he writes is
more ------- than the one before.

  (A) dull . . inspired
  (B) exceptional . . hackneyed
  (C) artistic . . informed
  (D) imaginative . . creative
  (E) original . . lackluster

Here's How to Crack It

The sentence doesn't have clues for the individual blanks, so let's look for triggers that will tell us whether the relationship between the blanks is the same or different. First, there is a semicolon, which tells us the two parts of the sentence go in the same direction. Also, the words *reliably* and *every book he writes* are clearly describing a relationship of similarity between the blanks. So we would note that the words should be the same, and go through our answer choices. (A), (B), and (E) are clearly opposites, and the words in (C) don't really have a relationship, so we're left with (D) as our best answer.

Final Words

As the questions get harder, you'll probably find harder words in the answer choices. Although you'll have a word of your own to compare to the answers and use POE, you might find many or most of the answer choices are words you don't know. When this happens, get rid of whatever you can quickly and take a guess. If you can't come up with your own word using the two questions we discussed earlier, then you should skip that question altogether. For example, some harder questions might also use a tough vocabulary word in the clue. If you don't know what the clue means you won't be able to fill in the blank with your own word and you're most likely going to get it wrong. If it's a two-blank question and you can fill in one of the blanks, you might try to eliminate a few and guess, but only if you've worked through the whole section and have run out of questions you can do with certainty.

Summary

- The first step on Sentence Completion questions is to cover the answer choices with your hand.

- Next, speak for yourself: Read the sentence, and put your own word in the blank.

- To help you figure out the meaning of the word that goes in the blank, find the clues in the sentence. Also, pay close attention to trigger words.

- Only after you've come up with your own word for the blank should you look down at the answer choices. Pick the word that comes closest to the word that you created. Be sure to use POE and evaluate every answer choice.

- On two-blank questions, just do one blank at a time.

Chapter 6
Critical Reading

This chapter deals only with passage-based reading questions. You'll see a passage followed by questions about the content of the passage. These questions are supposed to measure how well you understand what you read, but in reality they mostly measure how efficiently you can locate specific pieces of information. There are two types of passages—long ones and short ones—and we're going to look at them both.

LONG PASSAGES—WHAT TO EXPECT

Critical Reading long passages are generally from 40 to 100 lines, with six to twelve questions for each passage. The questions will be numbered 13–24 on Section 1 and 34–48 in Section 3. Unlike Sentence Completions, passage-based reading questions are not arranged in a set order of difficulty, so it will be up to you to identify which questions will be easiest for you to do. But don't worry; we'll show you what to expect and how to pick the best questions for your skills.

AN OPEN-BOOK TEST

Answering passage-based reading questions is like taking an open-book test; all of the information that you could be asked about is sitting right in front of you, so you never have to worry about any history, chemistry, or literature that you may (or may not!) have learned in school. Although you'll have to use the passage to answer the questions, there isn't really time to read the passage thoroughly, master all its details, and then painstakingly select the one choice that answers the question perfectly. What you need is a way to get in and out of this section with as little stress and as many points as possible.

If someone were to give you a ten-volume encyclopedia and ask you in what year Louis Pasteur invented pasteurization, would you begin reading at the A's and work all the way through to the P's? Probably not. You'd go right to the entry on Pasteur and read only the few lines that you needed to. That's how to approach passage-based reading questions on the PSAT.

THE METHOD

1. Read the blurb
2. Quickly read for the main idea
3. Choose a question and paraphrase it
4. Read what you need to answer the question
5. Answer in your own words
6. POE

Step 1: Read the Blurb

Long passages usually begin with a short introduction in italics which will give you a little background about the passage. If you see one, read it! It will give you some good context before you start reading the passage.

Step 2: Quickly Read for the Main Idea

Now take a minute to skim the passage. We're looking for the main idea here, so we don't want to get bogged down in the details. (We'll be coming back to the passage to answer the questions in step 4; we'll focus on the details then.) As we're reading we should be thinking about what the author is getting at; what's the big idea?

We're not just looking for this information so we can answer a main idea question later. In fact, knowing the main idea is central to answering all sorts of questions about the passage. Everything in the passage is there to support the main idea, so any time we start asking why the author did something, said something, or made some choice about what to say or what not to say, he or she did it because it has something to do with the main idea.

Once again, though, don't get wrapped up in the details of the passage. If something is confusing, leave it for now and stay focused on the big picture. There may not be any questions about that part of the passage anyway, and even if there are questions about it, they're probably going to be good questions to skip or save for last.

Passage Types

Critical Reading passages come from four broad subject areas:

1. Science: Discoveries, controversies, or other topics in physics, chemistry, astronomy, biology, medicine, botany, zoology, and the other sciences.
2. Humanities: Excerpts from essays about art, literature, music, philosophy, or folklore; discussions of artists, novelists, or historical figures.
3. Social sciences: Topics in politics, economics, sociology, or history.
4. Narrative: Usually excerpts from novels, short stories, or humorous essays. (We have yet to see a poem on the PSAT.)

ETS usually includes a passage involving a historically overlooked community or social group. This passage is usually either a social science or humanities passage.

Step 3: Choose a Question and Paraphrase It

All points are created equal, but not all questions are. The math sections and the sentence completions have an order of difficulty to help you make POOD decisions before you even read the question, but the reading passages don't give you this hint. You're going to have to use your judgment as you go along, taking into consideration such things as how long or complicated the question stem is and whether or not the things it asks about in the passage are hard to understand.

If the question is easy to understand, and therefore to paraphrase, then it may be a good question to attack right away. Questions that you have to spend time just trying to interpret and paraphrase should be put off until later. Or if the part of the passage that you need to read in order to answer the question is particularly difficult, then you should probably put off that question until later or skip it altogether. But if the reading is a breeze (or at least pretty straightforward), you probably want to do it now.

The question can still be tough if there are tricks in the answer choices, but we'll talk about what to watch out for when we get to POE.

Now that we've chosen a question it's time to paraphrase it. We'll do this so that we know what we're looking for when we go to the passage. We need to know this because we want to read actively, which means we're going to be actively searching for the information we need and thinking about it, not just passively letting photons hit our eyeballs as we daydream about sunny days at the beach.

Take a look at the following question:

> The author mentions the Israeli-Palestinian conflict in the
> last paragraph (lines 92-97) in order to

This question is asking us for the purpose of something, in other words, why did the author talk about something? What's the something? The Israeli-Palestinian conflict. When we read we're going to want to know what the author says about this and why, so the question is *Why does the author talk about the Israeli-Palestinian conflict?*

That was pretty simple, but we broke it into pieces anyway. This helps us to keep in mind how we'd paraphrase it if it were more complicated and to stay focused on the fact that we're trying to figure out why the author talks about something, not just what he says about it.

Remember back in step 2 we talked about getting the main idea of the passage? Here's where it starts to come in handy, because we know in most cases when we paraphrase a question like the one above, we really want to know what the thing we're being asked about has to do with the main idea of the passage.

Take a minute to read the questions below and think about what they're asking you to find out, then paraphrase them.

42. According to the passage, the parrot became
    uncooperative because

43. The author's use of irony in line 55 suggests that

44. The primary purpose of the passage is

45. The argument about crows in the third paragraph would
    be most strengthened if which of the following were
    true?

Explanations

42. The question is asking why the parrot became uncooperative, so we can paraphrase it as, *Why did the parrot become uncooperative?* How easy was that? Just make it into a question by starting with one of the "W" words. This question looks pretty simple, as it's not asking us to think about anything beyond what the passage says, so this is a question we'd certainly want to try on our first pass through the questions.

43. *What does the author's use of irony in line 55 tell us?* Questions that ask about what's *suggested* or *implied* can be pretty tough, because we don't really know what the question is after; it could be a number of things. Paraphrasing the question as above will get us focused on looking for whatever information is given on the topic in the passage, but we're going to have to focus on the answers and use POE carefully here. This would be a good question to hold off on for now and maybe come back to later.

44. *What is the primary purpose of the passage?* Another way to think about this question is, *Why did the author write this passage?* He's trying to get something across or convince us of something, so we should focus on trying to figure out what that is. We should probably hold off on general questions like this until we've worked more specific questions and therefore have more background.

45. This question is asking us to go outside of the information given in the passage. The answer must still be something we can derive from the passage or logically infer, but it's probably going to be pretty tough. The answer choices are going to present new information. Notice that the question stem says *if which of the following were true.* This is definitely a question to do last and only if we're going to attempt every question. To paraphrase it, we'll actually want to try to break it down into a few questions, rather than just one, as follows: *What is the third paragraph trying to convince us of about crows?* and *What kind of information would make this more likely?*

If you have to do this question, be sure to use bite-sized pieces to figure out what steps you'll need to take to answer the question. In fact, any time there's more than one question hidden in the question, see if you can break it down into a couple of questions, and don't forget to make one of them about how the main idea is related to whatever the question is asking about.

Step 4: Read What You Need to Answer the Question

The PSAT is a standardized test. That means that the answers can't just be a matter of opinion. If the folks at ETS are going to put a question on the test and say that the answer is (D), they need to be able to prove that (D) actually *is* the best answer and that no one who truly understood the question and the passage could disagree. They need to be able to point to a line in the passage and say, "See that sentence there? That means the answer *has* to be (D)." And because the test is designed this way, you absolutely cannot leave out Step 4. If you're about to pick an answer choice and you haven't found a line or lines in the passage that you can point to and prove that you've picked the right one, then you haven't picked the right one. Don't just choose based on your memory or on your gut. Don't depend on things you've learned in school, and under no circumstances should you make stuff up. ("Yeah, I guess the War of 1812 could've been fought against the Australians…") *FIND* the answer in the passage. It's in there!

Step 5: Answer in Your Own Words

Remember how we covered our answers and jotted down our own words for Sentence Completions, so we wouldn't be distracted by ETS's answer choices? The same goes for passage-based reading questions. It does you no good to know that the answer is in line 39 if you have no idea what line 39 means! You must translate the answer into your own words before you go to the choices. This often means taking a long-winded paragraph and condensing it down to a handful of words. (ETS often uses exact words from the passage to trick you into picking wrong answers, which is another good reason to substitute your own wording.) As you read the following paragraphs, consider what the key ideas are and how you might boil them down into a sentence or two.

1. We are told that the trouble with Modern Man is that he has been trying to detach himself from nature. He sits in the topmost tiers of polymer, glass, and steel, dangling his pulsing legs, surveying at a distance the writhing life of the planet. In this scenario, Man comes on as a stupendous lethal force, and the Earth is pictured as something delicate, like rising bubbles at the surface of a country pond, or flights of fragile birds.

2. When in the course of human events it becomes necessary for one people to dissolve the political bands which have connected them with another, and to assume among the powers of the earth the separate and equal station to which the Laws of Nature and of Nature's God entitle them, a decent respect to the opinions of mankind requires that they should declare the causes which impel them to the separation.

Answers

1. *Some say that the Earth is delicate and that Modern Man's detachment from it can really mess it up.*

2. *When people declare independence, they'd better tell the world why.*

Note that these answers are *short!* If you found yourself copying phrases such as "surveying at a distance" or "the course of human events," you are missing the point. Copying long phrases means that you don't understand them. You can't go to the choices and expect to get the right answer unless you comprehend what you've read.

Step 6: POE

Process of Elimination is the single most important step. After all, what good is understanding the passage and finding the correct answer if you don't fill in the correct little bubble? None, according to ETS; there is no partial credit on the PSAT. So you need to know what makes a good answer and what makes a bad answer in ETS-land. Some things to keep in mind:

PSAT Do's and Don'ts

- **Evaluate every answer choice.** The directions tell you to pick the "best" answer, and you can only do that if you've read through each one. Remember, ETS knows how to write answers that sound great but are actually wrong, and you're much more likely to avoid those traps if you work through each question completely.
- **Be aggressive.** There will be lots of things wrong in the answer choices, and if part of an answer choice is wrong, the whole thing is wrong. The "best" answer does not have to sound good or make you happy—it just has to be free of error, which means it's supported by the passage and answers the question, but may not be particularly impressive.
- **It's all about the passage.** If you know more about the War of 1812 than the author of the passage does, that's great...but it's not necessarily going to help you on the PSAT. Any answer choice that requires you to know outside information is wrong—everything you need is in the passage.

Cross It Off
On passage-based reading questions, it is very likely that you may need to read a few of the answer choices more than once. To avoid confusion, be sure you cross off each answer entirely when you eliminate something. That way, if you have two or three choices you are considering, you can easily tell which choices are left in the running and which you have eliminated.

POE Tips

Buzzwords

Beware answer choices that contain the following words:
must
always
impossible
never
cannot
each
every
totally
all
solely
only

- **Beware exact phrasing.** ETS often uses exact words from the passage in the wrong answers because they sound familiar and, therefore, test takers are likely to pick them. But correct answers to specific questions are usually *paraphrases* of information in the passage.
- **For General questions, pay attention to scope.** For example, if a passage gives a brief overview of the effects of the Industrial Revolution on city growth in England and you are asked for the primary purpose, you might find incorrect answers such as "detail the Bessemer process of steel manufacturing" (too specific) or "chart the spread of the Industrial Revolution throughout Europe" (too broad). Often, answers that are too specific are just mentioned once or twice in the passage, and answers that are too broad simply cannot be accomplished in 100 lines or fewer.
- **Avoid extremes and give no offense.** Last but certainly not least, ETS rarely makes extreme or offensive answer choices correct on its tests. If you see an answer choice that's extreme or potentially offensive to a certain group of people, eliminate it. The reason for this is simple: The more extreme an answer choice is, the easier it is to prove that answer choice wrong. The more offensive a passage is, the more likely it is that ETS will get sued. ETS doesn't like to be proven wrong or get sued, so "best" answers are wishy-washy and offend no one.

Here are some examples of extreme or offensive answer choices:

> Everyone believes that Shakespeare was the greatest writer in history.

> Nineteenth-century scientists were foolish and ignorant to believe in the existence of ether.

> The judges deliberately undermined the constitution in the landmark case.

In the first example, the passage would have to say that every single person in the world believes Shakespeare is the greatest, but if they wrote that in the passage this question would be pretty easy to answer, wouldn't it? Besides, how would they know? Can they read your mind? So it comes down to what can be supported by the passage once again.

In the second and third examples, an observation is made about some group that they (or their grandchildren) would probably be offended by. PSAT passages are very reasonable and wishy-washy, so offensive answers wouldn't be consistent with the passage.

Likewise, PSAT passages are usually not extreme in tone, so you can eliminate answer choices in questions that ask about the author's tone using extreme words like *condemnation, ridicule, adulation,* and *cynicism.*

Try It Yourself

Now that you know the steps for Critical Reading passages, it's time to try them out. Remember to look back to The Method on page 58 if you need a reminder of how to do something!

The following passage comes from a nineteenth-century British novel, The Picture of Dorian Gray, *about the influence of one member of the idle rich upon another. In the opening paragraph, Dorian Gray is speaking to Lord Henry Wotton about a portrait that's recently been painted of himself by another friend, Basil Hallward.*

"Dear Basil! I have not laid eyes on him for a week. It is rather horrid of me, as he has sent me my portrait in the most wonderful frame, specially designed by himself, and, though
Line I am a little jealous of the picture for being a whole month
5 younger than I am, I must admit that I delight in it. Perhaps you had better write to him. I don't want to see him alone. He says things that annoy me. He gives me good advice."

Lord Henry smiled. "People are very fond of giving away what they need most themselves. It is what I call the depth of
10 generosity."

"Oh, Basil is the best of fellows, but he seems to me to be just a bit of a Philistine. Since I have known you, Harry, I have discovered that."

"Basil, my dear boy, puts everything that is charming in
15 him into his work. The consequence is that he has nothing left for life but his prejudices, his principles, and his common sense. The only artists I have ever known who are personally delightful are bad artists. Good artists exist simply in what they make, and consequently are perfectly uninteresting
20 in what they are. A great poet, a really great poet, is the most unpoetical of all creatures. But inferior poets are absolutely fascinating. The worse their rhymes are, the more picturesque they look. The mere fact of having published a book of second-rate sonnets makes a man quite irresistible.
25 He lives the poetry that he cannot write. The others write the poetry that they dare not realize."

"I wonder is that really so, Harry?" said Dorian Gray, putting some perfume on his handkerchief out of a large, gold-topped bottle that stood on the table. "It must be, if you
30 say it. And now I am off. Imogen is waiting for me. Don't forget about tomorrow. Good-bye."

As he left the room, Lord Henry's heavy eyelids drooped, and he began to think. Certainly few people had ever interested him so much as Dorian Gray, and yet the lad's mad
35 adoration of some one else caused him not the slightest pang of annoyance or jealousy. He was pleased by it. It made him a more interesting study. He had been always enthralled by the methods of natural science, but the ordinary subject-matter of that science had seemed to him trivial and of no import.

40   And so he had begun by vivisecting himself, as he had ended
     by vivisecting others. Human life—that appeared to him
     the one thing worth investigating. Compared to it there was
     nothing else of any value. It was true that as one watched life
     in its curious crucible of pain and pleasure, one could not
45   wear over one's face a mask of glass, nor keep the sulphurous
     fumes from troubling the brain and making the imagination
     turbid with monstrous fancies and misshapen dreams. There
     were poisons so subtle that to know their properties one
     had to sicken of them. There were maladies so strange that
50   one had to pass through them if one sought to understand
     their nature. And, yet, what a great reward one received!
     How wonderful the whole world became to one! To note the
     curious hard logic of passion, and the emotional coloured
     life of the intellect—to observe where they met, and where
55   they separated, at what point they were in unison, and at what
     point they were at discord—there was a delight in that! What
     matter what the cost was? One could never pay too high a
     price for any sensation.

13. Dorian's statement about Basil in lines 6-8 ("I don't ...
    good advice.") implies that Dorian

    (A) wishes to avoid Basil
    (B) believes that Basil's advice does not apply to him
    (C) is jealous of Basil's skill as a painter
    (D) would prefer not to be reminded of his faults
    (E) does not wish to be without Sir Harry

Here's How to Crack It

This looks like a pretty straightforward inference question, which, hopefully, you would choose to do in your first pass through the questions. First, we'll paraphrase it: What is it asking? What does Dorian's statement tell us about him? This is kind of open-ended; we don't know exactly what we're looking for, so we'll go to the passage and, as we read, pay attention to the things we know for sure about Dorian based on what he's said and what he may be responding to in the context.

Remember, we want to read about five lines above and below the indicated lines, so we should start at the beginning of the passage and continue through the next couple of exchanges of dialogue. In fact, the statement in quotes can pretty much stand alone in this case. In the dialogue after the quote, Lord Henry doesn't really address Dorian's statement in a way that tells us anything about Dorian, so there's not much to be found there. In the statements themselves, Dorian says something a little surprising, doesn't he? Basil says things *that annoy him,* but what sort of things are these? Not advice of just any kind, but *good advice.* So Dorian is annoyed by good advice.

Let's take a look at the answers now. On our first pass through the answers, remember, we want to get rid of the answers that are just bad and then slow down and be a bit more careful once we're down to two. Also, because it's an inference the key part of the process is the one we're engaged in now, that is, we need to use POE to eliminate answers that are not supported by the passage. To think of it another way, we need to cross out answers that don't have to be true. (A) says Dorian wishes to avoid Basil. Does this have to be true? Not really. In fact, this is answer is a bit deceptive: Dorian says he *doesn't want to see him alone.* (B) also doesn't have any support in the passage. (C) is another deceptive answer; he says he's jealous of the painting, not of Basil. (D) looks pretty good, right? We decided that Dorian didn't like good advice. (E) has nothing to do with anything we read. So the answer is (D). There wasn't a close second, so we didn't need to slow down and agonize over the choice on this question. This is another indication that it was an easier question, but, of course, we didn't know that until after we'd finished.

14. The statement in lines 8-10 ("People are ... generosity.") implies that Sir Henry believes

    (A) that Basil is uncommonly generous
    (B) that Dorian should take Basil's advice
    (C) that Basil would benefit from some good advice
    (D) that giving advice is a foolish endeavor
    (E) one is not constrained from giving advice to
        others even if one needs it oneself

Here's How to Crack It

Here we want to figure out what Lord Henry believes about something or other. This is another inference question, so we want to pay attention to the evidence the passage gives us and try to decide for ourselves ahead of time, if we can. Although we read this part of the passage when we did number 17, we should read about five lines above and below again because now we're trying to answer a different question and we need to look for that answer. If you lost a sock and a favorite pen somewhere in your house and you searched for and found the sock in a corner of the living room, you might have to search that same area again when you started looking for the pen, because that's not what you were searching for before.

As we read, we can ask ourselves things about what we're reading, like who or what is Lord Henry talking about? He's talking about Basil. In fact, the whole subject of discussion here is Basil, so it's a good bet that this will be what the belief is about. What does he *say or imply* about Basil? In response to Dorian's observation about advice, Lord Henry says that *people are very fond of giving away what they're most in need of.* What people? He must mean Basil. This implies that Basil could use some of what he's giving away, which is *good advice.*

Let's take a look at the answers. Choice (A) is deceptive, the reference to generosity is there to tempt us. (B) is out because Lord Henry's belief appears to be about Basil, not Dorian. (C) looks pretty close to what we said. (D) is not supported, but might look tempting because Lord Henry's tone implies skepticism toward something, though we don't really know what he thinks of advice. What the heck is (E) trying to say? It seems like it could be relevant because it's talking about giving advice, but it's hard to tell how it relates to the passage.

15. Sir Henry's observation in lines 20-26 ("A great poet ... dare not realize.") depends most on the distinction between

(A) the temporary and the permanent
(B) subjective reflections and observations of others
(C) great poetry and the poet's writing ability
(D) one's social persona and the character of one's work
(E) relevant and irrelevant considerations

Here's How to Crack It

Remember to Read What You Need to answer the question.
This is usually about five lines above and below the lines they send you to, but if it doesn't seem like you have much information relevant to answering the question, then you probably haven't read enough.

This question should strike you as being a bit harder than some of the others we've seen. The question of what distinction something depends on is pretty abstract, as we'll need to think not only about what Sir Henry said and what he might have meant by it or what the author might have meant by it, but also what the underlying logic of his thought process was. We're going to need to paraphrase this using smaller bites rather than just one big gulp. First of all, what observation did he make? Let's plan to characterize or describe what the main idea of this part of the passage is. Then we'll need to think about what sorts of things he's comparing. Let's look at the first question. Reading just the lines in question is definitely not going to be enough context. To get at what Lord Henry is really talking about we're probably going to need to read the whole paragraph or so. As we read we should keep in mind what we're looking for, which, as we decided above, is the main idea of this paragraph. This sort of information is often stated directly somewhere in the vicinity of the lines we're interested in, just not necessarily in the lines the test sends us to. This is why reading enough context is so important at this point.

What is Lord Henry trying to convince us of in this paragraph? The information is in the first few sentences of the paragraph (where main ideas often appear), and it says that Basil puts all that's good about himself into his work, so there's nothing left for his personality. Then he goes further and says this is true of poets in general, that *the great ones are unpoetical,* whatever that means, while *the inferior ones are fascinating.* So the distinction is between work and personality.

Let's take a look at the answers. Choice (A) is totally irrelevant. Choice (B) seems to mean something, but we might not be sure what, so keep it for now. Choice (C) looks like it might be on target, it's talking about poetry and poetic abilities, that was certainly in what we were reading. Choice (D) talks about personality and work, that was what we decided was relevant to the answer in our analysis above. Choice (E) isn't related to anything we read in the passage, though it might look tempting because how could relevant things not be relevant to some distinction.

All right, we haven't managed to get all the way to the answer, so we're going to need to slow down and try to get rid of some of the answers we have left. Choice (B) looks pretty confusing, so let's leave it for now. When an answer is weird or unintelligible or uses garbled language, leave it alone for the time being. If there's nothing else left, we'll pick it, otherwise, we'll try to find a better answer. We're going to take a close look at choices (C) and (D), so if we can, we want to compare them and only pay attention to the parts that are different. The two have hardly anything in common, so we're going to want to focus instead on trying to find something wrong with each of the two remaining answers. Choice (C) we said was relevant, so let's take it apart and see if we can find a flaw. The question is about making a distinction, so every answer has two main parts; let's look at one side at a time. The first part says *great poetry*. That was definitely something that was being compared to something else, so it's probably okay. The right side says *the poet's writing ability*. Was that something that was under comparison in this paragraph? Take a look back at the paragraph. There are things that are kind of like that in there, but it's not about how they're different from poetry, it's really the same thing as the great poetry, so (C) is out. Notice, also, that this means that choice (C) doesn't answer the question. Choice (D) matched our expectation of what we were looking for, so we'll give it a quick check just because we still have that weird answer choice (B) lingering in the background. The first part of the answer talks about *one's social persona,* that means someone's outward personality in society, so that looks pretty good. The second part says *the character of one's work*, which seems to mean what kind of work someone does, good, bad, whatever, and that is what Lord Henry contrasts with personality, so this answer is both supported by the text and answers the question. We'll ignore the confusing answer (B) and pick choice (D).

This was a tough one. Take a closer look at what made it tough and remind yourself of what to look for when you see questions like these on the test. We'd definitely want to leave this question for later and only do it if our pacing goals said we were attempting nearly all of the questions in the section. Notice also that we didn't abandon POE when we were down to two and just pick something on a hunch. If we were really stuck we would have, but the possibility of getting stuck on a hard question and having to guess is part of the reason we'd save this one for last.

16. Dorian Gray's attitude toward Lord Henry can best be described as one of

(A) concealed distrust
(B) ironic irreverence
(C) sincere respect
(D) morbid fearfulness
(E) paralyzing awe

Here's How to Crack It

Questions about tone often have an extreme answer or two, and this one is no exception. There are a couple of answers we could get rid of almost without reading the passage. We're not going to do that if we can do the question, of course, and this question doesn't look too bad, but if we were totally out of time and had run out of any easier questions, we could get rid of (D) and (E) because they're pretty over the top. They use language like *morbid,* which means dying, and *paralyzing,* which would mean that Dorian is stunned frozen like a deer caught in headlights. We'd need some real evidence in the passage to justify something that extreme, but we're not going to find it.

To approach the question we need to look for something Dorian says or does that shows us how he feels about Lord Henry. In line 13 he suggests that Basil is a *philistine* compared to Lord Henry. Maybe we don't know what this means exactly, but, it sounds bad and in the surrounding lines Lord Henry and Dorian were criticizing Basil. In lines 29–30, Dorian acknowledges that *if you say something it must be true,* so it looks like he obviously has a positive view of Lord Henry. We can get rid of choices (A) and (B) because they don't match, and we're left with (C), so let's pick it.

17. The fact that Lord Henry's "eyelids drooped" indicates that

(A) he has grown tired due to the extensive conversation
(B) his attitude has become thoughtful
(C) he would like to join Dorian at the theater
(D) he is irritated that Dorian has become involved with an actress
(E) he is interested in what will occur when he and Dorian meet with Basil again

Here's How to Crack It

Why did Lord Henry's *eyelids droop*; what is the author trying to tell us about Lord Henry by telling us about this gesture? (Remember: Everything in the passage is there for a reason.) It's right there in the same sentence, *he began to think*. Checking out some more context we find Lord Henry doing a bunch more thinking. Let's take a look at the answers. (A) suggests he's grown tired, but we really have no evidence for this; this answer is there to trap people who don't go back and read the appropriate part of the passage. (B) looks like a match. There's no support for answers (C), (D), or (E), so get rid of them. (B) is the only answer left, so let's pick it and move on.

Now let's try a more complex question:

---

18. Lord Henry's reaction to Dorian's "mad adoration" implies that he views his relationship to Dorian as most akin to that of

    (A) an audience member to an actor in a play
    (B) a scientist to a laboratory animal
    (C) a detective to a criminal at large
    (D) an attorney to his client
    (E) a storyteller to the romantic hero

Here's How to Crack It

This question should set off some alarm bells. It's got the word *implies* in it, and it's asking us to compare something in the passage to some new information that might seem to have very little to do with the subject matter of the passage. A glance at the answer choices shows that we're being asked about some kind of weird analogy. We don't want to focus on the answers, but a glance can give us some useful information when we're confronted with a weird question or one in which we're really unsure of what the question is asking. The first thing we want to know here is, what *is* Lord Henry's reaction to Dorian's "mad adoration"? Then we'll need to characterize it in the abstract, that is, what *sort* of reaction is it? This way we'll be able to match it to the abstractness of the answers. In the passage we find that Lord Henry is untroubled by Dorian's fling, and for some reason likes that he doesn't mind. Then he goes on to talk about science and psychology and why people are interesting to study and a bunch of other tough language that has something to do with science. We really have to focus on looking for information about how Lord Henry thinks of Dorian in the last paragraph, and we're probably going to need to read the whole thing because not a lot of it seems to answer our question. Some things we can notice about the structure of the passage might help us, though—namely, that it starts with Lord Henry thinking about Dorian, and then turns to Henry's thoughts on science and studying things. What things? *Human life.* Choices (C) and (D) have nothing to do with this, so we can get rid of them. (A) is also unsupported, but if you happen to have read the book *The Picture of Dorian Gray*, by Oscar Wilde, you might remember that his crush is an actress. Outside information isn't necessary, and besides, Lord Henry is not a passive observer, as choice (A) implies. Choice (E) might look tempting because of the deceptive reference to Dorian's adoration of someone else, but that's a trick. Choice (B) matches what we've been looking for, so let's pick it.

19. To Lord Henry, "the mask of glass" and the "sulphurous fumes" most nearly represent

(A) a window to look through and a veil that obscures
(B) a defense and a danger
(C) objects to be studied
(D) tools of the scientific trade
(E) things that trouble the mind

Vocabulary or Not Vocabulary?

Some vocabulary questions, which we'll call "Vocab-in-Context" questions, ask you for the meaning of a word in the passage. Here's an example:

> The word "domestic" (line 43) most nearly means

Vocab-in-Context questions come in two flavors: Either they'll ask about difficult words (so you don't already know the meaning) or about secondary definitions of simple words (so you'll be tempted to pick a meaning that you're already familiar with). You should treat Vocab-in-Context questions like Sentence Completions questions—pretend the word is a blank and think about how to fill it based on the context of the sentence. So while it looks like these questions test your vocabulary, you're much better off depending on the context surrounding the word—again, it's an open-book test.

Here's How to Crack It

This question might be on the complicated side because it asks us what something *represents*, not merely what it *means*, as in a vocab-in-context question. We probably don't want to do this one on the first pass through the questions, but we might need to pick it up on the second pass, depending on what we need to reach our pacing goals. As we read, we'll want to consider what sort of things the objects mentioned are and what they're intended for. Once we've figured this out, we may have enough information to answer the question. The part of the passage that talks about this is pretty tough, as it turns out. There's some kind of extended metaphor being used and these objects are part of it. If this part of the passage is totally bewildering, we might want to bail at this point, especially if there are other easier questions to do. If we do decide to ditch this one we can cross out (A), (D), and (E), because they're all too literal for a question about a part of the passage that's this intensively figurative. (C) is deceptive, because we're not interested here in the things to be studied, but rather the reaction of the person doing the studying. (B) is supported because the mask of glass refers to something to protect someone's face and the sulphurous fumes, since they trouble the mind, are a danger, so the answer is (B).

20. The quote in lines 51-52 ("There were poisons... sicken of them.") most likely indicates an attempt to convey which of the following beliefs held by Lord Henry

(A) the study of life can be sickening and therefore not worth it

(B) there are things about man that are disturbing to consider and these qualities make him repellent

(C) the understanding of some complex subjects may require one's immersion in the subject

(D) some toxic chemicals have been found to be useful for study in the natural sciences

(E) there are dangers in the study of any subject, but those that occur in the natural sciences are not worth the risk

Here's How to Crack It

Here's another inference question in disguise. We need to figure out what Lord Henry believes, based on something stated in the passage, so we'll need to think about what we know from the passage and be sure to read enough context. The line in question refers to certain poisons as being subtle, but the passage really isn't about poisons, so there's a metaphor in use here. (In fact, the language is pretty tough in this part of the passage, so this is another question we should be doing later, during our second pass through the questions.) How did this come up in the first place? In the lines before, he's thinking about the fact that the study of people is the only interesting things to study when he says in lines 41–42, *human life— that appeared to him the one thing worth investigating*. In fact, this is the main point of the paragraph, and we've come back to it a few times to answer our questions about what he's thinking or why he brings up something else in the paragraph. But how is this related to the idea of poison and getting sick? It's not necessarily easy to figure this out, but notice in the sentence before that he says that *as one watched life ... one could not wear over one's face a mask of glass*. What would a mask do? It would protect. In the line we're asked about, he says that *to know the poisons ... one had to sicken of them*. So in general he seems to be saying that we can't be protected and would have to take the poison. He's talking about studying people, after all, so he must be saying that if you're going to study people, you're going to have to get involved and it might hurt. Whew! That was rough.

Let's check out the answers. Choice (A) looks pretty poor, since he clearly says at the end of the paragraph that any price is worth paying. Choice (B) is not supported, as he doesn't make any judgments about people in this section of the text. Choice (C) looks like it might be relevant, but it's not clear how, so keep it for now. Choice (D) is far too literal for something this figurative. Choice (E) might look tempting if you hadn't read carefully, but this part of the passage wasn't about the natural sciences, it was about the study of man, so get rid of this deceptive answer and pick (C). Fortunately, we didn't really have to figure out exactly what it meant, but if we had, we'd see that it's saying just what Lord Henry was getting at, that you can't stay apart from what you study sometimes.

21. The "great reward" referred to in line 51 is most likely

(A) good sensations
(B) a curious logic of the passions
(C) the knowledge of man's troubled nature
(D) a life of the imagination untroubled by monstrous dreams
(E) the keen understanding of human nature

Here's How to Crack It

The question is asking us *What's the great reward?* Reading that part of the passage we find a bunch of evidence in subsequent sentences like *to note* the curious hard logic of passion and *to observe* where they met and that *one can never pay too high a price for any sensation.* So the reward has something to do with *noting* and *observing* and *sensation.* Watch out for choice (A), that's a bit obvious and it doesn't give the full picture. Choice (B) should look suspicious because it just repeats something from the passage, that's deceptive and almost certain to be wrong. (C) looks all right, as it refers to knowledge, which is kind of what we're looking for. (D) is another deceptive answer that quotes the text, so let's get rid of that. (E) also looks like what we were looking for, so let's keep that as well. The two answers we have left, (C) and (E), are pretty similar, so let's compare them. How are they different? (C) refers to man's nature as *troubled*, but is otherwise nearly the same as (E), while (E) says a *keen understanding.* Does Lord Henry think of man's nature as troubled? He might. He does refer to poisons, maladies, and high prices to be paid, but is this the whole story? Let's leave it for the moment and take a look at choice (E). Certainly an understanding of human nature is supported and the same as the majority of choice (C), but what about a *keen* understanding? Going back to the portion of the passage that we read to get an answer of our own, we find that it spends several sentences describing the nature of the understanding that would be gained, as in, *to observe where they met, and where they separated, at what point they were in unison, and at what point they were in discord,* so the keen understanding seems to be pretty well supported. It might look like we're stuck now, but we have one more tool to try. Remember, the answer choice has to answer the question being asked. Does choice (C) do that? Not really, because the knowledge of man's troubles would only be half of the reward of understanding, whereas some of the paragraph clearly indicates that his reward would be an understanding of good *and* bad things, as, for example, *the emotional coloured life of the intellect,* and, of course, the passage also mentions that when one has the reward, *how wonderful the whole world became,* which does not match the tone of choice (C) either.

22. In line 53, "curious" most nearly means

(A) paradoxical
(B) interesting
(C) thoughtful
(D) excessive
(E) overly emotional

Here's How to Crack It

This is a Vocab-in-Context question, and we'll approach it the same way as a sentence completion. We'll go to the passage, cross out the word "curious," and use the evidence in that sentence (and the surrounding sentences, if necessary) to fill in a word of our own. Then we'll use POE to get rid of answers that don't match our word and, hopefully, pick the one remaining answer. Remember, when the word is an "easy" word, like curious, watch out for answers that are too obvious. What's too obvious? A lot of the time, Joe Bloggs doesn't bother to go back to the passage for his answers, so what would he pick if he just wanted something that means curious? Choices (B) and (C) look pretty suspicious now, don't they? We're not going to cross them out until we attempt the question, though. If we were to get stuck we could cross these two out, guess, and move on, but we want to use the approach if it's possible, especially in an easy question like this.

When we go back to the passage and cross out curious, we find it followed by the phrase *the hard logic of passion*. What do logic and passion have to do with each other? Isn't this a bit of a contradiction? So maybe we should use a word like *contradictory* or *paradoxical*. Hello! Paradoxical is there, so that looks pretty good. Check the other answers quickly, and if nothing else works, we'll pick (A). We had already decided to be wary of options (B) and (C), but *interesting* and *thoughtful* don't mean *contradictory*, so they're out. Neither *excessive* nor *overly emotional* means *contradictory* either, so we can get rid of them too. So (A) is the answer.

Notice, if we didn't know what paradoxical meant, we could still get the answer because we can POE our way there. Remember, if you don't know a word or understand an answer choice, you should keep it for the time being; it might be the right answer.

SHORT PASSAGES—WHAT TO EXPECT

About eight of the Critical Reading questions will be based on short, paragraph-long passages. They generally will not have a blurb or any introductory material, and they will usually be followed by only one or two questions per passage. But the object is the same: Answer the questions correctly, using as little time and effort as possible.

The Method

1. Read the passage for the general idea
2. Paraphrase the question
3. Read what you need above and below the line references to answer the question
4. Answer in your own words
5. POE

As you can see, the approach to the Short Reading is very similar to what we've been doing on the Long Reading. The key idea is that you're never reading the passage just to see what's there; you're always looking for the answer to the question you're working on. Let's try a couple:

Parkinson's disease is an incurable, progressive, degenerative brain disease that affects the way nerves control muscles. Since the disease has no cure, it becomes more
Line severe over time, and causes the gradual deterioration of cells
5 in the brain. Generally, Parkinson's disease is thought to be caused by a combination of unknown environmental and genetic factors. However, recent studies have linked some cases of early-onset Parkinson's (a rarer form of the disease that strikes patients under the age of 50) to specific genes
10 shared by sufferers. No such link has been found in patients over 50.

9. The author mentions "recent studies" in line 7 in order to

(A) explain a possible difference of one form of a disease
(B) to suggest that environmental factors are irrelevant
(C) highlight an error in common scientific wisdom
(D) connect two divergent theories on what factors cause a disease
(E) strengthen a controversial argument

Here's How to Crack It

The main point of this passage is that some ideas about Parkinson's may not apply to a particular form of the disease. We'll probably need to read most of the passage to get some context, because the question is asking us why the author talks about something, so we'll need to figure out how that something—*the recent studies*—relates to his main idea. Thankfully, we have a pretty good tool for getting a quick approximation. Remember we talked about trigger words in the Sentence Completions section? Well, they're equally useful in the passage reading sections. Notice the trigger word *however* in the beginning of the phrase *however, recent studies have linked....* That's just the thing we're interested in and it's telling us that there's a change in direction, so the new studies must tell us about an exception or a difference. We can get rid of (B), (C), and (E) on this basis. Now compare choices (A) and (D): what's different? Choice (D) mentions connecting the different things while (A) does not. Was there any mention of a connection between the two? No. So, (D) is out and the answer is (A).

Notice also that the use of the word *irrelevant* in choice (B) is too strong and the word *common* in choice (C) is not supported by the passage. Even if you don't figure out the magic bullet to answer the question every time, stay on the lookout for ways to get rid of answers. POE is king in the Critical Reading section.

10. It can be reasonably inferred from the discussion of the causes of Parkinson's disease that

   (A) the factors that cause Parkinson's disease in patients over 50 are only environmental
   (B) "degenerative" refers to a disease that becomes less severe over time
   (C) research has been done on the causes of early-onset Parkinson's
   (D) the cure for Parkinson's disease will eventually be found through genetic research
   (E) early-onset Parkinson's patients are exposed to the same environmental factors as patients over 50

Here's How to Crack It

We have another inference question here. Do we really have to see how each answer choice maps onto the passage? Nah. Remember, POE is your best friend! It tells you that it's safe to get rid of (A), because the phrase "only environmental" is too extreme to be a correct answer on the PSAT. (D) predicts the future, which is never a good idea—who says that a cure *will* be found? What if the planet gets hit by a comet first? Now we can go to the passage and discover that (B) is contradicted by the passage, which says that Parkinson's "becomes more severe over time," and (E) is not supported by the passage. But (C), on the other hand, must be true if recent studies have made discoveries about early-onset Parkinson's, as the passage indicates, and *must be true* is what we want on inference questions. (C) it is!

BEYOND THE BASICS

In addition to the techniques we've discussed so far, we have a few final points to round out our repertoire.

Literary Terms

There may be one or two questions on the test that ask about the literary devices the author uses to make a point. These aren't anything to be afraid of; they're usually relatively simple once you know the terminology, but they can be skipped if you're very uncomfortable with this question type. ETS tends to stick to the basics, so let's do some review:

- A **simile** (not to be confused with a smiley) is a comparison using "like" or "as." *The smoke curled out of the chimney like a snake being charmed out of its basket.*
- A **metaphor** is a figure of speech that is technically false but that suggests a likeness or analogy. When Romeo says that *Juliet is the sun*, he doesn't mean that she is literally a big ball of hydrogen gas 93 million miles away; he means that she *resembles* the sun in that she is radiant and makes him feel warm all over and stuff.
- An **extended metaphor** occurs when a metaphor is, you guessed it, extended to cover several comparisons. *From the top of the building, the people below were ants, scurrying to and fro with their parcels, stopping briefly to touch antennae in greeting, and disappearing back into their tunnels to continue their work.*
- **Personification** is the treatment of something inanimate as if it were alive. *The sun smiles down upon the trees and flowers.*
- **Hyperbole** is deliberate exaggeration. *I beat your PSAT score by about a trillion points.*
- **Verbal irony** occurs when there is a discrepancy between what someone says and what the situation indicates the speaker meant. *You dropped your car keys into the sewer? Smooth move!* Sarcasm is probably the most common type of verbal irony: It's verbal irony used to hurt someone's feelings.
- **Situational irony** occurs when people plan for events to turn out one way, but they turn out another. Contrary to the Alanis Morissette song, rain on your wedding day isn't ironic. It's a bummer, but there's no reason not to expect it. On the other hand, moving your wedding from Seattle to Phoenix to avoid the chance of rain, and then having a downpour in Phoenix on your wedding day while it's clear and sunny in Seattle—*that's* ironic.
- A **paradox** is a statement that looks like a contradiction, yet is actually true in a sense. *Less is more.*

Dual Passages

You will probably see one or more dual passages, which are passages that relate to each other somehow with questions that cover both of them. Dual passages can be short or long passages, and there will always be some differences in how the authors view the topic. Dual passages can have questions that ask about only one passage in addition to questions that ask about both passages; the questions that ask about both passages are usually more difficult, so the best strategy is:

1. Work Passage 1 and the questions that ask about only Passage 1.
2. Work Passage 2 and the questions that ask about only Passage 2.
3. Work the questions that ask about both passages.

It's especially important in dealing with the third step to get your own answers and write them down; just like two-blank Sentence Completions, these can be tricky if you try to deal with too much information at once. Below is an example of a typical dual passage and some questions that you might see on the PSAT.

Passage 1

Dreams of sending a manned mission to Mars are unlikely to come to fruition without the implementation of what NASA terms In Situ Resource Utilization (ISRU)
Line strategies: the use of Martian resources to support the
5 expedition. Scientists believe that the Martian landscape could yield the rocket fuel, energy, water, and oxygen necessary for a sustained human presence on the Red Planet. Without the use of ISRUs, the cost of transporting fuel, materials, and vital supplies from Earth would be prohibitive,
10 not to mention potentially dangerous. Despite the eagerness of scientists to explore Mars, no one would advocate sending explorers some forty million miles from Earth with no viable way of returning.

Passage 2

While sending a person to Mars would certainly represent
15 a triumph of human ingenuity and courage, the current state of technology makes such a mission unlikely in the near future. Some optimists argue that we can simply apply the lessons learned in sending people to the Moon to this more formidable situation. But there are forty million miles
20 separating Mars from Earth, a vast distance. As one scientist stated, "A distress message from the Moon would reach Earth in 1.8 seconds. But that same message would take almost 10 minutes to reach us from Mars. The time lag could be fatal." With so many pressing scientific issues here on Earth,
25 time and money should not be spent on a mission that would contribute more to human vanity than to scientific progress.

Let's begin with question 9.

_____○_____

9. The author of Passage 1 argues that ISRUs

(A) are prohibitively expensive
(B) reduce dangers of spaceflight
(C) can generate food and water
(D) will solve certain problems
(E) have not yet been built

Here's How to Crack It

The author of Passage 1 explains that ISRUs would allow humans on Mars to generate a variety of resources that would be too expensive to bring to Mars. Choice A is wrong because the author does not say that ISRUs are too expensive; *transporting needed resources* would be too expensive. Choice B doesn't quite work because author doesn't say that ISRUs reduce the dangers of spaceflight. Choice C is half right, which means all wrong—we are not told that ISRUs can generate food. There is no discussion of whether ISRUs have been built yet, so choice E is wrong. Choice D is the best answer.

_____○_____

Now let's try some questions about both passages.

_____○_____

10. The authors of both passages would most likely agree that

(A) a non-manned mission to Mars should be undertaken
(B) ISRUs are essential to certain manned space voyages
(C) scientific issues on Earth require immediate attention
(D) distress signals from the moon travel to Earth too slowly
(E) the distance between Mars and Earth poses challenges

Here's How to Crack It

For question 10, it's a good idea to deal with each author separately. Let's start with the author of Passage 1. Author 1 did not discuss non-manned missions, so we can eliminate choice A. Author 1 believes that ISRUs are necessary to a mission to Mars, so hold on to choice B. Author 1 does not discuss scientific issues on Earth, so we can eliminate choice C. Author 1 also doesn't discuss distress signals, so eliminate choice D. Author 1 certainly agrees with choice E: ISRUs are meant to address those challenges. So we've narrowed our answers down to choices B and E. Now let's examine whether the author of Passage 2 would agree with either of those. Author 2 does not address ISRUs, so eliminate choice B. Author 2 opposes manned travel to Mars because of certain challenges. Choice E is the best answer.

11. Compared to the author of Passage 1, the author of Passage 2 is more

(A) foreboding
(B) judgmental
(C) ambivalent
(D) optimistic
(E) sympathetic

Here's How to Crack It

Question 11, with its one-word answers, asks you to compare the attitudes of the two authors. The author of Passage 1 supports manned space travel to Mars with ISRUs. The author of Passage 2 opposes manned missions to Mars because of potentially fatal dangers. Choice A, *foreboding*, is a good description of Author 2's attitude and is correct. It would be difficult to call Author 2 judgmental, as opposed to worried, so choice B does not work. Certainly the more positive choices in D and E don't work. Authors are rarely ambivalent in PSAT passages, and Author 2 is no exception.

12. The author of Passage 2 would most likely respond to the author of Passage 1's proposal to use ISRUs by

(A) agreeing that ISRUs could make a manned trip to Mars possible
(B) questioning whether ISRUs are sufficiently developed at this time
(C) arguing that ISRUs do not address key risks of a manned Mars mission
(D) insisting that manned space travel should never be attempted
(E) claiming that scientific issues on the Moon should be resolved first

Here's How to Crack It

When asked what the author of one passage would say about the other passage, as in question 12, consider what the author *did* say on the topic referenced in the question. Here, although Author 2 does not explicitly discuss ISRUs, there is no question that the author is against manned space travel to Mars because of potentially fatal risks. So choice A is easy to eliminate as Author 2 does not support the use of ISRUs. Likewise, we don't know whether Author 2 believes ISRUs are developed enough or not, so eliminate choice B. Choice D is too extreme; Author 2 opposes manned space travel to Mars, but not necessarily *all* manned space travel ever. Choice E is wrong because of the reference to the Moon—Author 2 is interested in scientific issues on *Earth*. Choice C is the best choice: Author 2 specifically mentions the travel time of distress signals as a key risk; ISRUs can do nothing to address that risk.

Down to 2

Last but certainly not least, one final word about POE: Just about all test takers get to a point, particularly on passage-based reading questions, at which they're going back and forth between two answers, trying to decide which is better. At this point, stop yourself from arguing FOR each answer choice ("I like this one because…") and start actively finding a reason to eliminate one or the other ("This one doesn't sound right because..."). You can use the following steps in any order, together or separately, to help you get down to one answer choice.

- **Find the bad part.** Four out of five answer choices have *something* in them that makes them wrong, whether it is a word that's too extreme, a small phrase that's not supported by the passage, or something that's outside the scope of the passage. And usually, you're tempted to pick that answer choice anyway because the rest of it is exactly what you think the correct answer is. But you wouldn't buy a pair of shoes in which one fits really well and the other doesn't fit at all, would you? Well, the same goes for Critical Reading answer choices—find one part that's bad, and you can eliminate the whole answer choice.
- **Find the difference.** ETS won't put two identical answer choices on the PSAT. Either the answers will say different things, or they will say nearly the same thing in different ways; for example, one is phrased in a more extreme way than the other. Focus on the differences between the answers and you'll have an easier time figuring out which one is better supported by the passage and which one has the flaw. Don't be afraid to go back to the passage and look for flaws: Is the information really there? Does it answer the question?

Summary

o Long Passages
  - Read the blurb
  - Quickly read the passage for the main idea
  - Choose a question and paraphrase it
  - Read what you need to answer the question
  - Answer in your own words
  - POE

o Short Passages
  - Read the passage for the general idea
  - Paraphrase the question
  - Read what you need to answer the question
  - Answer in your own words
  - POE

o Dual Passages
  - First, attack questions about Passage 1 only
  - Next, do questions about Passage 2 only
  - Last, attempt questions about both passages

o Down to 2
  - Eliminate based on a careful reading of each answer to try to find the "bad part"
  - Eliminate based on the differences between the remaining answers

o Literary Terms
  - Remember to study them, even if it's just to be familiar enough to skip them!

Chapter 7
Math Basics

One of the more humiliating aspects of the PSAT (and the same applies to its big brother, the SAT) is that ETS claims that the Math section tests only sixth- to ninth-grade math. While this may be technically true—you'll see no trigonometry or calculus, only concepts that you'll have learned in algebra and geometry—what they don't tell you is that they will use these concepts in very sneaky ways. This chapter will help you lay the foundation to avoid the test writers' traps.

HOW TO CONQUER PSAT MATH

So what do you need to do? There are three important steps:

1. **Know the basic content.** Obviously you do need to know the basics of arithmetic, algebra, and geometry and to know this stuff cold. We'll cover what you need to know in this chapter.
2. **Learn some PSAT-specific problem-solving skills.** Since these basic concepts appear in ways you're probably not used to from math class, you need to prepare yourself with a set of test-specific problem-solving skills designed to help you solve PSAT Math problems. We'll cover the most important ones in the next chapter.
3. **Have a sound overall testing strategy.** This means knowing the order of difficulty of questions, and having a plan to pace yourself to get the maximum number of points in the time allotted. Be sure to read carefully the material in Chapter 4, to make sure you're using the strategy that will get you the greatest number of points in the time you have.

ORDER OF DIFFICULTY

The Math sections on the PSAT are Sections 2 and 4. Section 2 contains 20 multiple-choice questions. Section 4 is divided into multiple-choice and grid-in question types. Note that the order of difficulty goes from easy to hard within each of these types. For instance, on Section 4, number 28, the last multiple-choice question will be hard, but number 29, the first grid-in question, will be easy. This means that if you're going to skip some problems in Section 4, it's likely that you'll want to skip some of the questions numbered 27–28 and 36–38.

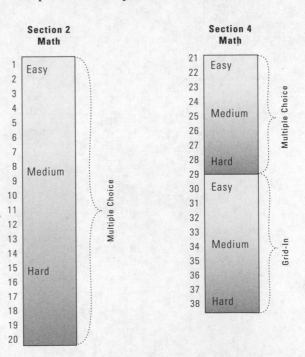

USING YOUR CALCULATOR

You are allowed to use a calculator on the PSAT, and you should definitely do so. You can use any graphing, scientific, or plain old four-function calculator, **provided that it doesn't have a keyboard**.

There are a few simple rules to remember when dealing with your calculator:

1. Use the calculator you're most comfortable with. You definitely don't want to be trying to find the right button on test day. Ideally, you should be practicing with the same calculator you'll use on test day.
2. Change your batteries the week before the test. If they run out during the test, there's nothing you can do about it.
3. Be sure to hit the "clear" or "on/off" button after each calculation to reset the calculator after an operation. A common mistake to make when using your calculator is to forget to clear your last result.
4. Your calculator is very good at calculating, but watch out for mis-keying information. (If you type the wrong numbers in, you'll get the wrong result.) Check each number on the display as you key it in.
5. Remember that, while it's nice to have all those funky scientific functions (like sine, cosine, etc.), you'll never need them on the PSAT. The most you'll need is the basic operations of addition, subtraction, multiplication, and division; the ability to convert fractions to decimals and vice versa; and the ability to do square roots and exponents.
6. Then, there's one really big, important rule whenever you think about using your calculator:

> A calculator can't think; it can only calculate.

What does this mean? It means that a calculator can't think through a problem for you. You have to do the work of understanding and setting up the problem correctly to make sure you know what the right calculation will be to get the answer. Only then can you use the calculator to calculate the answer. A calculator can't replace good problem-solving skills. It can only help make sure that you do basic calculations correctly.

Also, your calculator can't help you set up a problem in the way pencil and paper can. You should always be sure to set up the problem in your test booklet—writing it down is still the best method—this will help you catch any errors you might make and allow you to pick up where you left off if you lose focus.

That doesn't mean you won't use your calculator, though…far from it. Once you have set up a math problem, move quickly to your calculator to chug your way through the arithmetic, and be careful to enter each number and operator correctly. Remember, using your calculator is already saving you time—don't rush and lose the advantage that it gives you.

Drill 1

DEFINITIONS

One of the reasons that good math students often don't get the credit they deserve on the PSAT is that they've forgotten one or more of these definitions—or they read too fast and skip over these "little" words. Be sure you know them cold and watch out for them!

Match the words with their definitions, and then come up with some examples. Answers can be found in Part III.

1. integers

2. positive numbers

3. negative numbers

4. even numbers

5. odd numbers

6. factors

7. multiples

8. prime numbers

9. distinct

a. numbers that a certain number can be divided by, leaving no remainder
   Examples: _____

b. numbers in a row
   Examples: _____

c. the result of multiplication
   Examples: _____

d. numbers that are greater than zero
   Examples: _____

e. having a different value
   Examples: _____

f. integers that can be divided by 2 evenly (with no remainder)
   Examples: _____

g. the result of addition
   Examples: _____

h. a number's distance from zero; always a positive value
   Examples: _____

i. numbers that can be divided by a certain number with no remainder
   Examples: _____

10.	digit	j.	a figure from 0 through 9 that is used as a placeholder Examples: _____
11.	consecutive numbers	k.	numbers that are less than zero Examples: _____
12.	divisible		
13.	remainder	l.	a whole number that is left over after you divide Examples: _____
14.	sum		
15.	product	m.	the result of subtraction Examples: _____
16.	difference		
17.	quotient	n.	can be divided with no remainder Examples: _____
18.	absolute value		
		o.	numbers that have exactly two distinct factors: themselves and one Examples: _____
		p.	integers that cannot be divided evenly by 2 Examples: _____
		q.	the result of division Examples: _____
		r.	numbers that have no fractional or decimal parts Examples: _____

Finding Factors

The easiest way to find the complete list of the factors of a number is to begin trying all the integers beginning with 1, and see which of the integers go into that number without remainders. For instance, let's find the factors of 36.

Negative Land
Think of integers as steps on a staircase leading up from the cellar (the negatives), through a doorway (zero), and above the ground (the positives). Five steps down (–5) is farther below ground than four steps down (–4) because you're one step farther away from the cellar door (0). Integers are like stairs because when climbing stairs, you can't use a fraction of a step.

Factor List:
Does 1 go into 36? Yes, 1 times 36.
Does 2 go into 36? Yes, 2 times 18.
Does 3 go into 36? Yes, 3 times 12.
Does 4 go into 36? Yes, 4 times 9.
Does 5 go into 36? No.
Does 6 go into 36? Yes, 6 times 6.

Once you get to an integer that you've already seen in the factor list (in this case, 6) you know you're finished. So the factors of 36 are 1, 2, 3, 4, 6, 9, 12, 18, and 36.

Let's try this once more. What are all the factors of 40?

Does 1 go into 40? Yes, 1 times 40.
Does 2 go into 40? Yes, 2 times 20.
Does 3 go into 40? No.
Does 4 go into 40? Yes, 4 times 10.
Does 5 go into 40? Yes, 5 times 8.
Does 6 go into 40? No.
Does 7 go into 40? No.

Remember
Every positive integer is its own greatest factor and least multiple.

We don't have to try 8, since the number 8 has already appeared in our list of factors. So the factors of 40 are 1, 2, 4, 5, 8, 10, 20, and 40.

Having trouble remembering the difference between *factors* and *multiples*? Try this mnemonic:

Factors are Few, Multiples are Many.

Twelve is a number that has a relatively large number of *factors*, but it still has only six of them. The *multiples* of 12, on the other hand, go on forever. Every number has an infinite number of multiples.

Prime Factors

When you need to find the **prime factors** of a number, you can make a prime factor tree. Let's say you need to find the prime factors of 60.

Start by writing down the number you're going to factor.

Then factor out the primes one at a time. The first prime number is 2, so that's where we'll start. 60 divided by 2 is 30, so we can draw branches for the 2 and 30.

Now let's move on to 30. 30 is also divisible by 2 (30 ÷ 2 = 15), so we can draw branches for 2 and 15.

Fifteen is not divisible by 2, so we move on to the next prime number: 3. Fifteen divided by 3 is 5, so we can draw branches for 3 and 5.

Five is prime, so we're done! The prime factors of 60 are 2, 2, 3, and 5. Remember, though, if a problem asked for the *distinct* prime factors of 60, your answer would be 2, 3, and 5.

Managing Multiples

One type of question you'll see frequently on the PSAT involves finding common multiples. The easiest way to find a common multiple is to start listing out the multiples of the numbers you're given until you find which ones they have in common.

Here are some examples.

---

4. If a number p is a positive multiple of both 3 and 8,
    p must also be a multiple of

    (A)   5
    (B)   11
    (C)   12
    (D)   14
    (E)   18

Here's How to Crack It

Let's start by listing the multiples of 3: 3, 6, 9, 12, 15, 18, 21, 24, 27…. Now let's list the multiples of 8: 8, 16, 24, 32, 40….

Which numbers belong to both groups? 24 does. So the numbers that are multiples of both 3 and 8 must be multiples of 24. Of course, 24 itself isn't listed as an answer (that would be too easy.) But 24 (and every multiple of 24) will have a factor of 12 in it, so the answer is (C).

5. How many integers between 1 and 100 are multiples of both 4 and 6 ?

    (A)   8
    (B) 12
    (C) 18
    (D) 22
    (E) 24

Here's How to Crack It

Let's start by listing the multiples of 4: 4, 8, 12, 16, 20, 24, 28…. Now the multiples of 6: 6, 12, 18, 24, 30….

After just a few multiples, you should be able to see the pattern. The numbers 12 and 24 (and likewise, every multiple of 12: the numbers 36, 48, etc., will also work) are the common multiples of both 4 and 6. So the real question is, how many multiples of 12 are there between 1 and 100? That's not too difficult to figure out. We can list them out with the help of a calculator: 12, 24, 36, 48, 60, 72, 84, 96. So there are a total of 8, and that's (A).

Drill 2

Answers can be found in Part III.

a. What are 3 consecutive odd integers whose sum is 15?
_____ _____ _____

b. What are the factors of 10? _____ _____ _____ _____

c. What are the prime factors of 10? _____ _____

d. What are the factors of 48? _____ _____ _____ _____ _____ _____
_____ _____ _____ _____

e. What are the prime factors of 48? _____ _____

f. What are the first 7 positive multiples of 6? _____ _____ _____
_____ _____ _____ _____

g. What are the first 7 positive multiples of 4? _____ _____ _____
_____ _____ _____ _____

h. Numbers that are multiples of both 6 and 7 are also multiples of _____.

i. The product of two positive integers x and y is 30 and their sum is 11.
What are x and y? _____ and _____

j. The product of two positive integers x and y is 30 and their difference
is 13. What are x and y? _____ and _____

1. Which of the following does NOT have a remainder of 1 ?

    (A) $\dfrac{15}{7}$

    (B) $\dfrac{17}{8}$

    (C) $\dfrac{51}{3}$

    (D) $\dfrac{61}{4}$

    (E) $\dfrac{81}{10}$

2. Which of the following numbers has the digit 4 in the
thousandths place?

    (A) 4000.0
    (B)   40.0
    (C)   0.4
    (D)   0.04
    (E)   0.004

3. Which of the following numbers is NOT prime?

(A) 11
(B) 23
(C) 27
(D) 29
(E) 31

4. Which of the following is the least of 3 consecutive integers if their sum is 21 ?

(A) 4
(B) 5
(C) 6
(D) 7
(E) 8

5. If a, b, c, d, and e are consecutive even integers, and $a < b < c < d < e$, then $d + e$ is how much greater than $a + b$?

(A) 10
(B) 12
(C) 14
(D) 16
(E) 18

6. All numbers divisible by both 3 and 14 are also divisible by which of the following?

(A) 6
(B) 9
(C) 16
(D) 28
(E) 32

Exponents and Square Roots

Exponents are just a shorthand for multiplication. Instead of writing $3 \times 3 \times 3 \times 3$, you can write 3^4. Thus, you can handle exponents by expanding them out if necessary.

$$y^2 \times y^3 = y \times y \times y \times y \times y = y^5$$

$$\frac{y^4}{y^2} = \frac{y \times y \times y \times y}{y \times y} = y \times y = y^2$$

However, you can also multiply and divide exponents that have the same base using a shortcut called MADSPM. MADSPM also helps you remember how to deal with raising exponents to another power. Let's see the breakdown:

- **MA** means when you see a MULTIPLICATION sign, ADD the exponents. So $y^2 \times y^3 = y^{2+3} = y^5$.
- **DS** means when you see a DIVISION sign (or fraction), SUBTRACT the exponents. So $\frac{y^5}{y^2} = y^{5-2} = y^3$.

- **PM** means when you see an exponent raised to a POWER, MULTIPLY the exponents. So $(y^2)^3 = y^{2 \times 3} = y^6$. (This is really easy to confuse with multiplication, so watch out!)

Be careful, because the rules of MADSPM don't work for addition and subtraction. For example, $3^2 + 3^5$ does NOT equal 3^7. (Crunch it on your calculator if you want to prove it.)

Here are some additional rules to remember about exponents:

- Anything to the zero power equals 1: $3^0 = 1$. Mathematicians argue about whether 0^0 is 1 or is undefined, but that won't come up on the PSAT.
- Anything to the first power equals itself: $3^1 = 3$.
- 1 to any power equals 1: $1^{3876} = 1$.
- A negative exponent means to take the reciprocal of what would be the result if the negative weren't there: $2^{-2} = \frac{1}{2^2} = \frac{1}{4}$.
- A fractional exponent has two parts (like any other fraction), the numerator, which is the power the base is raised to, and the denominator, which is the root of the base. For example, $8^{2/3} = \sqrt[3]{8^2} = \sqrt[3]{64} = 4$

Warning
The rules for multiplying and dividing exponents do not apply to addition or subtraction:
$2^2 + 2^3 = 12$
$(2 \times 2) + (2 \times 2 \times 2) = 12$
It does not equal 2^5 or 32.

Remember that in calculating the value of a root, you're looking for what number multiplied by itself results in the number under the radical. In the above example, $\sqrt[3]{64} = 4$ because $4 \times 4 \times 4 = 64$.

When you see the square root sign, that means to take the positive root only. So, $\sqrt{9} = 3$, but not -3.

Square roots work just like exponents: You can *always* multiply and divide roots, but you can only add and subtract with the *same* root.

Multiplication and Division:

$$\sqrt{8} \times \sqrt{2} = \sqrt{8 \times 2} = \sqrt{16} = 4$$

$$\sqrt{\frac{1}{4}} = \frac{\sqrt{1}}{\sqrt{4}} = \frac{1}{2}$$

$$\sqrt{300} = \sqrt{100 \times 3} = \sqrt{100} \times \sqrt{3} = 10\sqrt{3}$$

Addition and Subtraction:

$$2\sqrt{2} + 3\sqrt{2} = 5\sqrt{2}$$

$$4\sqrt{3} - \sqrt{3} = 3\sqrt{3}$$

$2\sqrt{3} + 3\sqrt{2}$ *Cannot be added without a calculator since the terms do not have the same root.*

Drill 3

Answers can be found in Part III.

a. $3^3 \times 3^2 = $ _____

b. $\dfrac{3^3}{3^2} = $ _____

c. $\left(3^3\right)^2 = $ _____

d. $x^6 \times x^2 = $ _____

e. $\dfrac{x^6}{x^2} = $ _____

f. $\left(x^6\right)^2 = $ _____

3. If $3^4 = 9^x$, then $x = $

    (A) 2
    (B) 3
    (C) 4
    (D) 5
    (E) 6

5. If $\left(3^x\right)^3 = 3^{15}$, what is the value of x ?

    (A) 3
    (B) 5
    (C) 7
    (D) 9
    (E) 12

11. If $x^y x^6 = x^{54}$ and $\left(x^3\right)^z = x^9$, then $y + z = $

    (A) 10
    (B) 11
    (C) 12
    (D) 48
    (E) 51

Equations and Inequalities

An **equation** is a statement that contains an equals sign, such as $3x + 5 = 17$.

To solve an equation, you want to get the variable x alone on one side of the equals sign and everything else on the other side.

The first step is to put all of the variables on one side of the equation and all of the numbers on the other side, using addition and subtraction. As long as you perform the same operation on both sides of the equals sign, you aren't changing the value of the variable.

Then you can divide both sides of the equation by the *coefficient*, which is the number in front of the variable. If that number is a fraction, you can multiply everything by its reciprocal.

For example: $3x + 5 = 17$

$$
\begin{array}{rcl}
3x + 5 & = & 17 \\
\underline{-5 \qquad -5} & & \text{Subtract 5 from each side.} \\
3x & = & 12 \\
\underline{\div 3 \qquad\quad \div 3} & & \text{Divide each side by 3.} \\
x & = & 4
\end{array}
$$

Always remember the rule of equations:

> *Whatever you do to one side of the equation, you must also do to the other side.*

An **inequality** is any statement with one of these signs:

- $<$ (less than)
- $>$ (greater than)
- $\leq$ (less than or equal to)
- $\geq$ (greater than or equal to)

You can solve inequalities in the same way you solve equations, with one exception: Whenever you multiply or divide an inequality by a negative value, you must change the direction of the sign: $<$ becomes $>$, and $\leq$ becomes $\geq$.

For example: $3x + 5 > 17$

$$
\begin{array}{rll}
3x + 5 & > & 17 \\
-5 & & -5 \quad \text{Subtract 5 from each side.} \\
\hline
3x & > & 12 \\
\div 3 & & \div 3 \quad \text{Divide each side by 3.} \\
\hline
x & > & 4
\end{array}
$$

In this case, we didn't multiply or divide by a negative value, so the direction of the sign didn't change. However, if we were to divide by a negative value, we would need to change the direction of the sign.

$$
\begin{array}{rll}
-4x + 3 & > & 15 \\
-3 & & -3 \quad \text{Subtract 3 from each side.} \\
\hline
-4x & > & 12 \\
\div -4 & & \div -4 \quad \text{Divide each side by } -4. \\
\hline
x & < & -3
\end{array}
$$

Simultaneous Equations

Simultaneous equations occur when you have two equations at the same time. They're easier to deal with than they appear. All you have to do is stack the equations, and then add or subtract them.

12. If $x - 2y = 10$ and $3x + 4y = 5$, then $4x + 2y =$

(A) 5
(B) 9
(C) 15
(D) 24
(E) 30

Here's How to Crack It

Just stack the equations, making sure that all the x variables are lined up, all the y variables are lined up, and all the numbers are lined up.

$$
\begin{array}{r}
x - 2y = 10 \\
3x + 4y = 5 \\
\hline
\end{array}
$$

Now you need to decide whether to add the two equations together or subtract one from the other. The question is asking for $4x + 2y$ in this case, so that tells you to add, since $x + 3x = 4x$ and $-2y + 4y = 2y$.

$$
\begin{array}{r}
x - 2y = 10 \\
+ \quad 3x + 4y = 5 \\
\hline
4x + 2y = 15
\end{array}
$$

That's your answer: 15. The question doesn't ask for the values of each variable, so you don't need to worry about figuring out anything else.

———————◯———————

Let's try one more.

———————◯———————

9. If $3x + 2y = 7$ and $2x + 2y = 9$, what is the value of x ?

(A)   −2
(B)   2
(C)   7
(D)   9
(E)   16

Here's How to Crack It
Again, stack your equations.

$$
\begin{array}{l}
3x + 2y = 7 \\
2x + 2y = 9
\end{array}
$$

This time the question asks for the value of x. Would adding the equations or subtracting them give you x alone? Subtracting the second equation from the first one would, because the coefficients for y are the same.

$$
\begin{array}{r}
3x + 2y = 7 \\
- \quad 2x + 2y = 9 \\
\hline
x = -2
\end{array}
$$

The y variables cancel out, and you get −2 for your answer.

———————◯———————

GEOMETRY DEFINITIONS

Lines and Angles

Common sense might tell you what a line is, but for this test you are going to have to learn the particulars of a line, a ray, and a line segment.

A **line** continues on in each direction forever. You need only two points to form a line, but that line does not end at those points. A straight line has 180 degrees on each side.

A **ray** is a line with one distinct endpoint. Again, you need only two points to designate a ray, but one of those points is where it stops—it continues on forever in the other direction. A ray has 180 degrees as well.

A **line segment** is a line with two distinct endpoints. It requires two points, and it is the length from one point to the other. A line segment has 180 degrees.

Whenever you have angles on a line, remember *the rule of 180*: The angles on any line must add up to 180. In the figure below, what is the value of x? We know that $2x + x$ must add up to 180, so we know that $3x = 180$. This makes $x = 60$.

If two lines cross each other, they make *vertical angles*. These angles will always have the same measure. In the figure below, we know that z must equal 50, since $130 + z$ must equal 180. We know that y is 130, since it is across from the angle 130. We also know that x is 50, since it is across from z.

Any time you have two parallel lines and a line that crosses them, you have two kinds of angles: big angles and small angles. All of the big angles have the same measure, and all of the small angles have the same measure. In the following figure, angles a, d, e, and h all have the same measure; angles b, c, f, and g also all have the same measure.

Four-Sided Figures

Thinking Inside the Box
Here's a progression of quadrilaterals from least specific to most specific:
quadrilateral = 4-sided figure
↓
parallelogram =
a quadrilateral in which opposite sides are parallel
↓
rectangle =
a parallelogram in which all angles equal 90°
↓
square =
a rectangle in which all sides are equal

A figure with two sets of parallel sides is a **parallelogram**. In a parallelogram, the opposite angles are equal, and any adjacent angles add up to 180 degrees. (In the figure above, $x + y = 180$ degrees.) Opposite sides are also equal.

If all of the angles are also right angles, then the figure is a **rectangle**. And if all of the sides are the same length, then the figure is a **square**.

The *area* of a square, rectangle, or parallelogram is *length* × *width*. (In the parallelogram above, the length is shown by the dotted line.)

The *perimeter* of any figure is the sum of the lengths of its sides. A triangle with sides 3, 4, and 5 has a perimeter of 12.

Triangles

The sum of the angles inside a triangle must equal 180 degrees. This means that if you know two of the angles in a triangle, you can always solve for the third. Since we know that two of the angles in the following figure are 90 and 60 degrees, we can solve for the third angle, which must be 30 degrees.

An **isosceles triangle** is a triangle that has two sides that are equal. Angles that are opposite equal sides must be equal. In the figure below, we have an isosceles triangle. Since $AB = BC$, we know that angles x and y are equal. And since their sum must be 150 degrees (to make a total of 180 degrees when we add the last angle), they each must be 75 degrees.

The **area** of a triangle is $\frac{1}{2}$ *base × height*. Note that the height is always perpendicular to the base.

$$\text{Area} = \frac{1}{2} \times 10 \times 4 = 20 \qquad\qquad \text{Area} = \frac{1}{2} \times 6 \times 4 = 12$$

An **equilateral triangle** has all three sides equal and all of its angles equal to 60 degrees.

Here's a typical example of a PSAT question on triangles.

---

13. In triangle *ABC* above, *x* =

(A) 30
(B) 40
(C) 50
(D) 60
(E) 70

Here's How to Crack It
We know that the angle adjacent to the 100-degree angle must equal 80 degrees since we know that a straight line is 180 degrees. Fill it in on your diagram. Now, since we know that the sum of the angles contained in a triangle must equal 180 degrees, we know that $80 + 60 + x = 180$, so $x = 40$. That's (B).

Third Side Rule

Suppose you don't know anything about a triangle except the lengths of two of its sides. You can also then figure out that the third side must be between certain values, that is, the length of the third side must be less than the sum of the other two and greater than the difference.

> *The third side of a triangle is always less than the sum of the other two sides and greater than the difference between them.*

Why? Consider a triangle that looks like this:

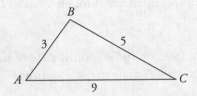

The shortest distance between two points is a straight line, right? And yet in this figure, the straight-line distance from *A* to *C* is 9, yet the scenic route from *A* to *B* to *C* is…8? That can't be right! And it isn't. The crooked path must be longer than the straight path, and thus any two sides of a triangle added together must be longer than the third side. In this example, 2 < *AC* < 8.

---

14. Which of the following is a possible perimeter of a triangle with sides 5 and 8 ?

    (A) 15
    (B) 16
    (C) 17
    (D) 26
    (E) 30

No Figures?
Draw one before you do anything else.

Here's How to Crack It

To find the perimeter of a triangle, you just need to add up the sides of the triangle, so let's see what we know about the sides. We know that the two given sides add up to 13, so the perimeter will be 13 + the third side. The third side will be between the sum and difference of those other two sides. 8 + 5 = 13 and 8 − 5 = 3, so the third side will be greater than 3 and less than 13. Add these to the sum of the sides we already know (13), and the perimeter must be between 16 (13 + 3) and 26 (13 + 13). The only answer choice that fits the bill is (C).

Circles

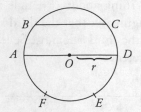

The **radius** of a circle is the distance from the center to the edge of the circle. In the figure above, *OD* is a radius. So is *OA*.

The **diameter** is the distance from one edge, through the center, to the other edge of the circle. The diameter will always be twice the measure of the radius and will always be the longest line you can draw through a circle. In the figure above, *AD* is the diameter.

A **chord** is any line drawn from one point on the edge of the circle to the other. In the figure above, *BC* is a chord. A diameter is also a chord.

An **arc** is any section of the circumference (the edge) of the circle. *EF* is an arc in the figure above.

The **area** of a circle with radius r is πr^2. A circle with a radius of 5 has an area of 25π.

The **circumference** is the distance around the outside edge of the circle. The circumference of a circle with radius r is $2\pi r$. A circle with radius of 5 has a circumference of 10π.

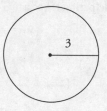

Area = 9π

Circumference = 6π

Area = 25π

Circumference = 10π

THE COORDINATE PLANE

You'll probably see one or two questions on the PSAT that involve the coordinate plane. The biggest mistake that people make on these questions is getting the *x*- and *y*-axes reversed. So let's just review:

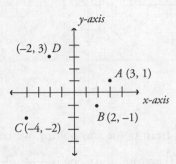

The *x*-axis is the horizontal axis, and the *y*-axis is the vertical axis. Points are given on the coordinate plane with the *x*-coordinate first. Positive *x*-values go to the right, and negative ones go to the left; positive *y*-values go up, and negative ones go down. So point *A* (3, 1) is 3 points to the right on the *x*-axis and 1 point up from there. Point *B* (2, –1) is two points to the right on the *x*-axis and 1 point down from there.

Slope is a measure of the steepness of a line on the coordinate plane. On most slope problems you need to recognize only whether the slope is positive, negative, or zero. A line that goes up and to the right has positive slope; a line that goes down and to the right has negative slope, and a flat line has zero slope. In the figure below, line 1 has positive slope, line 2 has zero slope, and line 3 has negative slope.

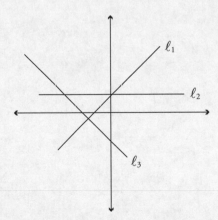

If you do need to calculate the slope, and the graph is drawn for you, here's how: slope = $\dfrac{y_2 - y_1}{x_2 - x_1}$. The *slope* of a line is equal to $\dfrac{rise}{run}$. To find the slope, take any two points on the line and count off the distance you need to get from one of these points to the other.

In the graph above, to get from point x to point y, we count up (rise) 3 units, and count over (run) 3 units. Therefore, the slope is $\frac{rise}{run} = \frac{3}{3} = 1$. Always remember to check whether the slope is positive or negative when you use $\frac{rise}{run}$.

If you're not given a figure and you can't draw one easily using the points given, you can find the slope by plugging the coordinates you know into the slope formula. The slope formula is $slope = \frac{y_2 - y_1}{x_2 - x_1}$. Just remember to plug the numbers into the formula carefully!

Drill 4

Answers can be found in Part III.

a. What is the area of square *ABCD* above? _____

b. What is the area of triangle *XYZ* above? _____

c. If the area of the triangle above is 400, what is the length of *AC* ?
_____

d. What is the area of the circle above with center *O* ? _____
e. What is its circumference? _____

f. If *ABCD* is a rectangle, *x* = _____ *y* = _____
g. What is the perimeter of rectangle *ABCD* ? _____

h. If the above figure is composed of two rectangles, what is the perimeter of the figure? _____

i. How many units do you count up (rise) to get from point *B* to point *A* ? _____

j. How many units must you count over (run) to get from point *A* to point *B* ? _____

k. What is the slope of the line above? _____ (Remember, the line is going down to the right so it must have a negative slope.)

17. If *ABCD* is a square, what is the area of the square?

(A) 2
(B) 4
(C) 20
(D) 25
(E) 36

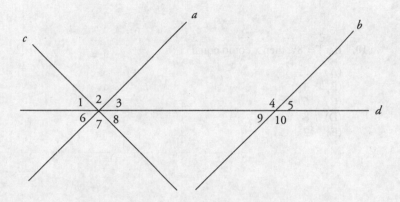

10. In the figure above, lines *a* and *b* are parallel. Which of the following pairs of angles must have equal degree measures?

  I. 1 and 5
 II. 2 and 7
III. 3 and 9

(A) None
(B) I only
(C) II only
(D) III only
(E) II and III only

$$x + 2y = 12$$
$$2x + y = 9$$

19. Given the system of equations above, what is the value of $x + y$?

(A) 3

(B) 7

(C) $\dfrac{21}{2}$

(D) 21

(E) It cannot be determined from the information given.

10. If $x^{\frac{5}{2}} = 8x$, then x could equal

(A) 2
(B) 4
(C) 6
(D) 8
(E) 12

PROBABILITY AND COUNTING

Probability refers to the chance that an event will happen, and is always given as a fraction between 0 and 1, inclusive. A probability of 0 means that the event will never happen; a probability of 1 means that it is certain to happen.

$$\text{Probability} = \frac{\text{number of outcomes you want}}{\text{number of possible outcomes}}$$

For instance, if you have a die with faces numbered 1 to 6, what is the chance of rolling a 2? There is one face with the number 2 on it, out of 6 total faces. Therefore, the probability of rolling a 2 is $\frac{1}{6}$.

What is the chance of rolling an even number on one roll of this die? There are 3 faces of the die with an even number (the sides numbered 2, 4, and 6) out of a total of 6 faces. Therefore, the probability of rolling an even number is $\frac{3}{6}$, or $\frac{1}{2}$.

Let's try one.

7. In a jar there are 3 green gumballs, 5 red gumballs, 8 white gumballs, and 1 blue gumball. If one gumball is chosen at random, what is the probability that it will be red?

(A) $\dfrac{5}{17}$

(B) $\dfrac{5}{16}$

(C) $\dfrac{1}{17}$

(D) $\dfrac{1}{12}$

(E) $\dfrac{1}{10}$

Here's How to Crack It

To solve this problem, we take the number of things we want (the 5 red gumballs) and place it over the number of possible things we have to choose from (all 17 gumballs in the jar). This gives us choice (A).

1, 2, 3, ... , 1000

Some questions may ask you how many ways something can happen. The trick here is to draw an underline representing each of the spots you need to fill, then for each spot, write in the number of things that could fill that spot. When you're done with all the spots, multiply them.

Let's take a look at an example:

14. Ms. Grady will choose one boy and one girl from her class to be the class representatives. If there are 3 boys and 7 girls in her class, how many different pairs of class representatives could she pick?

(A) 10
(B) 13
(C) 21
(D) 23
(E) 25

Here's How to Crack It

How many spots do we need to fill? Ms. Grady wants a pair of representatives, so we need to fill two spots. One will be a boy and the other a girl, so we need to fill one spot with the number of boys that we have to choose from and the other with the number of girls we have to choose from, then multiply them, so it's $3 \times 7 = 21$, which is choice (C).

Let's try another.

12. Sandra has six trophies, but only has room for three of them on her mantle. How many possible ways can she arrange three of the six trophies on her mantle?

   (A)   18
   (B)   54
   (C)   80
   (D)   120
   (E)   216

Here's How to Crack It

How many places does Sandra have on her mantle in which she can put trophies? She has three, so draw that many underlines. How many choices does she have for what to place in the first spot? She has six, so fill a six into the first underline. Then she has five left to choose from for the second spot and four left to choose from for the last spot; we'll fill in the spots and multiply, $6 \times 5 \times 4 = 120$, so the choice is (D).

Keep Left

No matter how many
digits in your answer,
always start gridding in
the leftmost column. That
way, you'll avoid omitting
digits and losing points.

GRID-INS: THE BASICS

You will see 10 questions on the PSAT that ask you to bubble in a numerical answer on a grid, rather than answer a multiple-choice question. These questions are arranged in order of difficulty and can be solved according to the methods outlined for the multiple-choice problems on the test. Don't worry that there are no answer choices—your approach is the same.

The only difficulty with grid-ins is getting used to the way in which you are asked to answer the question. For each question, you'll have a grid like the following:

We recommend that you write the answer on top of the grid to help you bubble, but it's important to know that the scoring machine only reads the bubbles. *If you bubble incorrectly, the computer will consider the answer to be incorrect.*

Here are the basic rules of gridding:

1. If your answer uses fewer than four boxes, you can grid it anywhere you like.

   To avoid confusion, we suggest that you start at the leftmost box. For example:

2. You can grid your answer as either a fraction or a decimal, *if* the fraction will fit.

You can grid an answer of .5 as either .5 or $\frac{1}{2}$.

or

Relax
If your answer is a fraction and it fits in the grid (fraction bar included), don't reduce it. Why bother? ETS won't give you an extra point. However, if your fraction doesn't fit, reduce it or turn it into a decimal on your calculator.

3. You do not need to reduce your fractions, *if* the fraction will fit.

If your answer is $\frac{2}{4}$, you can grid it as $\frac{2}{4}$, $\frac{1}{2}$, or .5.

or

or

4. If you have a decimal that will not fit in the spaces provided, you *must grid as many places as will fit.*

If your answer is $\frac{2}{3}$, you can grid it as $\frac{2}{3}$, .666, or .667 but .66 is *not* acceptable.

You do *not* need to round your numbers, so we suggest that you don't. There's no reason to give yourself a chance to make a mistake if you don't have to.

or

or

Don't Mix
Never grid in a mixed number. Change it into an improper fraction or decimal.

5. You cannot grid mixed numbers. Convert all mixed numbers to ordinary fractions.

If your answer is $2\frac{1}{2}$, you must convert it to $\frac{5}{2}$ or 2.5, otherwise the computer will read your 2 1/2 as 21/2.

or

6. You can't grid π, square roots, variables or negative numbers, so if you get an answer with one of those terms, you've made a mistake. Check your work.

Drill 5

Answers can be found in Part III.

Note: Figure not drawn to scale.

33. In triangle *ABC* above, if *AB* = *BC,* then *x* =
    (Disregard the degree symbol when gridding your answer.)

34. The sum of five consecutive integers, arranged in order from least to greatest, is 100. What is the sum of the next four consecutive integers?

35. If $5x^2 = 125$, what is the value of $5x^3$?

36. What is the sum of the distinct prime factors of 140 ?

Summary

o   The Math sections are arranged in Order of Difficulty, which can make it easier to spot the less difficult problems. However, remember that the test writers' idea of "easier" problems is not necessarily the same as your idea. Let your Personal Order of Difficulty be your guide.

o   Write in your test booklet to set up problems, and then use your calculator for figuring. And remember to type carefully—your calculator won't check for mistakes.

o   Review basic definitions again before the test to make sure you don't get stuck on the "little words."

o   To tell the difference between factors and multiples, remember that Factors are Few and Multiples are Many.

o   When you have to manipulate exponents, remember your MADSPM rules.

o   Inequalities can be worked just like equations, until you have to divide by a negative. Then you need to flip the inequality sign.

o   Got several equations to work with at once? Just follow the guidelines of Simultaneous Equations: Stack the equations and add or subtract to get what you're looking for.

o   Be sure to review your basic geometry rules before the test; often, problems hinge on knowing that vertical angles are equal or that a quadrilateral has 360 degrees.

o   On all geometry problems, draw figures out and aggressively fill in everything you know.

o   The third side rule says that any side of a triangle must be between the sum and the difference of the other two sides.

o   Probability is always a fraction between 0 and 1 (inclusive), and it is equal to the number of outcomes the question is asking for divided by the total number of possible outcomes.

o   When doing Grid-Ins, be sure to keep to the left, and don't bother reducing fractions if they fit.

Chapter 8
Math Techniques

In the previous chapter, we mentioned that one of the keys to doing well on the PSAT is to have a set of test-specific problem-solving skills. This chapter discusses some powerful strategies, which—though you may not use them in school—are specifically designed to get you points on the PSAT. Learn them well!

PLUGGING IN

One of the most powerful problem-solving skills on the PSAT is a technique we call Plugging In. Plugging In will turn nasty algebra problems into simple arithmetic and help you through the particularly twisted problems that you'll often see on the PSAT. There are several varieties of Plugging In, each suited to a different kind of question.

Plugging In Your Own Numbers

The problem with doing algebra is that it's just too easy to make a mistake.

> Whenever you see a problem with variables in the answer choices, PLUG IN.

Start by picking a number for the variable in the problem (or for more than one variable, if necessary), solve the problem using your number, and then see which answer choice gives you the correct answer.

Take a look at the following problem:

When to Plug In
- Phrases like "in terms of k" in the question
- Variables in the answers

2. If x is a positive integer, then 20% of $5x$ equals

    (A) x
    (B) $2x$
    (C) $5x$
    (D) $15x$
    (E) $20x$

Here's How to Crack It

Let's start by picking a number for x. Let's plug in a nice round number such as 10. When we plug in 10 for x, we change every x in the whole problem into a 10. Now the problem reads:

2. If 10 is a positive integer, then 20% of 5(10) equals

    (A)   10
    (B)   2(10)
    (C)   5(10)
    (D) 15(10)
    (E) 20(10)

Look how easy the problem becomes! Now we can solve: 20 percent of 50 is 10. Which answer says 10? (A) does.

That was a number 2, which means it was an easy problem. Let's try it again on a harder question.

---

8. If $-1 < x < 0$, then which of the following has the greatest value?

   (A) x

   (B) x^2

   (C) x^3

   (D) $\dfrac{1}{x}$

   (E) $2x$

Here's How to Crack It

This time when we pick a number for x, we have to make sure that it is between -1 and 0, because that's what the problem states. So let's try $-\dfrac{1}{2}$. If we make every x in the problem equal to $-\dfrac{1}{2}$, the problem now reads:

8. If $-1 < -\dfrac{1}{2} < 0$, then which of the following has the greatest value?

   (A) $-\dfrac{1}{2}$

   (B) $\left(-\dfrac{1}{2}\right)^2$

   (C) $\left(-\dfrac{1}{2}\right)^3$

   (D) $\dfrac{1}{-\dfrac{1}{2}}$

   (E) $2\left(-\dfrac{1}{2}\right)$

Plugging In Quick Reference
- When you see *in terms of* and variables in the answers choices, you can plug in.
- Pick your own number for an unknown in the problem.
- Do the necessary math to find the answer you're shooting for, or the target. Circle the target.
- Use POE to eliminate every answer that doesn't equal the target.

Now we can solve the problem. Which has the greatest value? Choice (A) is $-\dfrac{1}{2}$, choice (B) equals $\dfrac{1}{4}$, choice (C) equals $-\dfrac{1}{8}$, choice (D) equals -2, and choice (E) equals -1. So choice (B) is the greatest.

Plugging In is *such* a great technique because it turns hard algebra problems into medium and sometimes even easy arithmetic questions. Remember this when you're thinking of your POOD and looking for questions to do among the hard ones; if you see variables in the answers, there's a good chance it's one to try.

Don't worry too much about what numbers you choose to plug in; just plug in easy numbers (small numbers like 2, 5, or 10 or numbers that make the arithmetic easy like 100 if you're looking for a percent). Also, be sure your numbers fit the conditions of the questions (if they say $x \leq 11$, don't plug in 12).

What If There's No Variable?

Sometimes you'll see a problem that doesn't contain an x, y, or z, but which contains a hidden variable. If your answers are percents or fractional parts of some unknown quantity (total number of marbles in a jar, total miles to travel in a trip), try using Plugging In.

Take a look at this problem:

8. In a certain high school, the number of seniors is twice the number of juniors. If 60% of the senior class and 40% of the junior class attend the last football game of the season, approximately what percent of the combined junior and senior class attends the game?

    (A) 60%
    (B) 53%
    (C) 50%
    (D) 47%
    (E) 40%

Here's How to Crack It

What number, if we knew it, would make the math work on this problem incredibly easy? The number of students. So let's plug in a number and work the problem. Suppose that the number of seniors is 200 and the number of juniors is 100.

If 60% of the 200 seniors and 40% of the 100 juniors go to the game, that makes 120 seniors and 40 juniors, or 160 students. What fraction of the combined class went to the game? $\frac{160}{300}$, or about 53%. So the answer is (B).

Try another one.

────────────────○────────────────

10. Paolo sells cars at a certain dealership. On Monday,
    Paolo sells one-third of the cars on the lot. On Tuesday,
    Paolo sells one-fourth of the remaining cars. If Paolo
    sells half of the cars left on the lot on Wednesday, and
    no new cars were added to or taken from the lot, what
    percent of the original cars did Paolo sell?

    (A) 4.2%
    (B) 65%
    (C) 75%
    (D) 85%
    (E) 95.8%

Here's How to Crack It

Clearly Paolo is selling his share of cars, but notice that you're missing a very important piece of information in the problem: How many cars are on the lot? That's your hidden variable!

In a problem that deals with fractions, you can find a good number to plug in by multiplying the denominators in the problem. Since we're taking $\frac{1}{3}$ of the number, then $\frac{1}{4}$ of it, and then $\frac{1}{2}$ of it, we want something that will divide evenly by 3, 4, and 2. Whatever we get when we multiply 3 by 4 by 2 will certainly fit the bill! This turns out to be 24. This quick technique can save you a lot of headaches once you get to the math.

Now let's work through the problem, using 24 for the number of cars on the lot:

First, Paolo sells one-third of the cars on the lot. If we start with 24 cars, that's 8 cars Paolo sold and 16 cars left on the lot. On Tuesday, Paolo moves one-fourth of what's left, or 4 cars; that raises Paolo's tally to 12 cars and leaves 12 on the lot. Finally, Paolo sells half of the remaining cars. That equals 6 cars and brings Paolo up to 18 cars sold for the week. To figure out the percentage, divide the cars Paolo sold (18) by the total number of cars on the lot (24). Thus, 18 ÷ 24 is .75, or 75%, which is answer choice (C).

────────────────○────────────────

Drill 1

4. On Tuesday, Martha does $\frac{1}{2}$ of her weekly homework.

On Wednesday, she does $\frac{1}{3}$ of the remaining homework.

After Wednesday, what fractional part of her homework

remains to be done?

(A) $\frac{1}{6}$

(B) $\frac{1}{5}$

(C) $\frac{1}{4}$

(D) $\frac{1}{3}$

(E) $\frac{1}{2}$

14. If $a = \dfrac{b}{c^2}$ and $c \neq 0$, then $\dfrac{1}{b^2} =$

(A) ac^2

(B) a^2c^4

(C) $\dfrac{1}{ac^2}$

(D) $\dfrac{1}{a^2c^4}$

(E) $\dfrac{a^2}{c^4}$

12. If $p \neq 0$, then $\dfrac{\dfrac{1}{8}}{2p} =$

(A) $\dfrac{1}{16p}$

(B) $\dfrac{p}{4}$

(C) $\dfrac{4}{p}$

(D) $\dfrac{4p}{3}$

(E) $4p$

18. Jodi has x dollars in her bank account. She withdraws $\dfrac{1}{6}$ of the money in her account to pay her rent and another $\dfrac{1}{6}$ of the money in her account to make her car payment. Jodi then deposits her paycheck of y dollars into her account. A week later, she withdraws $\dfrac{1}{2}$ of the money in her account to spend on a new set of knives. In terms of x, how many dollars are left in Jodi's account?

(A) $\dfrac{(4x-3y)}{6}$

(B) $\dfrac{(3x-5y)}{6}$

(C) $\dfrac{(2x+2y-3)}{6}$

(D) $\dfrac{(3x-y)}{6}$

(E) $\dfrac{(2x+3y)}{6}$

Plugging In the Answers

You can also plug in when the answers to a problem are actual values, such as 2, 4, 10, or 20. Why would you want to do a lot of complicated algebra to solve a problem, when the answer is right there on the page? All you have to do is figure out *which* choice it is.

How can you tell which is the correct answer? Try every choice *until you find the one that works*. Even if this means you have to try all five choices, PITA is still a fast and reliable means of getting the right answer.

But if you use your head, you almost never have to try all five choices. When you plug in the answer choices, begin with choice (C), the middle number. If choice (C) works, you're done. If choice (C) doesn't work because it's too small, try one of the larger numbers. If choice (C) doesn't work because it's too big, try one of the smaller numbers. You can almost always find the answer in two or three tries.

Let's try PITA on the following problem.

PITA = Plugging In the Answers

Don't try to solve problems like this by writing equations and solving for *x* or *y*. Plugging In the Answers lets you use arithmetic (and your calculator!) instead of algebra, so you're less likely to make errors.

4. If the average (arithmetic mean) of 8 and x is equal to the average of 5, 9, and x, what is the value of x ?

    (A) 1
    (B) 2
    (C) 4
    (D) 8
    (E) 10

Here's How to Crack It

Let's start with choice (C) and plug in 4 for x. The problem now reads:

4. If the average (arithmetic mean) of 8 and 4 is equal to the average of 5, 9, and 4 . . .

Does this work? The average of 8 and 4 is 6, and the average of 5, 9, and 4 is also 6. Therefore, (C) is the answer.

Neat, huh? Of course, (C) won't always be the right answer. Let's try one more.

———————————○———————————

10. If $(x - 2)^2 = 2x - 1$, which of the following is a possible value of x ?

   (A) 1
   (B) 2
   (C) 3
   (D) 6
   (E) 7

Here's How to Crack It

If we try plugging in (C), 3, for x, the equation becomes 1 = 5, which is false. So (C) can't be right. If you're not sure which way to go next, just pick a direction. It won't take very long to figure out the correct answer. If we try plugging in (B), 2, for x, the equation becomes 0 = 3, which is false. If we try plugging in (A), 1, for x, the equation becomes 1 = 1, which is true. There's no need to try other answers, because there are no variables; only one answer choice can work. So the answer is (A).

———————————○———————————

Plugging In More Than Once

Some Problem Solving questions will require you to plug in more than once. They look like regular Plugging In problems, usually with variables in the answer choices, but they also have the word *must* or *always* in the question. You can treat these problems like normal Plugging In problems, but you will probably have to plug in more than one number before you can get down to the correct answer choice.

What you should do first is plug in an easy number and eliminate any answer choices that contradict what the question is looking for. Plugging in easy numbers will usually rule out two or three answer choices, but to get down to the just one, we'll probably have to resort to something less obvious, like the weird numbers in the box.

Let's give it a try.

When Numbers Get Weird
Weird numbers include the following:

- Zero
- One
- Negatives
- Extreme numbers (such as 1,000,000)
- Fractions

(The acronym ZONEF can help you remember the kinds of numbers to use.)

7. If $f < g < h$, which of the following must be true?

(A) $fg < h$
(B) $f < gh$
(C) $fgh > 0$
(D) $h - g > 0$
(E) $fg < gh$

Here's How to Crack It

There are variables in the answers and the word *must* in the question means *always*, so be prepared to plug in more than once!

For the first pass, we'll use easy, small numbers: $f = 2$, $g = 3$, and $h = 4$. Now we'll plug those values into each choice. (A) gives us $(2)(3) < 4$, which is false. Get rid of (A). (There's no point in trying it again with different numbers. If it doesn't work once it will *never* work. Move on quickly!) (B) works out to $2 < (3)(4)$, which is true, so we'll keep that one around for the time being. (C) says that $(2)(3)(4) > 0$, which is also true, so (C) sticks around. (D) claims that $4 - 3 > 0$, and rightly so. (D) stays. And (E) states that $(2)(3) < (3)(4)$, which is true. (E) survives to the second round.

Hmm, looks like we only got rid of one choice. That means it's time to break out the weird numbers. How about if we make $f = -5$, $g = 0$, and $h = 1$? Back to the choices! (A) is already gone, so we go straight to (B): $-5 < (0)(1)$. That's still true, so (B) still survives. But (C) now says that $(-5)(0)(1) > 0$, which is false. Eliminate (C). (D) now works out to $1 - 0 > 0$, which is true, so (D) sticks around, but (E) says that $(-5)(0) < (0)(1)$, which is false: they're equal. Eliminate (E).

At this point you might be tempted to choose between (B) and (D) by flipping a coin (in your head—if you actually flip a coin during the PSAT, the proctor may kick you out). But we haven't tried all of our weird numbers. Nothing in the problem says these numbers have to be integers! What if we tried $f = 0.5$, $g = 0.6$, and $h = 0.7$? Now (B) works out to $0.5 < (0.6)(0.7)$, which is false, because $(0.6)(0.7)$ is only 0.42! Eliminate (B), and that just leaves (D), which still works: $0.7 - 0.6$ is greater than 0. Select (D), and you're done.

Plugging In on Geometry

You can also plug in on geometry questions, just as you can for algebra. Any time that you have variables in the answer choices, or hidden variables, plug in! As long as you follow all the rules of geometry while you solve, you'll get the answer.

Take a look at this problem.

---

8. In the figure above, what is the value of $x + y$?

  (A) 120
  (B) 140
  (C) 180
  (D) 190
  (E) 210

Here's How to Crack It

We could solve this problem using algebra, but why? We can plug in whatever numbers we want for the other angles inside the triangle—as long as we obey the rule of 180, and make sure that all the angles in the triangle add up to 180 degrees. So let's plug in 60 and 90 for the other angles inside that triangle. Now we can solve for x and y: If the angle next to x is 60 degrees, then x will be equal to 120. If the angle next to y is equal to 90 degrees, then y will be equal to 90. This makes the sum $x + y$ equal to $120 + 90$, or 210. No matter what numbers we pick for the angles inside the triangle, we'll always get the same answer, (E).

Drill 2

8. If $3^{x+2} = 243$, what is the value of x ?

(A) 1
(B) 2
(C) 3
(D) 4
(E) 5

14. If $\dfrac{24x}{4} + \dfrac{1}{x} = 5$, then $x =$

(A) $-\dfrac{1}{6}$

(B) $\dfrac{1}{6}$

(C) $\dfrac{1}{4}$

(D) $\dfrac{1}{2}$

(E) 2

15. In the figure above, what is the value of b in terms of a ?

(A) $30 - a$
(B) $30 + a$
(C) $60 + a$
(D) $80 - a$
(E) $90 + a$

THE AVERAGE PIE

You probably remember the average formula from math class, which says:

Average (arithmetic mean) = $\dfrac{\text{total}}{\text{\# of things}}$. However, the PSAT rarely will ask you

to take a simple average. Of the three parts of an average problem—the average, the total, and the number of things—you're usually given two of these parts, but often in tricky combinations.

Therefore, the most reliable way to solve average problems is always to use the average pie:

What the pie shows you is that if you know any two of these parts, you can always solve for the third. Once you fill in two of the elements, the pie shows you how to solve for the third part. If you know the total and the number, you can solve the average (total divided by number); if you know the total and the average, you can solve for the number (total divided by average); if you know the number and average, you can solve for the total (number times average).

Let's try this example.

○

9. The average (arithmetic mean) of 3 numbers is 22 and the smallest of these numbers is 2. If the remaining two numbers are equal, what are their values?

   (A) 22
   (B) 32
   (C) 40
   (D) 64
   (E) 66

Total
When calculating averages, always find the total. It's the one piece of information that ETS loves to withhold.

Here's How to Crack It

Let's start by filling in our average pie. We know that 3 numbers have an average of 22. So we can fill in our pie, and the pie shows us that the sum total of these numbers must be 22 × 3, or 66.

We know that one of the numbers is 2, so we can subtract it from the total we've just found, which leaves 64. What else do we know from the question? That the remaining two numbers are equal, so 64/2 = 32. So the answer is (B).

Try one more.

8. Caroline scored 85, 88, and 89 on three of her four history tests. If her average (arithmetic mean) score for all four tests was 90, what did she score on her fourth test?

   (A) 90
   (B) 93
   (C) 96
   (D) 98
   (E) 99

Here's How to Crack It

Let's start with what we know: We know that the average of all 4 of her tests was 90. So we can fill in an average pie with this information:

Now the pie tells us that the sum total of the scores on these 4 tests will be 4 × 90, or 360. Since 3 of these tests have a sum of 85 + 88 + 89, or 262, we know that the score on the fourth test must be equal to 360 − 262, or 98. This makes the answer (D).

MEDIAN AND MODE

There are two more terms you should know: median and mode. You'll see at most one question on the PSAT that tests these ideas, but you might as well get it right.

The **median** of a group of numbers is the number in the middle, just as the "median" is the large divider in the middle of a road. To find the median, here's what you do:

- First, put the elements in the group in numerical order from lowest to highest.
- If the number of elements in your group is *odd*, find the number in the middle. That's the median.
- If you have an *even* number of elements in the group, find the two numbers in the middle and calculate their average (arithmetic mean).

Try this on the following two problems:

11. If the 5 students in Ms. Jaffray's math class scored 91, 83, 84, 90, and 85 on their final exams, what is the median score for her class on the final exam?

(A) 84
(B) 85
(C) 86
(D) 88
(E) 90

Here's How to Crack It

First, let's place these numbers in order from lowest to highest: 83, 84, 85, 90, 91. The number in the middle is 85, so the median of this group is 85 and the answer is (B).

The **mode** of a group of numbers is the number that appears the most. (Remember: *Mode* sounds like *most*.) To find the mode of a group of numbers, simply see which element appears the greatest number of times.

Finding a Median
To find the median of a set containing an even number of items, take the average of the two middle numbers after putting the numbers in order.

33. If the 7 students in Ms. Holoway's math class scored 91, 83, 92, 83, 91, 85, and 91 on their final exams, what is the mode of her students' scores?

Here's How to Crack It

Since the number 91 is the one that appears most often in the list, the mode of these numbers is 91. Pretty simple!

PERCENTS

Percent just means "divided by 100." So $20\% = \dfrac{20}{100} = \dfrac{1}{5}$ or .2 .

Likewise, $400\% = \dfrac{400}{100} = \dfrac{4}{1} = 4$.

Any percent question can be translated into algebra—just use the following rules:

Percent	÷ 100
Of	×
What	x (or any variable)
Is, Are, Equals	=

Take a look at some examples of phrases you might have to translate on the PSAT:

8 percent of 10		$.08 \times 10 = .8$
10 percent of 80		$.1 \times 80 = 8$
5 is what percent of 80?	becomes	$5 = \dfrac{x}{100} \times 80$
5 is 80 percent of what number?		$5 = \dfrac{80}{100}x$
What percent of 5 is 80?		$\dfrac{x}{100} \times 5 = 80$

Percent Increase or Decrease

Percent Increase or *Percent Decrease* = $\dfrac{change}{original\ amount} \times 100$.

For example: If an $80 item is reduced to $60 during a sale, the percent decrease is the change in price ($20) divided by the original amount ($80), or 25%.

RATIOS AND PROPORTIONS

Ratios

Ratios are about relationships between numbers. Whereas a fraction is a relationship between a part and whole, a ratio is about the relationship between parts. So, for example, if there were 3 boys and 7 girls in a room, the fraction of boys in the room would be $\dfrac{3}{10}$. But the ratio of boys to girls would be 3 : 7. Notice that if you add up the parts, you get the whole. 7 + 3 = 10. That's important for PSAT ratio problems, and you'll see why in a moment.

Ratios vs. Fractions

$\text{Fraction} = \dfrac{\text{part}}{\text{whole}}$

$\text{Ratio} = \dfrac{\text{part}}{\text{part}}$

Ratio problems usually aren't difficult to identify: the problem will tell you that there is a "ratio" of one thing to another, such as a 2 : 3 ratio of boys to girls in a club. When you see a ratio problem, drawing a ratio box will help you organize the information in the problem and figure out the correct answer.

For instance, suppose a problem tells you that there is a ratio of 2 boys to 3 girls in the physics club, which has 40 members total. Here's how you would put that information in a ratio box so that you can answer the question being asked:

Boys		Girls		Whole	
2	+	3	=		← Ratio
×		×		×	
=		=			← Multiplier
=		=		=	
				40	← Actual #s

The first line of a ratio box is where you put the *ratio* from the problem. These are parts of the whole; they're not actual numbers of people, animals, books, or anything else. By themselves, they don't tell you *how many* of anything you have.

The second line of a ratio box is for the **multiplier**. The multiplier tells you how much you have to multiply the ratio by to get an actual number of something. The multiplier is the same all the way across; it doesn't change from column to column. And usually, the multiplier isn't in the problem; you have to figure it out yourself.

The third line is for *actual numbers*, so when the problem gives you a number of people (or animals, books, or whatever), that information goes in the third line.

One more thing to notice: See how there's a column for "whole"? This is where you add up the numbers in the ratio row and actual numbers row. Don't forget to add a column for the whole—it's usually key in figuring out the problem.

Now that you know some information from the problem and you know how the ratio box works, you can fill in the rest of the box.

Boys		Girls		Whole	
2	+	3	=	5	← Ratio
×		×		×	
8	=	8	=	8	← Multiplier
=		=		=	
16	+	24	=	40	← Actual #s

The first step is adding the ratio columns to find the whole, which is 5. Then you can find the multiplier by figuring out what you need to multiply 5 by to get 40. Once you fill in 8 for the multiplier all the way across the middle row, finding the actual number of boys and girls in the club is a snap.

Now you can answer all kinds of questions about the membership of the physics club. There are 16 boys and 24 girls. Take the $\frac{part}{whole}$ from the ratio row to figure out that $\frac{3}{5}$ of the members are girls. That means $\frac{2}{5}$, or 40%, of the members are boys.

Try this one.

Gridding In
A ratio is usually expressed as 2 : 3 or 2 to 3, but if you need to grid a ratio, grid it as $\frac{2}{3}$.

---

3. If a certain kind of lemonade is made by mixing water and lemon juice in a ratio of $3\frac{1}{2}$ cups of water for every $\frac{1}{2}$ cup of lemon juice, how many cups of lemon juice will there be in 24 cups of lemonade?

    (A) 3
    (B) 8
    (C) 16
    (D) $16\frac{1}{2}$
    (E) 21

Here's How to Crack It

Water		Lemon	Whole
$3\frac{1}{2}$	+	$\frac{1}{2}$	4
×		×	×
6		6	6
=		=	=
21		3	24

Let's set up our ratio box. We have $3\frac{1}{2}$ cups of water and $\frac{1}{2}$ cup of lemon juice, which makes a total of 4 cups of lemonade; that's our "whole." Now we need to figure out how much lemon juice is in 24 cups of lemonade, so if we put 24 into the box, we can see that we need to multiply each part by 6. This means that there will be a total of 3 cups of lemon juice in 24 cups of lemonade. This makes (A) the correct answer.

―――――――○―――――――

Direct Proportion/Variation

Direct Proportion problems generally ask you to make a conversion (such as from ounces to pounds) or to compare two sets of information and find a missing piece. For example, a proportion problem may ask you to figure out the amount of time it will take to travel 300 miles at a rate of 50 miles per hour.

> To solve proportion problems, just set up two equal fractions. One will have all the information you know, and the other will have a missing piece that you're trying to figure out.

$$\frac{50 \; miles}{1 \; hour} = \frac{300 \; miles}{X \; hours}$$

Be sure to label the parts of your proportion so you'll know you have things in the right place; the same units should be in the numerator on both sides of the equal sign and the same units should be in the denominator on both sides of the equal sign. Notice how using a setup like this helps us keep track of the information we have and to find the information we're looking for, so we can use bite-sized pieces to work through the question.

Now we can cross-multiply and then solve for x: $50x = 300$, so $x = 6$ hours.

Let's try the following problem.

―――――――○―――――――

2. John receives $2.50 for every 4 pounds of berries he picks. How much money will he receive if he picks 90 pounds of berries?

   (A) $27.00
   (B) $36.00
   (C) $42.25
   (D) $48.50
   (E) $56.25

Here's How to Crack It

To solve this, set up a proportion.

$$\frac{\$2.50}{4 \; pounds} = \frac{x}{90 \; pounds}$$

Now we can cross-multiply. $4x = 2.50 \times 90$, so $4x = 225$, and $x = 56.25$. The answer is (E).

$\smallfrown$

Occasionally, you may see a problem that tells you there are two equal ratios. For example, if a problem says that the ratio of 24 to 0.6 is equal to the ratio of 12 to y, you can solve for y by setting up a proportion. A proportion, after all, is really just two ratios set equal to each other.

$$\frac{24}{0.6} = \frac{12}{y}$$

Then you can cross-multiply and solve to get 0.3 for your answer.

Indirect Proportion/Variation

Indirect Proportion is simply the opposite of a direct, or ordinary, proportion. In a direct proportion when one variable increases, so does the other; however, in an indirect variation or proportion, when one variable *increases*, the other variable *decreases*, or vice versa. These types of problems are generally clearly labeled and all you have to do is apply the indirect variation formula:

$$x_1 y_1 = x_2 y_2$$

Once you memorize the formula, applying it will become second nature to you.

Other Names
Indirect Proportion is sometimes called Inverse Proportion or Inverse Variation.

Now try this one.

18. On a particular survey, the percentage of people answering a question with the same response is inversely proportional to the number of the question. If 80% of the people surveyed answered the same response to the eighth question, then, approximately, what percentage of the people surveyed answered the same answer to the 30th question?

(A) 3%
(B) 13%
(C) 18%
(D) 21%
(E) 36%

Here's How to Crack It

The problem tells us that the numbers are inversely proportional, so we need to figure out what to put into the formula. The first piece of information is that 80 percent of the people answered the eighth question correctly; we need to know the percent of people who answered the 30th question correctly. Let's make x the percent and y the question number. Your equation should look like this:

$$(80)(8) = (x_2)(30)$$

When you solve the equation, you should end up with $\dfrac{640}{30}$ or $21\dfrac{1}{3}$, which is answer choice (D) (remember, when the problem says "approximately," you'll probably have to round up or down).

Drill 3

a. If a student scores 70, 90, 95, and 105, what is the average (arithmetic mean) for these tests? _____

b. If a student has an average (arithmetic mean) score of 80 on 4 tests, what is the total of the scores received on those tests? _____

c. If a student has an average of 60 on tests, with a total of 360, how many tests has the student taken? _____

d. If the average of 4 and x is equal to the average of 2, 8, and x, what is the value of x? _____

e. What percent of 5 is 6? _____

f. 60 percent of 90 is the same as 50 percent of what number? _____

g. Jenny's salary increased from $30,000 to $33,000. By what percent did her salary increase? _____

h. In 1980, factory X produced 18,600 pieces. In 1981, factory X only produced 16,000 pieces. By approximately what percent did production decrease from 1980 to 1981? _____

i. In a certain bag of marbles, the ratio of red marbles to green marbles is 7 : 5. If the bag contains 96 marbles, how many green marbles are in the bag? _____

4. The average (arithmetic mean) of 4 numbers is 80. If two of the numbers are 50 and 60, what is the sum of the other two numbers?

11. 60% of 80 is equivalent to 40% of what number?

(A) 100
(B) 105
(C) 110
(D) 120
(E) 140

14. A group of 30 adults and 20 children went to the beach. If 50% of the adults and 80% of the children went swimming, what percent of the group went swimming?

(A) 30%
(B) 46%
(C) 50%
(D) 62%
(E) 65%

Sets

Sets are basically lists of distinct numbers. The numbers in a set are called **elements** or **members**.

For example, if a problem asks for the set of even integers greater than 0 but less than 12, the set would be {2, 4, 6, 8, 10}.

Let's try one.

---

4. If set $X = \{2, 3, 5, 7\}$ and set $Y = \{3, 6, 8\}$, then which of the following represents the union of X and Y?

(A) {3}
(B) {2, 3}
(C) {2, 3, 5, 7}
(D) {3, 6 , 7, 8}
(E) {2, 3, 5, 6, 7, 8}

Here's How to Crack It

The question asks for the union of the two sets, so you need to combine the elements into one big set, as in (E). Watch out for (A), which is the tricky answer; it's the intersection, not the union.

Summary

o   The test is full of opportunities to use arithmetic instead of algebra—just look for your chances to use Plugging In and Plugging In the Answers.

o   If a question has *in terms of* or variables in the answer choices, it's a Plugging In problem. Plug in your own number, do the math, find the target, and use POE to get down to one correct answer.

o   If a question doesn't have variables but asks for a fraction or a percent of an unknown number, you can also plug in there. Just substitute your own number for the unknown and take the rest of the problem step by step.

o   If a question has an unknown and asks for a specific amount, making you feel like you have to write an equation, try Plugging In the Answers instead.

o   When plugging in with geometry problems, remember to use your knowledge of basic geometry rules, e.g., there are still 180 degrees in a triangle when you're using Plugging In.

o   The Average Pie can help you tackle any question about the average (arithmetic mean)—just fill what you know from the problem into the correct spots for *Total*, *Number of Things*, and *Average*.

o   Use the ratio box on questions that ask about a ratio. Fill in the ratio box with information from the problem, calculate the missing piece, then solve for whatever the problem is asking for.

o   Remember that there's a difference between direct and indirect (inverse) proportions. First, figure out which one you're dealing with, and then set up the correct formula and fill in the information the problem gives you.

o   Sets are groups of distinct numbers.

Chapter 9
Advanced Math Principles

So far we've covered basic knowledge and some PSAT-specific problem-solving skills. Now we'll look at some of the more advanced skills tested on the PSAT.

FUNCTIONS

The first of our topics takes us back to school. While much of this test isn't based on the math you've seen in high school recently, this is one topic that you'll most likely recognize. The functions on the PSAT mostly look like this:

$$f(x) = x^2 + 6x + 24$$

Just Follow the Instructions

Functions are like recipes. Each one is just a set of directions for you to follow. ETS provides the ingredients and you work your magic.

Most questions of this type will give you a specific value to plug in for x and then ask you to find the value of the function for that x. Each function is just a set of instructions that tells you what to do to x—or the number you plug in for x—in order to find the corresponding value for $f(x)$ (a fancy name for y). Just plug your information into that equation and follow the instructions.

Let's try an easy one.

5. If $f(x) = x^2 + 3x - 3$, then $f(7)$ equals
    (A) 14
    (B) 20
    (C) 32
    (D) 67
    (E) 83

Here's How to Crack It

Function questions are just trying to see if you can follow the directions, so follow them! The instructions, in this case, are in the equation. So plug 7 into the equation and it should look like this: $f(7) = 7^2 + 3(7) - 3$. Do the math and $f(7) = 67$. Therefore, the answer is (D).

FUNCTIONS WITH WEIRD SYMBOLS

If you ever see a strange symbol on the PSAT—& or @, for example—don't worry. There are no special symbols you should have learned in school that the PSAT requires you to know. What you're looking at is another type of function problem.

> A function problem is just ETS's way of testing whether you can follow directions. And the key is always to plug in numbers.

For instance, you might see a question like this one:

If $@x = 2x + 2$, what is the value of $@3$?

What ETS is asking you to do is to plug in the number that follows the @ symbol everywhere you see the variable x. So to solve for $@3$, you plug in 3 for x in the expression $2x + 2$, and get $2(3) + 2$, or 8.

To figure out the value of a function, all you have to do is plug in a value for x and solve.

Try the following:

---

5. If $x \# y = 4x - y$, what is the value of $3 \# 4$?

    (A) 6
    (B) 8
    (C) 10
    (D) 12
    (E) 14

Here's How to Crack It

In this case, we need to plug in whatever is to the left of the # for x, and whatever is to the right of the # for y. This means that we plug in 3 for x and 4 for y. So $3 \# 4$ will be equal to $4(3) - 4$, or 8. This makes (B) the answer.

EXPANDING, FACTORING, AND SOLVING QUADRATIC EQUATIONS

Ah, factoring. You're likely to see at least one problem on the PSAT that asks you to do this sort of complex algebraic manipulation. It may have been a little while since you've done this, so let's review.

Expanding

Most often you'll be asked to expand an expression simply by multiplying it out. When working with an expression of the form $(x + 3)(x + 4)$, multiply it out using the following rule:

FOIL = First Outer Inner Last

Start with the *first* figure in each set of parentheses: $x \times x = x^2$

Now do the two *outer* figures: $x \times 4 = 4x$

Next, the two *inner* figures: $3 \times x = 3x$

Finally, the *last* figure in each set of parentheses: $3 \times 4 = 12$

Add them all together, and we get $x^2 + 4x + 3x + 12$, or $x^2 + 7x + 12$

Factoring

If you ever see an expression of the form $x^2 + 7x + 12$ on the PSAT, there is a good chance that factoring it will be the key to cracking it.

The key to factoring is figuring out what pair of numbers will multiply to give you the constant term (12, in this case) and add up to the coefficient of the x term (7, in this question). (It could be more complicated if the x^2 term had a coefficient, but that rarely happens on the PSAT.)

Let's try an example:

Step 1: Draw two sets of parentheses next to each other and fill an x into the left side of each. That's what gives us our x^2 term.

Step 2: 12 can be factored a number of ways: 1×12, 2×6, or 3×4. Which of these adds up to 7? 3 and 4, so place a 3 on the right side of one parenthesis and a 4 in the other.

Step 3: Now we need to figure out what the correct signs should be. They should both be positive in this case, because that will sum to 7 and multiply to 12, so fill plus signs into each parenthesis.

$$x^2 + 7x + 12$$

$$(x \quad)(x \quad)$$

$$(x \quad 3)(x \quad 4)$$

$$(x + 3)(x + 4)$$

If you want to double-check your work, try expanding out $(x + 3)(x + 4)$ using FOIL and you'll get the original expression.

Now try the following problem.

⎯⎯⎯⎯⎯⎯⎯ ◯ ⎯⎯⎯⎯⎯⎯⎯

13. If $\dfrac{x^2 + 5x - 6}{x - 1} = 2$, then what is the value of x ?

(A) -4
(B) -1
(C) 5
(D) 6
(E) 8

Here's How to Crack It

Since we know we can factor $x^2 + 5x - 6$, we should do so. When we factor it, we get $\dfrac{(x-1)(x+6)}{(x-1)} = 2$. Now we can cancel the $(x - 1)$ and we're left with $x + 6 = 2$. If we solve for x, we find $x = -4$ and our answer is (A).

Don't forget that we can also just Plug In the Answers!

⎯⎯⎯⎯⎯⎯⎯ ◯ ⎯⎯⎯⎯⎯⎯⎯

Solving Quadratic Equations

Sometimes you'll want to factor to solve an equation. In this case, there will be two possible values for x, called the roots of the equation. To solve for x, use the following steps:

Step 1: Make sure that the equation is set equal to zero.

Step 2: Factor the equation.

Step 3: Set each parenthetical expression equal to zero. So if you have $(x + 2)(x - 7) = 0$, you get $(x + 2) = 0$ and $(x - 7) = 0$. When you solve for each, you get $x = -2$ and $x = 7$. Therefore, -2 and 7 are the solutions or roots of the equation.

Try the following problem.

————————————————◯————————————————

14. If $x^2 + 2x - 15 = 0$, then the possible values of x are

(A)   2 and 4
(B)   -13 and -4
(C)   5 and -4
(D)   -5 and 3
(E)   6 and 3

Here's How to Crack It

Let's try the steps:

Step 1: The equation is already set equal to zero.

Step 2: We can now factor the left side of the equation, to get $(x + 5)(x - 3) = 0$.

Step 3: When we set each parenthetical expression equal to zero, we get $x = -5$ and $x = 3$. Therefore, the answer is (D).

————————————————◯————————————————

Drill 1

Answers can be found in Part III.

5. If a function f is defined by $f(x) = \dfrac{5x+9}{x-1}$ where $x \neq 1$, what is the value of $f(3)$?

(A) 8
(B) 12
(C) 14
(D) 20
(E) 24

10. For all values of a and b, $a \blacklozenge b = \dfrac{a}{2} + 3b - 7$. What is the value of $6 \blacklozenge 8$?

(A) 14
(B) 20
(C) 27
(D) 33
(E) 37

12. If -3 is one of the solutions of the quadratic equation $x^2 + 8x + k = 0$, what is the other value of x ?

(A) -15
(B) -5
(C)   3
(D)   5
(E)   15

15. If $\dfrac{x^2 + 2x - 8}{x^2 - 7x + 10} = 4$, what is the value of x?

(A) -4
(B)   0
(C)   2
(D)   5
(E)   8

19. For all values of x, a function f is defined by $f(x) = x^2 + 7x + 12$. If $f(a) = 2$, what could be a value of a ?

(A) -5
(B) -3
(C)   2
(D)   5
(E) 30

THE PYTHAGOREAN THEOREM

Whenever you have a right triangle, you can use the Pythagorean theorem. The theorem says that the sum of the squares of the legs of the triangle (the sides next to the right angle) will equal the square of the hypotenuse (the side opposite the right angle).

$$a^2 + b^2 = c^2$$

Two of the most common ratios of sides that fit the Pythagorean theorem are $3 : 4 : 5$ and $5 : 12 : 13$. Since these are ratios, any multiples of these numbers will also work, such as $6 : 8 : 10$, and $30 : 40 : 50$.

Try the following example.

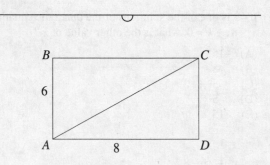

33. If *ABCD* is a rectangle, what is the perimeter of triangle *ABC* ?

	⑦	⑦	
⊙	⊙	⊙	⊙
	⓪	⓪	⓪
①	①	①	①
②	②	②	②
③	③	③	③
④	④	④	④
⑤	⑤	⑤	⑤
⑥	⑥	⑥	⑥
⑦	⑦	⑦	⑦
⑧	⑧	⑧	⑧
⑨	⑨	⑨	⑨

Here's How to Crack It

We can use the Pythagorean theorem to figure out the length of the diagonal of the rectangle—since it has sides 6 and 8, its diagonal must be 10. (If you remembered that this is one of those well-known Pythagorean ratios, you didn't actually have to do the calculations.) Therefore, the perimeter of the triangle is 6 + 8 + 10, or 24.

Let's try another one.

13. Gerald and Frank work in the same office. To drive home, Gerald drives 12 miles north, then 5 miles east. Frank drives 16 miles west, then 12 miles south. What is the distance between Gerald's to Frank's house?

    (A) 17
    (B) 24
    (C) 33
    (D) 45
    (E) 60

Here's How to Crack It:

The easiest way to solve this would be to draw the directions and the distances that both Gerald and Frank travel. If we place a point that represents their office, we should draw Gerald's directly up 12 miles and to the right for 5. Frank travels from the same point of origin directly to the right for 16 miles and then down for 12. A drawing of this should look like the following:

We can then see that we have two right triangles formed. Using the common ratios, we can fill in the hypotenuse of the triangle with sides 5 and 12 with 13 and the hypotenuse of the triangle with sides 12 and 16 with 20. We then have a continuous line between the two hypotenuses. We can add 20 and 13 to get 33 in choice (C).

SPECIAL RIGHT TRIANGLES

There are two specific right triangles, the properties of which may play a role in some harder PSAT math problems. They are the right triangles with angles 45-45-90 and 30-60-90.

An isosceles right triangle has angles that measure 45, 45, and 90 degrees. Whenever you have a 45-45-90 triangle with sides of x, the hypotenuse will always be $x\sqrt{2}$. This means that if one of the legs of the triangle measures 3, then the hypotenuse will be $3\sqrt{2}$.

This right triangle is important because it is half of a square. Memorizing the 45-45-90 triangle will allow you to easily find the diagonal of a square from its side, or find the side of a square from its diagonal.

Here's an example.

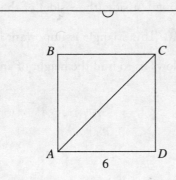

13. In square *ABCD* above, what is the perimeter of triangle *ABC* ?

   (A) $6\sqrt{2}$

   (B) 8

   (C) $12 + \sqrt{2}$

   (D) $12 + 6\sqrt{2}$

   (E) 18

Here's How to Crack It

Remember we mentioned disguised figures a few pages back? Here's an example. This question looks like a question about a square, and it certainly is, in part, but it's really more about the two triangles formed by the diagonal.

In this square, we know that each of the triangles formed by the diagonal AC is a 45-45-90 right triangle. Since the square has a side of 6, using the 45-45-90 right triangle rule, each of the sides is 6 and the diagonal is $6\sqrt{2}$. Therefore, the perimeter of the triangle is $6 + 6 + 6\sqrt{2}$, or $12 + 6\sqrt{2}$ and the answer is (D).

The other important right triangle to memorize is the 30-60-90 right triangle.

A 30-60-90 triangle with a short side of x will have a hypotenuse of $2x$ and a middle side of $x\sqrt{3}$. If the smallest side (the x side) of the triangle is 5, then the sides measure 5, $5\sqrt{3}$, and 10. This triangle is important because it is half of an equilateral triangle, and it allows us to find the height of an equilateral triangle.

Try the following.

13. Triangle *ABC* above is equilateral, with sides of length 4. What is its area?

(A) 3

(B) $4\sqrt{2}$

(C) $4\sqrt{3}$

(D) 8

(E) $8\sqrt{3}$

Here's How to Crack It

To find the area of the triangle, we need to know the base and the height. The question tells you that the base (line segment *AC*) is 4; now we need to find the height, which is *perpendicular* to the base. You can create a height by drawing a line from angle *B* straight down to the base, as you can see in the drawing above. Now you have two 30-60-90 triangles, and you can use the rules of 30-60-90 triangles to figure out the height. Half of the base would be 2, and that's the side across from the 30 degree angle, so you would multiply it by $\sqrt{3}$ to get the height.

Now we know that the base is 4 and the height is $2\sqrt{3}$, so plugging those numbers into the formula for area of a triangle, we get $A = \dfrac{1}{2} \times 4 \times 2\sqrt{3}$, which equals 4 $\sqrt{3}$. Thus, (C) is the correct answer.

OVERLAPPING FIGURES

Very often on a harder geometry problem you'll see two figures that overlap: a triangle and a square, a triangle and a circle, or a square and a circle.

> The key to solving overlapping figure problems is figuring out what the two figures have in common. This may be something you have to draw in yourself.

Take a look at the following problem.

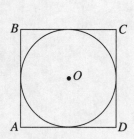

16. In the figure above, the circle with center O is drawn in square $ABCD$. If the area of square $ABCD$ is 36, what is the area of circle O ?

(A) 18
(B) 24
(C) 9π
(D) 12π
(E) 36π

Here's How to Crack It

Go ahead and draw a diameter in the figure through point O and parallel to the base. We mentioned earlier that we want to write down things we know about the figure, so let's write the formulas for both of the figures we've been given. The questions mentions the area of the square and the area of the circle, so write $A = s^2$ for the square and $A = \pi r^2$ for the circle.

Now let's take the information we've been given and take bite-sized pieces to crack it. Since we know that the area of the square is 36, we can solve the first equation and to get $s = 6$, so $d = 6$ as well. Let's take that information to the other formula, that of the circle, which is what we're being asked to find. The radius is half of the diameter, so $A = \pi 3^2 = 9\pi$, so that's our answer, choice (C).

Let's try another one.

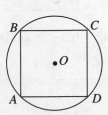

19. In the figure above, *ABCD* is a square drawn in the circle with center *O*. If the area of the circle is 16π, what is the area of square *ABCD* ?

(A) 4
(B) 16
(C) 16√2
(D) 32
(E) 32√2

Here's How to Crack It

What do the square and the circle have in common? A diagonal of the square is a diameter of the circle. Go ahead and draw that on the figure now. Once again, we have two formulas we might need here, $A = s^2$ for the square and $A = \pi r^2$ for the circle. We know something about the circle, so let's use that information to take the next bite: subbing in 16π for the area, we can solve and get $r = 4$. This tells us that the diameter is 8 and so is the diagonal of the square. What now? We could use the Pythagorean theorem to solve for the sides, but if you remember your special right triangles, you might remember that when you draw a diagonal in a square it divides it into two 45-45-90 triangles. Since we multiply the length of the side by $\sqrt{2}$ in these special right triangles to find the diagonal, we can just divide by $\sqrt{2}$ to find the side, which gives us $8/\sqrt{2}$ as the length of a side of the square. We won't bother getting the decimal equivalent or rationalizing because if we put this right into the formula we get $\left(8/\sqrt{2}\right)^2 = 64/2 = 32$, which is the answer, so we'll pick choice (D).

Quick Review
- An interior angle is an angle formed by two radii.
- A sector is the portion of the circle between the two radii.

PROPORTIONALITY IN A CIRCLE

Here's one more rule that plays a role in more advanced circle problems.

> Arc measure is proportional to interior angle measure, which is proportional to sector area.

This means that whatever fraction of the total degree measure is made up by the interior angle, the arc described by that angle is the same fraction of the circumference, and the pie piece created has the same fraction of the area.

Take a look at the figure below:

If angle x is equal to 90 degrees, which is one-quarter of 360 degrees, then the arc AB is equal to one-quarter of the circumference of the circle and the area of the sector of the circle enclosed by radii OA and OB is equal to one-quarter of the area of the circle.

To see how this works in a question, try number 18.

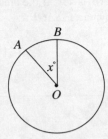

18. The circle above with center O has a radius of 4. If $x = 30$, what is the length of arc AB ?

(A) $\dfrac{\pi}{6}$

(B) $\dfrac{2\pi}{3}$

(C) 3

(D) $\dfrac{3\pi}{2}$

(E) 3π

Here's How to Crack It

Since the interior angle x is equal to 30 degrees, which is $\dfrac{1}{12}$ of 360 degrees, we know that the arc AB will be equal to $\dfrac{1}{12}$ of the circumference of the circle. Since the circle has radius 4, its circumference will be 8π. Therefore, arc AB will measure $\dfrac{1}{12} \times 8\pi$, or $\dfrac{2\pi}{3}$, choice (B).

11. Points A and B lie on a circle with center O such that the measure of $\angle OAB$ is 45°. If the area of the circle is 64π, what is the perimeter of $\triangle AOB$?

(A) $8 + 8\sqrt{2}$
(B) $16 + 8\sqrt{2}$
(C) $16 + 16\sqrt{2}$
(D) $32 + 16\sqrt{2}$
(E) $64 + 16\sqrt{2}$

Here's How to Crack It

This time a diagram isn't given, so drawing the circle should be your first step. Since points A and B lie on the circle, $\overline{OA}$ and $\overline{OB}$ are both radii, and equal in length, making $\triangle AOB$ isosceles. The problem indicates that $\angle OAB$ is 45 degrees, which means that $\angle OBA$ is also 45 degrees, which makes $\triangle AOB$ a 45-45-90 triangle (remember those special right triangles?).

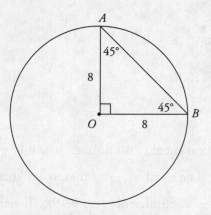

Given the circle's area of 64π, the radii of the circle (which are the legs of the isosceles right triangle) are 8, and the hypotenuse is $8\sqrt{2}$, making the perimeter $8 + 8 + 8\sqrt{2}$, or $16 + 8\sqrt{2}$, which is answer choice (B).

TANGENTS TO A CIRCLE

A tangent is a line that intersects the edge of a circle at exactly one point. A radius drawn to the point of tangency forms a 90 degree angle with the tangent line. This comes up occasionally on hard problems, so take a look at the example below. As you work through this question, if you're thinking that you'd never know how to do it yourself, there's still a valuable lesson here, and it's that this question is not in your POOD, so you should look instead for a plug in or something you're more familiar with, even if it's a number 19 or 20.

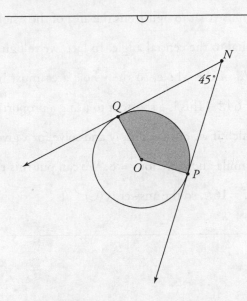

18. In the figure above, $\overrightarrow{NP}$ and $\overrightarrow{NQ}$ are tangent to the circle with center O at points P and Q, respectively. If the area of the shaded region is 24π, what is the circumference of the circle?

(A) 8π
(B) 12π
(C) 16π
(D) 40π
(E) 64π

Here's How to Crack It

The key is remembering that any line or line segment drawn tangent to a circle is perpendicular to a radius drawn from the center of the circle to that tangent point; this means both $\angle OQN$ and $\angle OPN$ equal 90 degrees. With $\angle QNP$ given as 45 degrees, that leaves the central $\angle QOP$ of quadrilateral $QNPO$. Since all quadrilaterals contain 360 degrees and since 45 of the remaining 180 degrees are accounted for, that remaining angle must be 135 degrees. As all circles contain 360 degrees of arc, this means the shaded area represents $\dfrac{135}{360}$ or $\dfrac{3}{8}$ of the area of the entire circle.

Remember, we want to write down the formulas for quantities the question talks about, so that's $A = \pi r^2$ and $C = 2\pi r$. So far we don't have anything we can put directly into a formula, so what do we know? We're told that the area of the shaded sector is 24π, so we can use that to figure out the area of the whole circle, because we know it's proportional to the central angle. In fact, we've figured out that this part of the circle is 3/8 of the whole, so the whole area must be 8/3 times the sector, so $8/3 \times 24\pi = 64\pi$ (This is a shortcut to using a proportion, which looks like this: $\dfrac{3}{8} = \dfrac{24\pi}{x}$, which if we cross-multiply and solve for x gives us 64π.) Now we can use the first formula and solve for $r = 8$. We can put this right into the second formula and get $C = 16\pi$, so the answer is (C).

Drill 2

Answers can be found in Part III.

13. If two sides of a triangle are 3 and 7, which of the following could be the perimeter of the triangle?

(A) 4
(B) 10
(C) 15
(D) 20
(E) 21

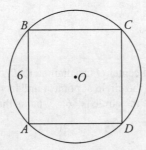

8. In the figure above, rectangle *ABCD* is inscribed in circle *O*. If the length of side *AB* is 6 and the area of the rectangle is 48, what is the area of circle *O* ?

(A) 10
(B) 10π
(C) 25π
(D) 50π
(E) 100π

14. In the figure above, if triangle *ABC* is isosceles, what is the perimeter of the triangle?

(A) 12.5
(B) $10\sqrt{2}$
(C) $10 + 5\sqrt{2}$
(D) $15\sqrt{2}$
(E) 25

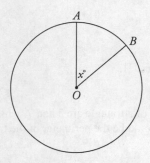

16. The circle shown above has its center at *O*. If *x* = 60 and the length of arc *AB* is 2π, what is the area of circle *O*?

(A)   4
(B)   6
(C) 6π
(D) 12π
(E) 36π

18. A circle with center *O* has diameter $\overline{AB}$. Segment $\overline{AC}$ is tangent to the circle at point *A* and has a length of 5. If the area of the circle is 36π, what is the perimeter of triangle *ABC*?

(A)   13
(B)   15
(C)   25
(D)   30
(E)   60

Summary

o   On Functions questions, just take the formula they give you and plug in the numbers they give you. Anyone adept at Plugging In will do great, whether the problem has $f(x)$ or weird symbols.

o   Quadratics generally require that you *expand* or *factor*—the general rule is, if you see a quadratic in one form, switch it to the other.

o   There is no trigonometry on the PSAT—the Pythagorean theorem, common right triangles (such as 3 : 4 : 5 and 5 : 12 : 13), and Special Right Triangles (45-45-90 and 30-60-90) are the only tools you need to figure out angles and lengths in a right triangle.

o   When you see overlapping figures, figure out which measurement the two figures have in common.

o   Circles that show an interior angle (an angle that extends from the center of the circle) have proportionality. The interior angle over the whole degree measure (360 degrees) equals the same fraction as the arc enclosed by that angle over the circumference. Likewise, both of these fractions are equal to the area of the segment over the entire area of the circle.

o   When you see a line that is "tangent to" a circle, remember two things:
    •   The line intersects the circle at exactly one point.
    •   The radius of the circle that intersects the tangent line is perpendicular to that tangent line.

Chapter 10
Writing Skills

For some of you, taking a test of your writing skills would be a good thing; for others, it's not so appealing. But don't worry—there is no essay. What this section really tests is a few grammar rules and your skill at correcting sentences using those rules. Even if you haven't had much grammar in school, this chapter will teach you what you need to know and help you approach the Writing Skills section like a pro.

WHAT TO EXPECT

The Writing Skills section contains 39 questions, including 14 Error Identification questions, 20 Improving Sentences questions, and 5 Improving Paragraphs questions. If these questions don't sound like anything you've studied in school about writing, you're not mistaken. The Writing Skills section is much more about test-taking skills than it is about actual writing skills. It will be the last section of the PSAT, and you will be allotted 30 minutes to complete it.

PSAT Grammar

The grammar ETS chooses to test on the PSAT is pretty basic. Even if you haven't done much grammar in school, don't sweat it; learning just a few rules will take you a long way. While we can't cover every single scenario that you might see on test day, ETS is actually quite predictable and likes to test the same few rules over and over. We'll cover those rules in this chapter, and if you need more in-depth work in any of the areas covered here, pick up a copy of The Princeton Review's *Grammar Smart* for a more comprehensive review.

> How to Do Well
> - Review/learn PSAT grammar
> - Know how to attack each question type
> - Know which questions to do and which ones to skip

Question Strategy

Every question type on the PSAT can be cracked, and the Writing Skills questions are no exception. While reviewing the basic grammar you need, you will also learn how to crack Error ID and Improving Sentences questions. After you solidify your approach to these question types, you'll learn how to crack Improving Paragraphs questions by employing the grammar and skills you've already mastered.

To Do or Not To Do

The Writing Skills section is arranged in a rough order of difficulty, with the exception of the Improving Paragraphs questions, which are the last five questions of the section. As usual, this means that the early questions will have fairly obvious answers that you shouldn't second guess, the middle third will be fairly straightforward but will contain some tricks, while the last third should be approached with caution. The Writing Skills sections are a little different than the other two sections, though, because they're more about knowing the rules that are tested and less about having to think hard about how to solve something or what the passage means.

If you spot the mistake in a sentence right off the bat, you're already close to getting the answer. Stay focused on what kind of error ETS is testing in that question, and use POE. If you don't spot an error, you'll have to proceed more carefully; don't trust your ear, especially on the later (hard) questions.

SNEAK PREVIEW

Error IDs

Before we begin reviewing ETS's grammar, let's take a peek at the two main question types you'll see on the Writing Skills section.

21. This is an example of an Error ID question that has no
       A   B   C D
    error. No error
            E

An Error ID question gives you a sentence that has four words or phrases underlined, each with a corresponding letter underneath. At the end of each sentence will be "No error"—choice (E). There are some important things you need to know about Error IDs:

- There is never more than one error per sentence.
- If there is an error, it's always underlined.
- Approximately 20 percent of all Error ID questions are correct as written, so don't be afraid to pick choice (E).
- Error IDs are short and therefore quick; you should usually be able to eliminate at least one answer choice, so you should plan to attempt most Error ID questions, but be extra careful or skip the last couple of questions.

Improving Sentences

15. This is an example of an Improving Sentences question that does not contain an error.

    (A) that does not contain
    (B) that has not been containing
    (C) which has not been contain
    (D) which is not being with
    (E) about which there is nothing to indicate it being with

Improving Sentences questions give you a sentence, part or all of which is underlined. The underlined part may or may not contain a grammatical error. There are some important things you need to know about Improving Sentences questions:

- Answer choice (A) always repeats the underlined portion exactly as it appears in the initial sentence. Thus, you never need to read answer choice (A)—you already did when you first read the sentence.

- Approximately 20 percent of the sentences will be correct as written, so don't be afraid to choose answer choice (A) if you've eliminated the other choices.
- The non-underlined portion of the sentence is always correct. Make sure to read it carefully. Many students focus only on the underlined part since that's where the error has to be (if there is one); however, often you can only find the underlined error by focusing carefully on the sentence as a whole.
- Don't try to revise the sentence in your head; you never know how ETS is going to fix it, and your perfect revision probably won't be listed. Work with the answer choices they give you and look for the *best* answer.

THE METHOD

There are many similarities in the way we approach Error IDs and Improving Sentences. Here are some things to keep in mind for both question types:

- **Don't make decisions based on sound.** One of the biggest ways the test writers try to trip you up is to use an error that sounds correct to you because you hear it so often in everyday life. For example, the sentence "Everyone should bring their own lunch" sounds perfectly normal, yet it contains a grammatical error (pronoun agreement, which you'll hear more about later). Alternatively, ETS can put in words that sound odd because you're not used to hearing them, but are, in fact, perfectly correct. The important thing is to move beyond "It sounds bad" or "It sounds okay" as the sole reason you eliminate or choose an answer choice. Learn the rules ETS tests, and look for them.
- **Use POE aggressively.** Focus on eliminating everything you can, based on the rules of grammar, not on picking something that stands out as a "good" sentence.
- **Trim the fat.** One technique that will help you decide if an answer choice contains an error is "trimming the fat." This means taking a sentence and getting rid of the extraneous words and phrases that are just there for distraction. For example, take the following sentence: "Japan, since the early part of the 1980s when Japanese products became popular with consumers, have been able to export the high-quality technology demanded by foreign markets." There is a long, distracting phrase separating *Japan* and *have* so that it's easy to forget that these two words have to agree in number to be correct—and they don't. It should be *Japan...has,* because Japan is *one* country. So when you see prepositional phrases or phrases offset by commas, ignore them while you figure out if the surrounding words are correct. You can even cross them off, but don't make it so that it's hard to read; you may need to see those words later.

Error IDs

When you first read an Error ID, one of two things will happen: Either you will spot an error immediately, or you won't. It doesn't really matter if you do or not; there are ways to get the correct answer regardless.

Plan A: If You Spot an Error Immediately

1. Try to articulate to yourself what the error is, so that you avoid picking an answer solely by using your ear. For instance, say to yourself, "There is a subject/verb agreement error, because *Japan* is singular and *have* is plural."
2. Check the other answers just to be safe.
3. Select your original answer if you're confident it truly is an error.

Plan B: If You Don't Spot an Error Immediately

1. Check each underlined portion individually, thinking about the grammar rules that might apply to it. For example, if the word *everyone* is underlined, say to yourself, "*Everyone* is a pronoun, so I need to check for agreement, ambiguity, and case."
2. Eliminate answers that you know are grammatically correct.
3. Select the answer that violates a rule, or (E) if there is no error.

Improving Sentences

Again, when you first read the sentence, either you will spot an error or you won't. What you *don't* want to do, above all, is read the sentence five or six times, replacing the underlined portion with each of the answer choices. This is a huge waste of time and will end in your picking an answer based on what you remember sounding the best—not a great way to go through these problems. Remember, ETS knows how to trick your memory and your ear.

Plan A: If You Spot an Error Immediately

1. Again, try to articulate to yourself what the error is, so that you avoid picking an answer solely by ear. If you're confident it's an error, then eliminate (A) and any answer choices that make the same error.
2. Compare the remaining answer choices and note how they differ. Eliminate any answer choices that contain new errors or change the intended meaning of the original sentence. If you get down to two answers that both seem grammatically correct, pick the more concise (usually shorter) answer.
3. Repeat Step 2 until you're down to one answer choice, and pick it.

Plan B: If You Don't Spot an Error Immediately

1. Compare the answer choices and note how they differ. Eliminate any answer choices that contain errors.
2. Repeat Step 1 until you have one answer choice left.

Now that we've talked about how to do each question type, we're going to move on to reviewing the grammar. We'll do problems as we go along to practice the techniques.

Grammar? Ugh!

To do well on the Writing Skills section, you need to remember some basic grammar rules. Now, don't get worked up about being tested on grammar. PSAT grammar is not difficult, nor is it extensive. In fact, the PSAT really tests only five basic grammatical concepts:

1. verbs
2. nouns
3. pronouns
4. prepositions
5. other little things

These are the five areas in which a sentence can "go wrong." They will function as a checklist for you—every time you read a sentence, you will look at these five areas to find the error. If you don't find one after checking these five things, then there probably isn't one.

No Error?

As we've mentioned, about 20 percent of Error ID questions and Improving Sentences questions contain no error. If you've used your checklist and can't find a mistake, chances are there isn't one. Don't be afraid to pick *No error*—choice (E) on Error ID or choice (A) on Improving Sentences questions.

VERBS

A **verb** is an action word. It tells what the subject of the sentence is doing. There are three types of errors you can see with verbs:

- agreement
- parallelism
- tense

Agreement

> Verbs must always *agree* in number with the subjects with which they are paired: singular with singular, plural with plural.

Subject-verb agreement is heavily tested on the PSAT, so whenever you see a verb in the underlined portion of a sentence make sure it agrees in number with the subject it refers to. That is, plural with plural, singular with singular. Remember, the subject is the thing the sentence is talking about. If you are given a singular subject (*Jake, the car, she, Europe*), it must be paired with a singular verb (*is, was, plays, rocks*). Singular verbs generally have an *s* on the end, like plural nouns.

Let's look at a question.

---

1. The statistics released by the state department <u>makes the economic situation look bleaker than it really is</u>.

    (A) makes the economic situation look bleaker than it really is
    (B) makes the economic situation look bleaker than they really are
    (C) make the economic situations look bleaker than it really is
    (D) make the economic situation look bleaker than it really is
    (E) make the economic situation look more bleak than they really are

Here's How to Crack It

The verb *makes* appears in the underlined portion of the sentence, so we need to check the subject. This sentence is about *the statistics*, so the subject is plural. Don't be confused by all of the other words that appear after it, *released by the state department,* they're just there to distract us. We're only interested in the simple subject, which is plural. The verb *makes* is singular, though, so there's a problem with the sentence as it's written. Let's go ahead and cross out choice (A) now. Remember, we don't need to read it because it repeats the underlined portion of the sentence exactly. Let's also cross out (B) right away because it repeats the error.

Answer choices (C) and (D) are identical except for the words *situation* and *situations.* Which is correct? The verb it is paired up with is *is,* which is singular, so the singular *situation* is correct. We can eliminate (C). Comparing (D) and (E) we find that (E) uses *they...are,* which is plural, so we can get rid of that and choose (D).

Sometimes, though, you will have to do more work to figure out if the subject of the sentence is plural or singular. Here are some things to watch out for:

Collective Nouns

These can be a little tricky, but they have one thing in common: They are all *groups* of people, places, or things. Therefore, they are singular and take singular verbs.

> The *family* is
> The *jury* is
> The *group* is
> The *audience* is
> The *company* is
> The *government* is
> The *United States* (or any other country) is

Compound Subjects

Subjects joined by *and* are plural: Bill and Pat *were* going to the show. However, subjects joined by *or* can be either singular or plural (the same is true for *nor*). If the last noun given is singular, then the sentence takes a singular verb; if the last noun given is plural, it takes a plural verb.

The following pronouns also take singular verbs:

> Either *is*
> Neither *is*
> None *is*
> Each *is*
> Anyone *is*
> No one *is*
> Everyone *is*

Let's try a question.

_____○_____

27. Pam Cruise and Jim Braswell, neither of whom takes the
                                  ‾‾‾‾‾‾‾   ‾‾‾‾
                                    A   B
    bus to work, is secretly plotting to take over the world.
                 ‾‾   ‾‾‾‾‾‾‾‾
                  C   D
    No error
    ‾‾‾‾‾‾‾‾
       E

Here's How to Crack It

If you don't immediately spot the error, go through each answer choice and eliminate anything that contains no error. Answer choice (C) gives us the singular verb *is*. When we Trim the Fat to get rid of the phrase between the subject and the verb, we see that *is* has been paired up with a plural subject here: *Pam Cruise and Jim Braswell*. Therefore, the correct answer is (C).

Parallelism

The next thing you need to check when you see a verb is whether it is *parallel* to the other verbs in the sentence.

In other words, do the verbs use the same form? For example, *to run, to walk,* and *to sing* are in the same form, whereas *to walk* and *singing* are not. Be particularly careful to watch for parallelism when you see lists of verbs.

Now let's try out a question that tests our skills.

---

8. As a competitor in the Iron Man competition, Paula was required to swim 2.4 miles, bike 112 miles, and <u>running the last 26 miles</u>.

    (A)   running the last 26 miles
    (B)   to run the last 26 miles
    (C)   run the last 26 miles
    (D)   ran the last 26 miles
    (E)   she had to run the last 26 miles

Here's How to Crack It

We can tell from comparing the answer choices that it all boils down to which form the verb *run* should be in, so let's look at the sentence for clues. The first verb in the list is *to swim,* and the second one is *bike.* When a list starts with *to,* the rest of the verbs can start with *to,* or the rest of the verbs can leave off the *to,* like *bike* does in this sentence. *Running, to run,* and *ran* aren't parallel to *swim* and *bike,* so (A), (B), and (D) can be eliminated. (E) just repeats a lot of words from the sentence unnecessarily, so it can go too, leaving (C) as our best answer.

Just the Answer, Please
Remember, when solving Error ID questions, all you have to do is identify the error. Don't worry if you don't know exactly how to fix an error—ETS only cares if you can identify it.

Tense

> Finally, verbs need to be in the proper *tense,* such as past, present, or future. Verb tenses should generally be consistent in a sentence unless the meaning requires different tenses.

Let's try an example:

> Throughout the Middle Ages, women work
> $\underset{A}{}$ $\underset{B}{}$
> beside men, knowing that the effort of men and
> $\underset{C}{}$
> women alike was essential to survival. No error
> $\underset{D}{}$ $\underset{E}{}$

Here's How to Crack It

The verb *work* refers to something that happened *throughout the Middle Ages,* according to the sentence, and the Middle Ages definitely happened in the past. *Work,* though, is in the present tense, so it's erroneous, and (B) is the correct answer.

That's Just Perfect

If you see the verbs *have, has,* or *had* paired up with other verbs on the PSAT, you're probably looking at verbs in a *perfect* form, such as the past perfect or present perfect. Here's how and when you use those forms:

Past perfect verbs describe something in the past that took place *before another event in the past.* It uses the word *had,* then the verb. For example:

> I *had sung* all night until my neighbor called the police.
> Leigh *had skied* every day before she broke her leg.

Present perfect usually tells you about an event that started in the past and is continuing through the present. It can also refer to an event that happened at an unspecified time in the past. Present perfect uses the words *have* or *has,* depending on whether a singular or plural verb is needed, and then the verb. For example:

> The dogs *have sung* along with me before.
> My neighbor *has glared* at me ever since.

Verbs in the perfect form have to be constructed properly when used (*have sung* instead of *have sang*), and they should be used only if needed for the above situations; it's not okay to substitute them for simple past, present, and future verbs.

NOUNS

Nouns are words that indicate a person, place, thing, or idea. Anything you can touch, talk about, discuss, or think about is a noun in that context. PSAT sometimes tests noun agreement. When two or more nouns in a sentence refer to each other, they need to agree in number: singular with singular and plural with plural.

Give this question a try:

---

26. If your friends <u>are</u> not good students <u>now</u> <u>they will</u>
             A   B   C
   probably not be <u>a good student</u> in college. <u>No error.</u>
                    D   E

Here's How to Crack It

Did you see an error? In the first part of the sentence it says *students*, while in the later part of the sentence it says *student*. Are we to believe that your friends will morph into one person when they go to college? Maybe if they're headed to Comic Book University. The answer is (D).

PRONOUNS

Pronouns are words that take the place of nouns. As with verbs, there are three types of errors that pronouns can have:

* agreement
* ambiguity
* case

Agreement

> **Pronouns** must agree in number with the nouns they replace. Singular pronouns replace singular nouns; plural pronouns replace plural nouns.

After all the time we've spent on verb agreement this may seem obvious, but there are some additional tricks that ETS especially likes to pull with pronouns. To learn how to get around them, first we're going to look at some pronouns that are *always* singular.

Either *is*
Neither *is*
Each *is*
Anybody *is*
No one *is*
Everyone *is*
Everything *is*

Pronouns starting with *any* and *every* can be tricky because the words *any* and *every* seem to imply that there are several people or things, but just remember: If you see *one*, *body*, or *thing* at the end of the word, it's singular. Also, the word *none* can be singular or plural, but ETS prefers to treat it as singular, so you should too.

ETS also likes to write questions with the word *their* used as a singular pronoun, like many people do in everyday speech: *Everyone should clean up their stuff*. However, in ETS-land, *their* is still always considered plural. If it's being used to replace a singular pronoun (like *everyone*), it's wrong. (This is another way the test writers will try to trick you if you're using your ear, but it's easy to spot once you know about it!) Don't worry about whether *their* should be replaced with *his, his or her,* or some other option—you won't have to choose for the PSAT. You just need to know that *their* is plural and should replace only plural subjects, such as *the students, Al and Susan,* or *voters.*

Try this question.

―――――――――――○―――――――――――

Everyone <u>on the softball team</u> <u>who came up</u> to bat
        A   B
<u>squinted at the pitcher</u> in order to keep the sun's glaring
      C
rays out of <u>their eyes</u>. <u>No error</u>
        D   E

Here's How to Crack It

Is there an underlined pronoun late in this sentence? There sure is: *their eyes*. Whose eyes are being referred to? Let's Trim the Fat to check this sentence:

> "*Everyone*…squinted…to keep the sun's…rays…out of *their* eyes."

> *Everyone* is singular, but *their* is plural, so it cannot replace *everyone*.

The answer is (D).

―――――――――――○―――――――――――

Ambiguity

> When you see a pronoun in a sentence on the PSAT, you should make sure it's perfectly clear what the pronoun replaces.

For example:

> *After looking over the color samples, Mary agreed with Martha that her porch should be painted green.*

Whose porch is being painted green? Mary's or Martha's? This sentence has a problem with pronoun *ambiguity*, which means you can't tell which noun the pronoun is supposed to replace.

Whenever you spot a pronoun, especially late in a sentence, look to see what the pronoun is referring to. If there's more than one possibility, the pronoun has an ambiguity error. If it's perfectly clear what noun (or pronoun) the pronoun replaces, move on to checking for agreement and case. Let's try one:

The director told the star of the production that he was
        A   B
making far too much money to tolerate such nasty
                              C
treatment from the producer. No error
      D   E

Here's How to Crack It

When you identify answer choice (B) as a pronoun, you should immediately try to figure out which noun (or pronoun) it is referring to. Here, who is making too much money—the director or the star? From the sentence there's no way to tell, so (B) has a pronoun ambiguity error and is the correct answer. You might think the sentence would make more sense if the word *he* referred to the director—or the star. However, the sentence itself doesn't give you any clues pointing to either one, so the pronoun is ambiguous.

Subject Pronouns

Singular	**Plural**
I	we
you	you
he	they
she	they
it	they
who	who

Object Pronouns

Singular	**Plural**
me	us
you	you
him	them
her	them
it	them
whom	whom

Case

Pronouns come in two "flavors," or cases: **subjective** and **objective**. The subject is the person or thing performing the action in the sentence. The object is the person or thing *receiving* the action. Think of it this way: An object just sits there. It doesn't *do* anything—things are done to it. The subject, however, *does* something.

Subjects and objects are represented by different pronouns. For example, *I* is a subject pronoun, as in the sentence "I did it," while *me* is an object pronoun, as in "It happened to me." See how the subject does something, and the object has something done to it?

Try the following example:

The leading roles in the widely acclaimed play, a modern
                            A
version of an Irish folktale, were performed by Jessica
     B   C
and him. No error
    D   E

Here's How to Crack It

Look at the pronoun that comes at the end of the sentence. *Him* is in the object case, so we need to know if that's correct. In this case, *performed by...him* is correct. You'd need the subject case if you were going to say *he performed*, but as it stands, the pronoun is correct. The rest of the underlined portions of the sentence also check out, so the answer is (E).

The I/Me Thing

Are you always getting corrected on your use (or misuse) of *I* or *me*? When in doubt about whether a pronoun needs a subject or object case, Trim the Fat to figure out whether it is acting or being acted upon. Which of the following sentences is correct?

The book belongs to Jerry and I.
The book belongs to Jerry and me.

Let's trim the fat and take out *Jerry and*. Now we're left with *The book belongs to _____*. What goes in the blank, *I* or *me*? *Me* is correct, because *to* is a preposition (more on those in a moment) and we need an *object* pronoun to come after the preposition. Let's look at a trickier one:

Clare is more creative than I.
Clare is more creative than me.

Be careful. This may look as if the pronoun is an object, but actually the sentence is incomplete. What the sentence really says is, "Clare is more creative than I am." The *am* is understood. When in doubt, say the sentence to yourself, adding *am, is,* or *are*. If any form of *be* makes sense, the sentence requires a subject pronoun.

PREPOSITIONS

Prepositions add information about a noun, generally to give one noun's relationship to something else, either in time or space. (For example: *over, under, around, along, by, to, beside, near, with, beyond, before, after, at, in, on*, etc.)

Prepositions are *always* followed by a noun or pronoun, which is called the *object* of the preposition. In the sentence "I threw the ball to him," *to* is the preposition and *him* is the object. (Notice that *him* is an *object* pronoun.) Together they create the prepositional phrase *to him*. It's important to recognize prepositional phrases because they often appear as distractions on the PSAT, and you'll want to get rid of them when you trim the fat.

DRILL 1

Identify the prepositions and their objects in the following sentences: Answers can be found in Part III.

1. Lina walked over the bridge.
2. The ball went beyond the green.
3. Please shelve the dictionary with the other reference books.
4. I want to return the movie to her.

DRILL 2

Another reason prepositions are important is that some words have to be paired with certain prepositions. These word pairs are called *idioms,* and unlike subject/verb agreement and pronoun ambiguity, you won't have certain rules to fall back on to solve an idiom problem on the test; you'll just have to memorize them. Here are some questions involving idioms that are commonly tested on the PSAT; fill in the blanks, check your answers, and make flash cards to memorize any that you don't know. Answers can be found in Part III.

1. I am *indebted* _____ you.
2. I am *resentful* _____ you.
3. I am *delighted* _____ you.
4. I am *jealous* _____ you.
5. I am *worried* _____ you.
6. I am *astounded* _____ you.
7. The women had a *dispute* _____ politics.
8. You have a *responsibility* _____ take care of your pet.
9. My friends are not so *different* _____ your friends.
10. Scott is *considered* _____ the best composer at the conservatory.

Try an Error ID example:

---○---

28. Despite the poor weather, my sister and I were planning
     ‾‾‾‾‾   ‾‾‾‾‾‾‾‾‾‾‾   ‾‾‾‾‾‾‾
     A   B   C

on attending the festival. No error
‾‾‾‾‾‾‾‾‾‾‾‾‾‾‾‾‾‾‾‾‾‾   ‾‾‾‾‾‾‾‾
        D   E

Here's How to Crack It

Though we may hear similar sentences every day and not realize there is a grammar mistake, the word *planning* is part of an idiom: *planning to*. A correct use would read *planning to attend*, so (D) has an error and is the correct answer.

---○---

OTHER LITTLE THINGS

The final area of grammar we're going to cover is Other Little Things—some areas that are tested on the PSAT but don't fall into our other categories. The areas are:

- faulty comparisons
- misplaced modifiers
- adjectives/adverbs
- voice
- active/passive

Faulty Comparisons

Whenever you see a PSAT question that makes a comparison, check for these types of errors.

Apples to Apples

One type of error is comparing things that can't actually be compared. A correct comparison compares apples to apples, not apples to banana pudding. For example, look at the following sentence:

> *Larry goes shopping at Foodtown because the prices are better than Shop Rite.*

Even though it's pretty common to hear sentences like this in everyday speech, it's actually wrong and you will probably see something like this in a couple of test questions. This one can be tricky to spot for the very reason we stated above, that lots of people talk this way and we know what they mean, so we give them the benefit of the doubt and assume they're speaking correctly. But we can't do that on the PSAT. Remember, don't trust your ear; when you see comparison words like *like, as, compared to,* and so on, check to see if the things being compared are actually the same sort of thing. The two things being compared are *Foodtown's prices* and *Shop Rite,* instead of *Foodtown's prices* and *Shop Rite's prices.* Even though we would assume the speaker was comparing prices to prices if we heard that sentence on television, the comparison has to be made more clearly on the PSAT. Better sentences would read:

> *Larry goes shopping at Foodtown because the prices are better than Shop Rite's prices.*

or even

> *Larry goes shopping at Foodtown because the prices are better than Shop Rite's.*

Do You Count?

While we're on the subject of grocery stores, you've probably seen a sign that says *10 items or less* about a thousand times. Guess what? It's grammatically wrong. When items can be counted, the word *fewer* should be used instead of *less.*

For example:

> If you eat *fewer* French fries, you can use *less* ketchup.

Similar word pair include *many* (can be counted) versus *much* (can't be counted)...

> *Many* hands make *much* less work.

...and *number* (can be counted) versus *amount* (can't be counted).

> The same *number* of people ate different *amounts* of pudding.

Two's Company, Three or More Is...?

Finally, different words must be used when comparing two things versus comparing three or more things. The following examples will jog your memory:

- *More* (two things) versus *Most* (three or more things)
  Given vanilla and strawberry as ice cream flavor options, I think vanilla is the *more* appealing option.
  In fact, of all the flavors I've tried, I like vanilla the *most.*

- *Less* (two things) versus *Least* (three or more things)
  I am *less* likely to be chosen than Judy is.
  I am the *least* likely person to be chosen from the department.
- *Better* (two things) versus *Best* (three or more things)
  My math teacher is *better* than the one I had last year.
  My Princeton Review teacher is the *best* teacher I have ever had.
- *Between* (two things) versus *Among* (three or more things)
  Between you and me, I never liked her anyway.
  Among all the people here, no one likes her.

Misplaced Modifiers

A modifier is a descriptive word or phrase inserted in a sentence to add dimension to the thing it modifies. For example:

As a horse who talked in his sleep, Mr. Ed was unique.

"As a horse who talked in his sleep" is the modifying phrase in this sentence. It describes a characteristic of Mr. Ed. Generally speaking, a modifying phrase should be right next to the thing it modifies. If it's not, the meaning of the sentence may change. For example:

Walking down the road, my mood shifted from bitter to relaxed.

What is walking down the road? According to this sentence, *My mood,* because that's what comes right after the comma. Questions about this mistake can be tricky; we know what the sentence is trying to say and we're likely to give it the benefit of the doubt. But when you see a descriptive phrase in the beginning of a sentence and it's underlined, look closely at the words that come immediately after the comma to see if that's really what the phrase is describing.

Try the following example:

17. Perhaps the most beautiful natural vegetation in the world, the west of Ireland explodes each spring with a tremendous variety of wildflowers.

   (A) Perhaps the most beautiful natural vegetation in the world
   (B) In what may be the world's most beautiful natural vegetation
   (C) Home to what may be the most beautiful natural vegetation in the world
   (D) Its vegetation may be the world's most beautiful
   (E) More beautiful in its natural vegetation than anywhere else in the world

Here's How to Crack It

Is the west of Ireland a kind of vegetation? No, so cross off (A). We need an answer that will make the opening phrase modify *the west of Ireland*. Answer choice (B) is still modifying the vegetation, so cross it off. All three other choices fix the problem, but (C) does it the best. (D) makes the sentence a bit awkward, and (E) actually changes the meaning of the sentence by saying that the west of Ireland definitely has the most beautiful vegetation while the original sentence says *perhaps*. ETS's answer is (C).

Adjectives/Adverbs

Misplaced modifiers aren't the only descriptive errors ETS will throw at you. Another way they try to trip you up is by using adjectives instead of adverbs and vice versa. Remember that an **adjective** modifies a noun, while an **adverb** modifies verbs, adverbs, and adjectives. The adverb is the one that usually has *–ly* on the end. In the following sentence, circle the adverbs and underline the adjectives:

> The stealthy thief, desperately hoping to evade the persistent police, ran quickly into the dank, dark alley after brazenly stealing the stunningly exquisite jewels.

First, let's list the adjectives along with the nouns they modify: *stealthy* thief, *persistent* police, *dank* alley, *dark* alley, *exquisite* jewels. Now for the adverbs with the words they modify: *desperately* hoping (verb), ran (verb) *quickly*, *brazenly* stealing (verb), *stunningly* exquisite (adjective).

Now try the following Improving Sentences example:

---

15. Movie cameras are no longer particularly costly, but film, development, and editing equipment <u>cause the monetary expense of making a film to add up tremendous</u>.

   (A) cause the monetary expense of making a film to add up tremendous
   (B) add tremendously to the expense of making a film
   (C) much increase the film-making expenses
   (D) add to the tremendous expense of making a film
   (E) tremendously add up to the expense of making a film

Here's How to Crack It

Here we have an adjective/adverb error. What should the last word in the sentence be? Tremendous*ly*. Cross off (A) and also (D), since it doesn't fix the error and changes the meaning of the sentence. (C) is way out there, so cross it off too. In (E), the placement of the *tremendously* is awkward and slightly changes the meaning of the sentence. ETS's answer is (B).

Active/Passive Voice

Last but not least, ETS prefers sentences written in the active voice to sentences written in the passive voice. In the **active voice**, the subject of the sentence is doing something. In the **passive voice**, the main actor becomes the object, and is being acted upon. The word *by* often (but not always) highlights passive voice.

Active:	She took the PSAT.
Passive:	The PSAT was taken *by* her.

Passive voice isn't wrong, but when you see it in a PSAT question, there will generally be a choice that uses that active voice, so if that choice is grammatical, pick it.

TECHNIQUE REVIEW

Before we go to Drill 3, let's review some techniques.

For Error ID questions, read the sentence and determine whether you spot an error. If you do spot an error, try to articulate that error to yourself to make sure you're not basing your decision simply on sound. Check the other answers against the grammar rules you've learned, and if you're still sure your original error is the correct answer, pick it.

If you don't spot an error right off the bat on an Error ID question, check all answer choices against the grammar rules. Eliminate any choices that stand up to scrutiny until you find an error or until only (E) is left.

For Improving Sentences questions, read the sentence and ask the same question—do you spot an error? If you do, try to articulate it to yourself, and if you decide it violates one of the rules we've discussed, eliminate (A) and any answer choice that repeats the error. Compare the remaining answer choices, eliminating errors until you are down to one.

If you don't spot an error immediately on an Improving Sentences question, move straight to comparing answer choices. The differences among the answer choices give you clues to what rules are being tested, and you can eliminate answers based on the rules you've learned. Repeat until only one answer choice is left.

Drill 3

Before we move on to Improving Paragraphs questions, try putting together what you've learned. Do the following Error ID and Improving Sentences questions using your grammar checklist. Remember to trim the fat and use POE. On Improving Sentences, do not hesitate to check out the answer choices for a clue to help you spot the error. You may wish to jot down your grammar checklist before you begin. Answers can be found in Part III.

1. When the student council announced its intention to elect a minority representative, <u>neither the principal nor the superintendent were willing to comment on the issue</u>.

   (A) neither the principal nor the superintendent were willing to comment on the issue
   (B) neither the principal or the superintendent were willing to comment on the issue
   (C) neither the principal nor the superintendent was willing to comment on the issue
   (D) neither of the principal nor the superintendent was willing to comment on the issue
   (E) neither the principal or the superintendent was willing to comment on the issue

2. Artists can offer startling representations of the world <u>but with their responsibility</u> to elevate humanity.

   (A) but with their responsibility
   (B) with the responsibility
   (C) having also the responsibility
   (D) but ought to be responsible
   (E) their responsibility being as well

3. The patient began his difficult postsurgery <u>recovery, but he was</u> able to recover from the psychological effects of the injury.

   (A) recovery, but he was
   (B) recovery, where he was
   (C) recovery only when he was
   (D) recovery only when being
   (E) recovery, also he was

4. <u>It is a more difficult task to learn to type than mastering a simple word-processing program.</u>

   (A) It is a more difficult task to learn to type than mastering a simple word-processing program.
   (B) It is more difficult of a task to learn to type than mastering a simple word-processing program.
   (C) It is a more difficult task to learn to type than to have mastered a simple word-processing program.
   (D) It is a more difficult task to learn to type than simply to master a word-processing program.
   (E) It is a more difficult task to learn to type than to master a simple word-processing program.

5. In 1962, Jackie Robinson gained admission to the National Baseball Hall of Fame, he was the first Black baseball player in the major leagues.

(A) In 1962, Jackie Robinson gained admission to the National Baseball Hall of Fame, he was the first Black baseball player in the major leagues.

(B) In 1962, Jackie Robinson, the first Black major-league baseball player, gained admission to the National Baseball Hall of Fame.

(C) In the National Baseball Hall of Fame in 1962, Jackie Robinson, the first Black baseball player in the major leagues, was admitted to it.

(D) With admission to the National Baseball Hall of Fame in 1962, he was the first Black major-league player to do it, Jackie Robinson.

(E) The first Black major-league player was when he was Jackie Robinson, admitted to the national Baseball Hall of Fame in 1962.

6. A well-organized person can go through the day efficiently, wasting little time or they waste none at all.

(A) wasting little time or they waste none at all
(B) wasting little or no time
(C) wasting little time or wasting none at all
(D) wasting either little time or none
(E) either little or no time being wasted

7. When Michelle Shocked recorded her *Arkansas Traveler* album, regional American folk songs were used as inspiration, but it was never copied exactly by her.

(A) regional American folk songs were used as inspiration, but it was never copied exactly by her
(B) regional American folk songs were used as inspiration, but she never copied them exactly
(C) regional American folk songs were used as inspiration by her and not copied exactly
(D) she used regional American folk songs, but they were not exactly copied
(E) she used regional American folk songs as inspiration, but never copied them exactly

8. Educators and parents agree that a daily reading time will not only enhance a child's education but also will encourage the child to read independently.

(A) but also will encourage the child to read independently
(B) but also encouraging the child to read independently
(C) but encourage the child to read independently too
(D) but encourage children to read independently
(E) but also encourage them to read independently

21. Eric's new CD <u>were destroyed</u> when Paula Ann, running
    A

    <u>quickly</u> <u>through</u> the office, stepped on it. <u>No error</u>
    B   C   D   E

22. Because <u>their</u> class <u>was going</u> on a field trip that day,
    A   B

    James and Alice <u>each</u> needed <u>a lunch</u> to bring to school.
    C   D

    <u>No error</u>
    E

23. None <u>of the</u> students on the review board <u>is</u> qualified to
    A   B

    ascertain <u>whether</u> the money was <u>well spent</u>. <u>No error</u>
    C   D   E

24. Just <u>between</u> you and <u>I</u>, *Borat* was the dumbest movie I
    A   B

    <u>have ever seen</u>. <u>No error</u>
    C   D   E

25. If you <u>had looked</u> at the prices <u>closely</u>, you'll see that the
    A   B

    "economy size" of detergent is <u>actually</u> more expensive
    C

    than the <u>smaller</u> trial sizes. <u>No error</u>
    D   E

26. The <u>new</u> course schedule worked out <u>splendid</u> for all
    A   B

    of those <u>students</u> who <u>had been</u> concerned. <u>No error</u>
    C   D   E

27. <u>Many</u> young adults find it extremely difficult <u>to return</u>
    A   B

    home from college and <u>abide with</u> the rules <u>set down</u>
    C   D

    by their parents. <u>No error</u>
    E

28. I recently heard an <u>announcement where</u> the Rangers
    A   B

    <u>will be playing</u> a game at home <u>this</u> weekend. <u>No error</u>
    C   D   E

29. Just <u>last month</u>, two weeks after the announcement
    A

    <u>of elections</u> in Kazakhstan, 92-year-old Fydor <u>has cast</u> his
    B   C

    <u>first vote in</u> 70 years. <u>No error</u>
    D   E

Improving Paragraphs

Questions in the Improving Paragraphs section are not just about grammar, but also about the logical flow of the passage and its support of the main idea.

The five Improving Paragraphs questions require you to make corrections to a "first draft" of a student's essay. You will be given a passage composed of approximately three paragraphs. Each paragraph contains numbered sentences. Your job is to "edit" the rough draft to make it better. You're not going to be asked lots of tough questions about the content of the passage, so take about 30 seconds to skim it before going to the questions.

Here is a sample passage for you to skim:

> (1) Conservation and ecology are the hot topics at our school. (2) Students used to just throw everything out in one big garbage pail. (3) Sure, it was easy. (4) It wasn't good for the environment.
>
> (5) I volunteered to head up the conservation team. (6) My friends and I decided to map out our strategies. (7) First we needed to get students to become aware of the problem. (8) Educating was important. (9) A thing to do was implement a recycling program. (10) We checked with the local town government. (11) They would supply the recycling bins. (12) We had to supply the people who'd be willing to recycle. (13) The most important thing students had to learn to do was to separate their garbage. (14) Glass in one container. (15) Plastic in another.
>
> (16) Our final step was to get the teachers and administrators involved. (17) Paper can be recycled too. (18) We ran a poster contest. (19) The winners are hanging in our halls. (20) Reuse, recycle, renew. (21) That's our school's new motto.

Now, before you get out your red pencil and jump in, there are a few more things you need to know. Your passage may consist of 15 or more sentences, each potentially containing some kind of error. However, you will be asked only five questions. Don't spend time fixing errors for which there are no questions.

The Questions

There are three basic types of questions that you will be asked:

- **Revision questions:** These questions ask you to revise sentences or parts of sentences in much the same way as Improving Sentences questions do.
- **Combination questions:** These questions ask you to combine two or more sentences to improve the quality and/or flow of the paragraph.
- **Content questions:** These questions ask you about passage content, typically by asking you to insert a sentence before or after a paragraph.

Revision Questions

As we mentioned, these questions are very similar to Improving Sentences questions. Therefore, you can follow the same basic approach. One warning: There is normally no such thing as "No error" on Improving Paragraphs questions. Do not assume that (A) is merely a repeat of the given sentence.

Even though the sentence you are revising is provided for you, you may still need to go back to the passage to gain some context when trying to fix a sentence. Before going back, however, use POE. If you have spotted an error in the given sentence, cross off answers that don't fix it. Also, cross off answer choices that contain obvious errors. After doing some POE, go back and read a few sentences before and after the given sentence in the passage. This should be enough context for you to determine the best edit.

Try the following revision question, referring back to the sample passage.

37. In context, what is the best way to revise sentence 9 (reproduced below)?

    A thing to do was implement a recycling program.

    (A) Next, we needed to implement a recycling program.
    (B) Implementing a recycling program was a thing to do.
    (C) A recycling program needed to be implemented.
    (D) Implementing a program for recycling was the step that would be next.
    (E) A program would need to be implemented next for recycling.

Here's How to Crack It

The correct revision will be concise and unambiguous. It will also flow well. We can get rid of choices (B), (D), and (E) before going back to the passage. Choice (B) is as clunky as the given sentence; choices (D) and (E) are awkwardly written.

That leaves (A) and (C). Choice (C) is in the passive voice, which is a reason to be very wary of choosing it. But choice (A) also seems to have a problem: It starts with the word *Next*, and if we don't consider the surrounding context, that looks a little weird. But if we *do* consider the surrounding context, it makes perfect sense. Go back to line 7: "First, we needed to..." Oh, so this is a list! First we did this, and next we did that, and finally we did the other thing. All righty then. (A) it is.

Combination Questions

Combination questions are revision questions with a twist: You are working with two sentences instead of one. The sentences are almost always reprinted for you underneath the question. As with revision questions, go back to the passage to get context and a sense of flow first.

To combine sentences you will need to work with conjunctions. If the sentences are flowing in the same direction, look for an answer with words like *and, since, as well as*, etc. If the sentences seem to be flowing in opposite directions, look for trigger words in the answer choices such as *however, but, on the contrary*, etc.

Try the following question:

---

38. Which of the following represents the most effective way to combine sentences 20 and 21 (reproduced below)?

Reuse, recycle, renew. That's our school's new motto.

(A) Reuse, recycle, renew and you know our school's new motto.

(B) The new motto of our school is that: "Reuse, recycle, renew."

(C) "Reuse, recycle, renew" are the new motto of our school now.

(D) The new motto of our school is reusing, recycling, and renewing.

(E) "Reuse, recycle, renew" is our school's new motto.

Here's How to Crack It

First, the sentences are moving in the same direction. Your job is to find a clear, concise way to combine them. (A) and (B) are out because they are poorly worded. (C) is a trap: "Reuse, recycle, renew" *is* a motto. Don't be fooled into thinking you need a plural verb simply because there is no "and" in answer choice (C). Choice (D) changes the quoted portion, and therefore the meaning. ETS's answer is (E).

Try another:

---

36. Which of the following represents the best revision of the underlined portions of sentences 7 and 8 (reproduced below)?

First we needed to get students to become aware of the <u>*problem. Educating was important*</u>.

(A) problem for educating was important
(B) problem of educating. It was important
(C) problem to educate was important
(D) problem: education was important
(E) problem for education was important to us

Here's How to Crack It

Again, we have a same-direction combination going on. We need something that flows. (A) and (C) use the wrong prepositions, which slightly change the meaning of the sentence. Cross them off. (B) is as awkward or more awkward than the original sentence. (E) uses the wrong preposition and adds extra awkward stuff. ETS's answer is (D). The colon is a nice, neat way to continue a thought without using two sentences.

Content Questions

ETS will occasionally ask you a question regarding the content of the passage. These questions may ask:

1. Which sentence should immediately follow or precede the passage?
2. Which sentence should be inserted into the passage?
3. What is the best description of the passage as a whole?

If you are asked the third question, you will need to read the whole passage. However, you will more likely be asked one of the first two questions. To answer these, you will need to read the relevant paragraph.

Try this example using the sample passage from earlier in this section:

35. Which of the following sentences, if added after sentence 4, would best serve to link the first paragraph to the second paragraph?

(A) Unfortunately, the environment suffered.
(B) Clearly, we had to make a change.
(C) Easy things are often not good for the environment.
(D) However, people can be very lazy.
(E) The school was against any change.

Here's How to Crack It

The question wants us to link the first two paragraphs together, which makes sense only if there's currently a gap between them. So let's look for the gap. The first paragraph is about the wasteful practices that used to be in vogue at this writer's school. Then we hit the second paragraph and all of a sudden we find that the writer has "volunteered to head up the conservation team." What conservation team? Did a conservation team just drop out of the sky? Something's missing! It looks like the link we need to make is between realizing that there are problems and deciding to take action.

If we look at the choices, we find that (A), (C), and (D) all just talk more about the problems with how people at the school dispose of their trash. Those choices don't make the transition to taking action. For that matter, neither does (E), which hints that trying to change the way students throw away their trash will be a futile effort. Only (B) gets us from seeing the problem to doing something about it, so pick (B).

Time Is of the Essence

Now, keep in mind that this is the end of a 30-minute section at the end of a two-hour test. You may not have the time or the energy to do all the Improving Paragraphs questions. Therefore, do the shorter, easier questions first. Then, if you have the time, do the longer questions.

Drill 4

Try the following Improving Paragraphs drill to practice what you have learned. Answers can be found in Part III.

(1) Censorship in the media had been an extremely important issue throughout the twentieth century. (2) In the 1950s television programs and movies had to comply with codes that enforced strict standards of propriety. (3) Couples were shown sleeping in separate beds, and the concept of nudity or verbal profanity was unheard of. (4) In reaction to them, in the 1960s and 1970s the media abandoned the codes in favor of more realistic representations of relationships and everyday life. (5) Filmmakers and songwriters were able to express themselves more honestly and freely. (6) The idea that in the early 1960s the Rolling Stones had to change their lyrics from "let's spend the night together" to "let's spend some time together" seemed almost unlikely by the end of the decade.

(7) Yet in the mid-1980s a period of conservative reaction occurred, turning the cycle around. (8) Explicit song lyrics began to be censored. (9) Warning labels were added to the covers of albums. (10) The labels indicated that some of the language might be "offensive" to the consumer. (11) It is unfortunate that people feel the need to blame the media for societal problems instead of realizing that the media only brings to light the problems that already exist.

(12) Hopefully, our reactions will ultimately break free of all previous patterns. (13) Yet until this happens we must remain content to know that the good parts of the past, as well as the bad, repeat themselves.

35. In context, what is the best version of the underlined portion of sentence 1 (reproduced below)?

Censorship in the media had been an extremely important issue throughout the twentieth century.

- (A) (as it is now)
- (B) was extremely
- (C) was an extremely
- (D) has been extreme as an
- (E) will be an extremely

36. Which of the following would be the best subject for a paragraph immediately preceding this essay?

- (A) The types of movies most popular in the 1950s
- (B) The changing role of the media over the last ten years
- (C) The ways in which the economy affects society's political views
- (D) The role of the media in European countries
- (E) The roots of media censorship

37. The author wishes to divide the first paragraph into two shorter paragraphs. The most appropriate place to begin a new paragraph would be

- (A) between sentences 1 and 2
- (B) between sentences 2 and 3
- (C) between sentences 3 and 4
- (D) between sentences 4 and 5
- (E) between sentences 5 and 6

38. What word could best replace "unlikely" in sentence 6?

- (A) strange
- (B) conventional
- (C) unpopular
- (D) inconceivable
- (E) unbearable

39. Which would be the best way to revise and combine the underlined portions of sentences 9 and 10 (reproduced below)?

Warning labels were added to the covers of albums. The labels indicated that some of the language might be "offensive" to the consumer.

- (A) albums, indicating
- (B) albums, which indicated
- (C) albums, and they indicated
- (D) albums, the indication being
- (E) albums, being indicative

Final Words of Wisdom

As with all the sections of the PSAT, don't be afraid to do some POE and guess. You will almost always be able to eliminate some answer choices, so always try to knock out the questions you know you can do in your first run through the questions. If you need a couple more points to reach your pacing goals or if you've started to answer the question but gotten stuck, eliminate whatever you can *quickly*, guess, and move on.

Summary

o   About one-fifth of all Improving Sentences and Error ID questions are correct as is—(A) for Improving Sentences and (E) for Error ID.

o   Resist using your ear to pick a right or wrong answer. You can use it to guide you toward possible errors, but you should always make the decision to keep or eliminate an answer choice based on grammar rules.

o   Remember to use Plan A or Plan B on all Improving Sentences and Error ID questions, based on whether you spot an error immediately after reading the sentence.

o   Verbs have to agree in number, be parallel, and be in the proper tense to be correct.

o   Pronouns have to agree, be in the proper case, and not be ambiguous in order to be correct.

o   Prepositions are always followed by a noun or pronoun and have to be idiomatically correct, meaning that some words go together just because.

o   Comparisons must equate two (or more) things that can really be compared, use the correct comparison word based on whether the things being compared can be counted (*less* vs. *fewer*), and must use the correct words based on how many things are being compared (*more* vs. *most*).

o   Modifiers must be placed directly next to the words they are modifying, so check to see that the placement of a modifier makes sense (and isn't "misplaced").

o   Adjectives modify only nouns, whereas adverbs modify verbs, adjectives, or other adverbs.

o   The test writers prefer active voice over passive voice, so if an answer choice says that something was done by someone, look for a better answer.

Chapter 11
Vocabulary

As you've seen, vocabulary can be an important issue in the Critical Reading sections of the PSAT, particularly in Sentence Completions. This chapter is intended to help you further develop your vocabulary.

How to Learn Vocabulary

First, let's talk about how NOT to learn vocabulary. Some people assume that you should take a dictionary, and learn each word, one at a time, starting with the letter *A*. This, of course, is not a very well thought-out plan. The kind of vocabulary that appears on the PSAT is actually a fairly narrow range of what is considered by the test writers to be those words that a well-educated college student should know. These are the words that are typically used by good writers of English prose, scholars, and scientists (when they're writing for the public and not in scientific jargon).

To help with learning vocabulary, it's extremely important that you carry a pocket dictionary with you all the time so you can look up unfamiliar words. You can find inexpensive paperback dictionaries at any used bookstore. Carry one with you from now until the test!

The Hit Parade

The Princeton Review's Hit Parade is a list of the words that commonly appear on the PSAT and SAT. It starts on page 205 of this book. This list is useful not only because some of these words are likely to appear on your test, but also because it shows you what *kinds* of words are typically tested on the PSAT and SAT. These are the sorts of words that you should pay particular attention to when you're doing your daily reading. Write them down and learn them!

Flash Cards

Some people like using flash cards as a way to help them learn vocabulary. Flash cards are useful, but be sure to write down not only the word and its definition, but also an example sentence in which you use that word. If you need help, ask a teacher, parent, or friend to help you come up with a sentence.

Some Daily Reading

While you are preparing for these tests, it's important that you get in the habit of reading. This will not only help you on the reading passages, but also will help you improve your vocabulary. Make sure to set aside 20–30 minutes *every day* to do some reading.

What should you read? Anything. Everything. Pick your favorite magazine or book. Ideally, read something that is above, but not too much above, your current reading level, but *read something every day*. While you're reading, circle any words that you don't understand, and look them up. Then add them to your list of words to learn. In fact, you should start a vocab journal and plan to update and maintain it from now until after the SAT, at least.

Using These Words

One great way to learn vocabulary is to be annoying. No kidding! Here's how you do it:

Pick 5–10 words each day. Write them down, along with their definitions, on a small note card, which you can refer to if your memory fails you. Now go about your daily business, but use these words every chance you get. Instead of *outgoing*, use the word *gregarious*. Instead of *funny*, use the word *mirthful*. You will really annoy your friends, but you will certainly learn those words.

Mnemonics

Another great technique for learning words is to find a mnemonic device. *Mnemonic* is from the Greek word *mneme*, which means "memory," so a mnemonic device is something that is so stupid or funny that it's unforgettable, and will help remind you of the meaning of a word. (By the way—what other common English word comes from that same Greek root *mneme*? We'll tell you in a minute.)

For instance, for the word *excavate*, which means "to make a hole by digging," you can think of the word *cave*. A cave is a hole underground and part of the word ex**cave**te.

How about another one? Let's try the word *paramount*, which means "of chief importance." You can remember this word because it's like a **mount**ain—it's the biggest and most important thing on the horizon.

Try making mnemonics for each of the following words:

prosaic

flagrant

clandestine

timorous

Once you've made your own mnemonics for the above words, read our examples on the following page.

Prosaic
Rebecca made a **pro**saic **mo**saic—it consisted of only one tile.

Flagrant
Burning the **flag** shows **flag**rant disrespect for the country.

Clandestine

The **clan** of spies planned a **clan**destine maneuver that depended on its secrecy to work.

Timorous

Tiny **Tim** was **timorous**; he was afraid that one day a giant would crush him.

And the answer to the earlier question: What other common English word has the same root (*mneme*) as the word *mnemonic*? *Amnesia* (the prefix *a-* meaning "without," the word itself means "without memory").

If you want more help with mnemonics, check out some other books by The Princeton Review: *Word Smart, Word Smart II, Illustrated Word Smart, More Illustrated Word Smart,* and *How to Remember Everything.* All of them contain some great drills, visuals, or mnemonics to help you memorize more words.

The Hit Parade

Here is a list of the words most commonly found on the PSAT. We've grouped them by topic, so they'll be easier to memorize. Happy studying!

> ## Pronunciation Guide
>
> A is pronounced like the *a* in *hat*
>
> AH is pronounced like the *a* in *father*
>
> AI and AY are pronounced like the *a* in *game*
>
> AW is pronounced like the *aw* in *law*
>
> E is pronounced like the *e* in *hem*
>
> EE is pronounced like the *e* in *me*
>
> I and IH are pronounced like the *i* in *icky*
>
> IE and Y (as a vowel) are pronounced like the *ie* in *lie*
>
> J is pronounced like the *j* in *jam*
>
> O is pronounced like the *o* in *home*
>
> OO is pronounced like the *oo* in *boot*
>
> OR is pronounced like the word *or*
>
> OW is pronounced like the *ow* in *cow*
>
> S is pronounced like the *s* in *sad*
>
> U and UH are pronounced like the *u* in *hum*
>
> ZH is pronounced like the *ge* in *garage*

WEEK 1

ARE YOU TALKIN' TO ME?

candid   KAN did

completely honest, straightforward

Candace's candidness overwhelmed her business colleagues, who were not used to such honesty.

conjecture   kun JEK chur

inference; guesswork

At this point, Kimaya's hypothesis about single-cell biorhythms is still conjecture; she doesn't have conclusive evidence.

didactic   die DAK tik

instructive

The tapes were entertaining and didactic; they both amused and instructed children.

euphemism   YOO fuh miz um

a mild, indirect, or vague term substituting for a harsh, blunt, or offensive term

"To pass away" is a common euphemism for dying.

extrapolate   ek STRAP uh layt

to infer or estimate by extending or projecting known information

Seeing the wrecked bike and his daughter's skinned knees, Heath extrapolated that she had had a biking accident.

incoherent   in ko HAIR unt

lacking cohesion or connection

Maury's sentences were so incoherent that nobody understood a word.

insinuate   in SIN yoo ayt

to introduce or communicate stealthily

Sean insinuated that Grace stole the arsenic, but he never came out and said it.

lucid   **LOO sid**

easily understood; clear

Our teacher provides lucid explanations of even the most difficult concepts so that we can all understand them.

rhetoric   **RET uh rik**

the art of using language effectively and persuasively

Since they are expected to make speeches, most politicians and lawyers are well versed in the art of rhetoric.

WHAT'S UP, TEACH?

acumen   **AK yoo men**

quickness, accuracy, and keenness of judgment or insight

Judge Ackerman's legal acumen was so well regarded that he was nicknamed the "Solomon of the South."

adroit   **uh DROYT**

dexterous; deft

An adroit balloon-animal-maker, Adrianna became popular at children's parties.

ascertain   **as er TAYN**

to find out, as through investigation or experimentation

The private investigator had long suspected my dog; before long, he ascertained that Toto was indeed the murderer.

astute   **uh STOOT**

shrewd; clever

Stewart is financially astute; he invests wisely and never falls for scams.

circumspect   **SER kum spekt**

careful; prudent; discreet

Ned's circumspect manner makes him a wise appointment to the diplomatic corps.

disseminate   dis SEM uh nayt

to scatter widely, as in sowing seed

> The news about Dave's embarrassing moment at the party disseminated quickly through the school; by the end of the day, everyone knew what had happened.

erudition   er yuh DISH un

deep, extensive learning

> Professor Rudy's erudition was such that she could answer any question her students put to her.

husbandry   HUZ bun dree

the application of scientific principles to agriculture, especially to animal breeding

> After years of practicing animal husbandry, Marsha's husband was able to create a breed of dog that actually walked itself.

pedantic   puh DAN tik

excessively concerned with book learning and formal rules

> Pedro's pedantic tendencies prompted him to remind us constantly of all the grammatical rules we were breaking.

perspicacious   per spih KAY shus

shrewd; clear-sighted

> Persephone's perspicacious mind had solved so many cases that the popular private investagator was able to retire.

pragmatic   prag MAT ik

practical

> Never one for wild and unrealistic schemes, Matt took a pragmatic approach to research.

precocious   pre KO shus

exhibiting unusually early intellectual aptitude or maturity

> Bobby Fisher's precocious intellect made him one of the world's best chess players before he could even drive.

prospectus   pro SPEK tus

  formal proposal

    Before writing my thesis, I had to submit a detailed prospectus to the
    department for approval.

rudimentary   roo duh MEN tuh ree

  basic; elementary; in the earliest stages of development

    Josh's rudimentary golf skills were easily overpowered by Tiger Woods's
    amazing performance on the green.

WHEN THE GOING GETS TOUGH

abstruse   ab STROOS

  difficult to understand

    Abby found her professor's lecture on non-Euclidian geometry abstruse;
    she doubted anyone else in class understood it either.

callous   KAL us

  emotionally hardened; unfeeling

    Callie's callous remark about her friend's cluttered room really hurt his
    feelings.

convoluted   kon vo LOO tid

  intricate; complex

    The directions were so convoluted that we became hopelessly lost.

enigma   en IG ma

  a puzzle, mystery, or riddle

    The emu was an enigma; you could never tell what it was thinking.

inscrutable   in SKROOT uh bul

  difficult to fathom or understand; impenetrable

    The ancient poet's handwriting was so inscrutable that even the most
    prominent Latin scholars could not read the manuscript.

reticent   RET uh sint

inclined to keep silent; reserved

Rosanna's reticent behavior caused the interviewer to think her incapable of conversing with other students.

staid   STAYD

unemotional; serious

Mr. Estado was well known for his staid demeanor; he stayed calm even when everyone else celebrated the team's amazing victory.

CULTURAL ARTIFACTS

arcane   ar KAYN

known or understood by only a few

The dusty archive includes an arcane treasure trove of nautical charts from the Age of Discovery.

assimilate   uh SIM uh layt

to absorb or become absorbed; to make or become similar

Keisha assimilated so quickly at her new school that she was named head of the social committee a month after enrolling.

autonomy   aw TAHN uh mee

independence; self-determination

Candice gained autonomy upon moving out of her parents' house into her own apartment.

cosmopolitan   koz mo PAHL i tun

worldly; widely sophisticated

Inga was surprisingly cosmopolitan considering that she had never left her tiny hometown in Norway.

derivative   duh RIV uh tiv

something that comes from another source

Special Victims Unit and *Criminal Intent* are derivatives of the original *Law & Order* drama series.

entourage   AHN ter azh

  a group of attendants or associates; a retinue

  Top celebrities travel with extensive entourages, which often include
  security guards, assistants, stylists, managers, publicists, and more.

esoteric   es oh TAIR ik

  intended for or understood by only a small group

  Esme's play is extremely esoteric; someone not raised in Estonia would
  find it difficult to follow.

gaffe   GAF

  a clumsy social error; a faux pas

  Geoff committed the gaffe of telling his date that he'd gone out with
  her sister the night before.

idiosyncrasy   ID ee oh SINK ruh see

  characteristic peculiar to an individual or group

  She had many idiosyncrasies, one of which was washing her socks in
  the dishwasher.

insular   IN suh ler

  isolated; narrow or provincial

  The family was so insular that no one else could get near them.

orthodox   OR thuh doks

  adhering to the traditional and established, especially in religion

  My father held an orthodox view of baseball; he believed that the field
  should be outside and made of real grass.

potentate   PO tun tayt

  one who has the power and position to rule over others; monarch

  An omnipotent potentate is a person to be reckoned with; great power
  in the hands of a great leader is a powerful combination.

CAST OUT

castigate   **KAS tih gayt**

to scold, rebuke, or harshly criticize

Mr. Castile preferred not to castigate student misbehavior publicly; instead, he would quietly send the troublemaker to the principal's office.

censure   **SEN shur**

to issue official blame

In recent years the FCC has censured networks for the provocative antics of Super Bowl halftime acts; what goes on during the game, however, usually escapes the organization's notice.

denounce   **duh NOWNTS**

to condemn openly

In many powerful speeches throughout his lifetime, Martin Luther King, Jr. denounced racism as immoral.

reclusive   **ree KLOO siv**

seeking or preferring seclusion or isolation

Our neighbors were quite reclusive, hardly ever emerging from behind the closed doors of their home.

relinquish   **ree LING kwish**

to retire from; give up or abandon

Ricky relinquished his career in order to search for the source of the world's best relish.

renounce   **ree NOWNTS**

to give up (a title, for example), especially by formal announcement

Nancy renounced her given name and began selling records under the moniker "Boedicia."

vituperative   **vie TOOP ur uh tiv**

marked by harshly abusive condemnation

The vituperative speech was so cruel that the members left feeling completely abused.

THERE'S NO WAY AROUND IT

circumscribe   SER kum skryb
    to draw a circle around; to restrict
      The archeologist circumscribed the excavation area on the map.

contiguous   kun TIG yoo us
    sharing an edge or boundary; touching
      The continental United States consists of 48 contiguous states.

WEEK 2

I'LL BE THE JUDGE OF THAT!

conciliatory   kon SIL ee uh tor ee
    appeasing; soothing; showing willingness to reconcile
      After arguing endlessly with them for weeks, Connie switched to a more conciliatory tone with her parents once prom season arrived.

credible   KRED uh bul
    capable of being believed; plausible
      The shocking but credible report of mice in the kitchen kept Eddie up all night.

exonerate   eg ZON er ayt
    to free from blame
      Xena was exonerated of all charges.

incontrovertible   in kahn truh VERT uh bul
    indisputable; not open to question
      The videotape of the robbery provided incontrovertible evidence against the suspect—he was obviously guilty.

indict   in DITE
    to officially charge with wrongdoing or a crime
      President Nixon was indicted during the Watergate scandal.

litigious   luh TIJ us

prone to engage in lawsuits

Letitia was a litigious little girl; at one point, she tried to sue her dog.

partisan   PAR tiz un

devoted to or biased in support of a party, group, or cause

Today's partisan politics are so antagonistic that it's difficult to reach a successful compromise on any issue.

parity   PA ruh tee

equality, as in amount, status, or value (antonym: disparity)

The judges at the Olympics must score each athlete's performance with parity; such impartial treatment is hard since one always wants to root for one's own country.

rectitude   REK ti tood

moral uprightness; righteousness

Thanks to his unerring sense of fairness and justice, Viktor was a model of moral rectitude; his hometown even erected a statue in his honor.

remiss   ree MISS

lax in attending to duty; negligent

Cassie was remiss in fulfilling her Miss America duties; she didn't even come close to ending world hunger.

repudiate   ree PYOO dee ayt

to reject the validity or authority of

I repudiated the teacher's arguments about Empress Wu Zetian's reputation by showing him that the reports of her cruelty were from unreliable sources.

sanctimonious   sank ti MO nee us

feigning piety or righteousness

The sanctimonious scholar had actually been plagiarizing other people's work for years.

scrupulous   SKROO pyoo lus

principled, having a strong sense of right and wrong; conscientious and exacting

Evan's scrupulous behavior began to annoy his friends when he called the cops on them for toilet papering their teacher's house.

solicitous   so LIS it us

concerned

The parents asked solicitous questions about the college admissions officer's family.

sophistry   SAHF is tree

plausible but misleading or fallacious argument

The professor's sophistry misled the sophomore into incorrect beliefs.

substantiate   sub STAN shee ayt

to support with proof or evidence; verify

The argument was substantiated by clear facts and hard evidence.

veracity   vuh RA si tee

adherence to the truth; truthfulness

Since Vera was known for her veracity, it came as a complete shock when her family found out she'd lied on her application.

vindicate   VIN dih kayt

to free from blame

Mrs. Layton was finally vindicated after her husband admitted to the crime.

FLATTERY WILL GET YOU NOWHERE

cajole   kuh JOL

to urge with repeated appeals, teasing, or flattery

The sweet-talking senior cajoled an impressionable junior into seeing *Lord of the Rings* for the tenth time.

chicanery   chik AY ner ee
    trickery

      The candidate accused his debate opponent of resorting to cheap chicanery to sway the electorate.

obsequious   ob SEEK wee us
    fawning and servile

      Kevin was so obsequious that even his teachers were embarrassed; as a result, his sucking up rarely led to better grades.

sycophant   SIK uh fent
    insincere, obsequious flatterer

      Siggie is such a sycophant; he slyly sucks up to his teachers and reaps the rewards of his behavior.

ONE PERSON CAN CHANGE THE WORLD

altruism   AL troo iz im
    unselfish concern for the welfare of others; selflessness

      Alta, a model of altruism, gave her movie ticket to someone who needed it more.

eminent   EM uh nent
    distinguished; prominent

      Emeril Lagasse is one of the most eminent chefs working today; every TV-watcher knows how well known and highly regarded he is.

empathetic   em puh THET ik
    identification with and understanding of another's situation, feelings, and motives

      Emily is one of my most empathetic friends; she can always relate to my emotions.

extol   ek STOL
    to praise highly

      Tollivan extolled the virtues of the troll while his teacher looked on amazed.

laudatory   LAW duh tor ee

    full of praise

        The principal's speech was laudatory, congratulating the students on their SAT scores.

magnanimous   mag nan IM it ee

    courageously or generously noble in mind and heart

        The magnanimous prince cared deeply for his country and its people.

philanthropic   fil un THROP ik

    humanitarian; benevolent; relating to monetary generosity

        Phil was a philanthropic soul, always catering to the needy and the underprivileged.

reciprocate   ree SIP ro kayt

    to mutually take or give; to respond in kind

        The chef reciprocated his rival's respect; they admired each other so much that they even traded recipes.

GET RID OF IT

defunct   duh FUNKT

    no longer existing or functioning

        The theory that the world was flat became defunct when Magellan sailed to the West and didn't fall off the earth.

eradicate   er RAD i kayt

    to get rid of as if by tearing it up by the roots; abolish

        Radcliffe did her best to eradicate the radishes from her farm.

expurgate   ek spur GAYT

    to remove objectionable content before publication or release

        The Chinese government expurgates nearly all obscene matter from the nation's Internet.

extirpate   ek stir PAYT

    to destroy

        While the family was on vacation, the termites practically extirpated the house.

quell   KWEL

>*to put down forcibly; suppress*

Nell quelled the fight over the quiche by throwing it out the window—
she had long given up on reasoning with her sisters.

raze   RAYZ

>*to level to the ground; demolish*

It is difficult to raze a city building without demolishing other structures
around it.

squelch   SKWELCH

>*to crush as if by trampling; squash*

Sam wanted to keep squash as pets, but Quentin squelched the idea.

supplant   suh PLANT

>*to usurp the place of, especially through intrigue or underhanded tactics*

The ants prepared to supplant the roaches as the dominant insect in the
kitchen; their plan was to take the roaches by surprise and drive them
out.

stymie   STY mee

>*to thwart or stump*

Stan was stymied by the Sudoku puzzle; he just couldn't solve it.

IF YOU CAN'T SAY ANYTHING NICE

abase   uh BAYS

>*to lower in rank, prestige, or esteem*

Bayard's withering restaurant review was an attempt to abase his former
friend, the owner.

deride   duh RIDE

>*to mock contemptuously*

Derrick was derided for wearing two different colored socks, but he
couldn't help it—it was laundry day.

derogatory   duh RAH guh tor ee

   insulting or intended to insult

   The unethical politician didn't just attack his opponent's views; he
   also made derogatory remarks about the other candidate's family and
   personal hygiene.

disparage   dis PAR uj

   to speak of negatively; to belittle

   Wanda disparaged Glen by calling him a cheat and a liar.

effrontery   eh FRON ter ee

   brazen boldness; presumptuousness

   The attorney's effrontery in asking such personal questions so shocked
   Esther that she immediately ran from the office.

ignominy   IG nuh mi nee

   great personal dishonor or humiliation; disgraceful conduct

   Ignacio felt great ignominy after the scandal broke.

impugn   im PYOON

   to attack as false or questionable

   Instead of taking the high road, the candidate impugned his opponent's
   character.

mar   MAR

   to damage, especially in a disfiguring way

   The perfect day was marred by the arrival of storm clouds.

pejorative   puh JOR uh tiv

   disparaging, belittling, insulting

   Teachers should refrain from using pejorative terms as *numbskull* and
   jackass to refer to other teachers.

vex   VEKS

   to annoy or bother; to perplex

   Bex's mom was vexed when Bex was very vague about her whereabouts
   for the evening.

vindictive   vin DIK tiv

disposed to seek revenge; revengeful; spiteful

Vincenzo was very vindictive; when someone hurt him, he responded
by vigorously plotting revenge.

WEEK 3

OVERKILL

bombastic   bom BAS tik

given to pompous speech or writing

The principal's bombastic speech bombed in the eyes of the students; it
only furthered their impression of him as a pompous jerk.

ebullience   eh BOO li ents

intense enthusiasm

A sense of ebullience swept over the lacrosse fans crowd when their
team won the game.

exorbitant   eg ZOR bit int

exceeding all bounds, as of custom or fairness

I wanted to buy a Porsche, but the price was exorbitant, so instead I
purchased a used mail truck.

exuberant   eg ZOO bur ent

full of unrestrained enthusiasm or joy

William was exuberant when he found out that he'd gotten into the
college of his choice.

embellish   em BELL ish

to ornament or decorate; to exaggerate

One can never trust that Anwar's stories are realistic; his details are almost
always embellished so that his experiences sound more interesting than
they really are.

flagrant   **FLAY grent**
> *extremely or deliberately shocking or noticeable*
>> Burning the flag shows flagrant disrespect for the country.

gratuitous   **gruh TOO uh tus**
> *given freely; unearned; unnecessary*
>> The film was full of gratuitous sex and violence inessential to the story.

lavish (adj)   **LAV ish**
> *extravagant*
>> Lavanya's wedding was a lavish affair.

lugubrious   **luh GOO bree yus**
> *mournful, dismal, or gloomy, especially to an exaggerated or ludicrous degree*
>> Lucas's lugubrious eulogy for his pet lobster quickly became ridiculous.

opulent   **OP yoo lent**
> *displaying great wealth*
>> The ophthalmologist's opulent home was the envy of his friends; the crystal chandeliers, marble floors, and teak furniture must have cost a fortune.

ornate   **or NAYT**
> *elaborately decorated*
>> The wood carvings were so ornate that you could examine them many times and still notice things you had not seen before.

penchant   **PEN chent**
> *a strong inclination or liking*
>> Penny's penchant for chocolate-covered ants led her to munch on them all day.

redundant   **ree DUN dint**
> *needlessly repetitive*
>> The author's speech was terribly redundant, repeating the same phrases, saying the same thing over and over, and constantly reiterating the same point.

ubiquitous   yoo BIK wit us

being or seeming to be everywhere at the same time; omnipresent

Kenny had a ubiquitous little sister; wherever he turned, there she was.

THROUGH SOMEONE ELSE'S EYES

vicarious   vie KA ree us

felt or undergone as if one were taking part in the experience or feelings of another

Stan, who was never athletic but loved sports, lived vicariously through his brother, a professional basketball player.

vignette   vin YET

a short scene or story

The poodle vignette in my new film expresses the true meaning of Valentine's Day.

LOTS 'N' LOTS

amalgam   uh MAL gum

a combination of diverse elements; a mixture

The song was an amalgam of many different styles, from blues to hip hop to folk.

inundate   IN un dayt

to overwhelm as if with a flood; to swamp

The day after the ad ran, Martha was inundated with phone calls.

multifarious   mul ti FAYR ee us

diverse; various

The multifarious achievements of Leonardo da Vinci, ranging from architecture and painting to philosophy and science, are unparalleled in our century.

multiplicity   mul tuh PLI sit ee

state of being various or manifold; a great number

A multiplicity of views is essential to a healthy multicultural democracy.

IT'S GETTING BETTER ALL THE TIME

alleviate   **uh LEE vee ayt**

to ease a pain or burden

Alvin meditated to alleviate the pain from the headache he got after taking the SAT.

ameliorate   **uh MEEL yor ayt**

to make something better; improve

Winning a silver medal quickly ameliorated Amelia's angst at losing the gold.

beneficial   **ben uh FISH ul**

producing or promoting a favorable result; helpful

According to my doctor, tea's beneficial effects may include reducing anxiety.

curative   **KYUR uh tiv**

able to heal or cure

The aloe had a curative effect on my sunburn; within hours, the flaking had stopped.

palliative   **PAL lee uh tiv**

relieving or soothing the symptoms of a disease or disorder without effecting a cure

Watching professional polo on TV became a palliative for the screaming child; it was the only thing that would quiet him.

therapeutic   **thair uh PYOO tik**

having or exhibiting healing powers

The therapeutic air of the Mediterranean cured Thomas of his asthma.

MODEL BEHAVIOR

complement   KOM plem ent
   something that completes, goes with, or brings to perfection

   The lovely computer is the perfect complement to the modern
   furnishings in Abby's apartment.

epitome   ep IT o mee
   a representative or example of a type

   She is the epitome of selflessness; no matter how much or little she has,
   she always gives to others.

felicitous   fuh LIH sih tus
   admirably suited; apt

   Jamie Foxx made a felicitous speech when he won his Oscar.

LIAR, LIAR, PANTS ON FIRE

belie   bee LIE
   to misrepresent

   He smiled in order to belie his hostility.

debunk   duh BUNK
   to expose untruths, shams, or exaggerated claims

   The university administration debunked the myth that bunk beds are
   only for children by installing them in every dorm on campus.

dubious   DOO bee us
   doubtful; of unlikely authenticity

   Jerry's dubious claim that he could fly like Superman didn't win him
   any summer job offers.

duplicitous   doo PLIS uh tus
   deliberately deceptive

   The duplicitous man duplicated dollars and gave the counterfeits to
   unsuspecting vendors.

fabricate   **FAB ruh kayt**

to make up in order to deceive

Fabio fabricated the story that he used to play drums for Metallica; he has never actually held a drumstick in his life.

fallacy   **FAL uh see**

a false notion

The idea that there is only one college for you is a fallacy.

mendacious   **men DAY shus**

lying; untruthful

John's mendacious statements on the stand sealed his fate; he was found guilty of lying to the court about his role in the crime.

specious   **SPEE shus**

having the ring of truth or plausibility but actually false

Susie's specious argument seemed to make sense, but when I looked more closely, it was clearly illogical.

SITTIN' ON THE FENCE

ambiguous   **am BIG yoo us**

open to more than one interpretation

Big's eyes were an ambiguous color: in some lights they looked brown, and in others, green.

ambivalent   **am BIV uh lint**

simultaneously feeling opposing feelings; uncertain

Amy felt ambivalent about her dance class: On one hand, she enjoyed the exercise, but on the other, the choice of dances bored her.

apathetic   **ap uh THET ik**

feeling or showing little emotion

The apathetic students didn't even bother to vote for class president.

capricious   **kuh PREE shus**

impulsive and unpredictable

The referee's capricious behavior angered the players; he would call a foul for minor contact, but ignore elbowing and kicking.

equivocal   **e KWIV uh kul**

open to two or more interpretations and often intended to mislead; ambiguous (antonym: unequivocal)

> The politician made so many equivocal statements during the scandal that no one could be sure what, if anything, he had admitted to.

erratic   **e RAT ik**

markedly inconsistent

> Erroll's erratic behavior made it difficult for his friends to predict what he would do in a given moment.

impetuous   **im PET choo us**

suddenly and forcefully energetic or emotional; impulsive and passionate

> Mr. Limpet was so impetuous that we never knew what he would do next.

impetus   **IM pit us**

an impelling force or stimulus

> A looming deadline provided Imelda with the impetus she needed to finish her research paper.

sporadic   **spo RAD ik**

occurring at irregular intervals; having no pattern or order in time

> Storms in Florida are sporadic; it's hard to predict when they're going to occur.

vacillate   **VA sil ayt**

to sway from one side to the other; oscillate

> The cook vacillated between favoring chicken and preferring fish; he just couldn't decide which to prepare.

whimsical   **WIM zi kul**

characterized by whim; unpredictable

> Egbert rarely behaved as expected; indeed, he was a whimsical soul whose every decision was anybody's guess.

I JUST CAN'T TAKE IT ANYMORE

flag   **FLAG**

> to decline in vigor or strength; to tire; to droop

> After several few days climbing mountains in pouring rain, our enthusiasm for the hiking trip began to flag.

jaded   **JAY did**

> worn out; wearied

> Jade's experiences had jaded her; she no longer believed that the junk stacked in her garage was going to make her rich.

WEEK 4

SHE'S CRAFTY

ingenuous   **in JEN yoo us**

> lacking in cunning, guile, or worldliness (antonym: disingenuous)

> Janine was so ingenuous that it was too easy for her friends to dupe her.

subterfuge   **SUB ter fyoozh**

> a deceptive stratagem or device

> The submarine pilots were trained in the art of subterfuge; they were excellent at faking out their enemies.

surreptitious   **sir up TISH us**

> secretive; sneaky

> Sara drank the cough syrup surreptitiously because she didn't want anyone to know that she was sick.

JUST A LITTLE BIT

dearth   DERTH

scarce supply; lack

There was a dearth of money in my piggybank; it collected dust, not bills.

modicum   MAHD ik um

a small, moderate, or token amount

A modicum of effort may result in a small score improvement; in order to improve significantly, however, you must study as often as possible.

paucity   PAW sit ee

smallness in number; scarcity

The struggling city had a paucity of resources and therefore a high level of poverty.

squander   SKWAN der

to spend wastefully

Kerri squandered her savings on shoes and wasn't able to buy her apartment.

temperate   TEM per ut

moderate; restrained (antonym: intemperate)

Temperate climates rarely experience extremes in temperature.

tenuous   TEN yoo us

having little substance or strength; shaky

Her grasp on reality is tenuous at best; she's not even sure what year it is.

I WILL SURVIVE

diligent   DIL uh jint

marked by painstaking effort; hard-working

With diligent effort, they were able to finish the model airplane in record time.

maverick   MAV rik

one who is independent and resists adherence to a group

In the movie *Top Gun*, Tom Cruise played a maverick who often broke rules and did things his own way.

mercenary   MUR sin air ee

motivated solely by a desire for money or material gain

During the war, Mercer was a mercenary; he'd fight for whichever side paid him the most for his services.

obstinate   OB stin it

stubbornly attached to an opinion or a course of action

Despite Jeremy's broken leg, his parents were obstinate; they steadfastly refused to buy him an XBox.

proliferate   pro LIF er ayt

to grow or increase rapidly

Because fax machines, pagers, and cell phones have proliferated in recent years, many new area codes have been created to handle the demand for phone numbers.

tenacity   te NAS uh tee

persistence

With his overwhelming tenacity, Clark was finally able to interview Brad Pitt for the school newspaper.

vigilant   VIJ uh lent

on the alert; watchful

The participants of the candlelight vigil were vigilant, as they had heard that the fraternity across the street was planning to egg them.

CONNECT THE DOTS

extraneous   ek STRAY nee us

irrelevant; inessential

The book, though interesting, had so much extraneous information that it was hard to keep track of the important points.

juxtapose   JUK stuh pohz

to place side by side, especially for comparison or contrast

Separately the pictures look identical, but if you juxtapose them, you can see the differences.

superfluous   soo PUR floo us

extra; unnecessary

If there is sugar in your tea, honey would be superfluous.

synergy   SIN er jee

combined action or operation

The synergy of hydrogen and oxygen creates water.

tangential   tan JEN chul

merely touching or slightly connected; only superficially relevant

Though Abby's paper was well written, its thesis was so tangential to its proof that her teacher couldn't give her a good grade.

I WRITE THE SONGS

aesthetic   es THET ik

having to do with the appreciation of beauty

Aesthetic considerations determined the arrangement of paintings at the museum; as long as art looked good together, it didn't matter who had painted it.

aural   AW rul

of or related to the ear or the sense of hearing

It should come as no surprise that musicians prefer aural to visual learning.

cacophony   kuh KAH fuh nee

discordant, unpleasant noise

Brian had to shield his ears from the awful cacophony produced by the punk band onstage.

dirge   DERJ

a funeral hymn or lament

The dirge was so beautiful that everyone cried, even those who hadn't known the deceased.

eclectic   uh KLEK tik

made up of a variety of sources or styles

Lou's taste in music is quite eclectic; he listens to everything from rap to polka.

incongruous   in KAHN groo us

lacking in harmony; incompatible

My chicken and jello soup experiment failed; the tastes were just too incongruous.

sonorous   SAHN ur us

producing a deep or full sound

My father's sonorous snoring keeps me up all night unless I close my door and wear earplugs.

strident   STRY dent

loud, harsh, grating, or shrill

The strident shouting kept the neighbors awake all night.

DUDE, THIS SUCKS!

debacle   **duh BAHK ul**

disastrous or ludicrous defeat or failure; fiasco

Jim's interview was a complete debacle; he accidentally locked himself in the bathroom, sneezed on the interviewer multiple times, and knocked over the president of the company.

debilitate   **duh BIL i tayt**

impair the strength of; weaken

Deb ran the New York City marathon without proper training; the experience left her debilitated for weeks.

tumultuous   **tum UL choo us**

noisy and disorderly

The tumultuous applause was so deafening that the pianist couldn't hear the singer.

IT'S ALL IN THE TIMING

anachronistic   **ah nak ruh NIS tik**

the representation of something as existing or happening in the wrong time period

I noticed an anachronism in the museum's ancient Rome display: a digital clock ticking behind a statue of Venus.

archaic   **ar KAY ik**

characteristic of an earlier time; antiquated; old

"How dost thou?" is an archaic way of saying "How are you?"

dilatory   **DIL uh tor ee**

habitually late

Always waiting until the last moment to leave home in the morning, Dylan was a dilatory student.

ephemeral   uh FEM er ul

   lasting for only a brief time

   The importance of SAT scores is truly ephemeral; when you are applying,
   they are crucial, but once you get into college, no one cares how well
   you did.

redolent   RED uh lint

   fragrant; aromatic; suggestive

   The aroma of apple pie wafted into my room, redolent of weekends
   spent baking with my grandmother.

temporal   TEM per ul

   of, relating to, or limited by time

   One's enjoyment of a mocha latte is bound by temporal limitations; all
   too soon, the latte is gone.

WHO CAN IT BE NOW?

onerous   O ner us

   troublesome or oppressive; burdensome

   The onerous task was so difficult that Ona thought she'd never get
   through it.

portent   POR tent

   indication of something important or calamitous about to occur; omen

   A red morning sky is a terrible portent for all sailors—it means that
   stormy seas are ahead.

prescience   PRE shens

   knowledge of actions or events before they occur; foreknowledge; foresight

   Preetha's prescience was such that people wondered if she was psychic;
   how else could she know so much about the future?

BOOORING

austere   **aw STEER**

without decoration; strict

The gray walls and bare floors of his monastery cell provided an even more austere setting than Brother Austen had hoped for.

banal   **buh NAL**

drearily commonplace; predictable; trite

The poet's imagery is so banal that I think she cribbed her work from *Poetry for Dummies.*

hackneyed   **HAK need**

worn out through overuse; trite

All Hal could offer in the way of advice were hackneyed old phrases that I'd heard a hundred times before.

insipid   **in SIP id**

uninteresting; unchallenging; lacking taste or savor

That insipid movie was so predictable that I walked out.

prosaic   **pro ZAY ik**

unimaginative; dull (antonym: poetic)

Rebecca made a prosaic mosaic consisting of identical, undecorated tiles.

soporific   **sah puh RIF ik**

inducing or tending to induce sleep

The congressman's speech was so soporific that even his cat was yawning.

vapid   **VAP id**

lacking liveliness, animation, or interest; dull

Valerie's date was so vapid that she thought he was sleeping with his eyes open.

WEEK 5

IT ALL CHANGES SO FAST

brevity   BRE vi tee
> *the quality or state of being brief in duration*

   Brevity = briefness. (You can't get any shorter than that!)

expedient   ek SPEE dee ent
> *appropriate to a purpose; convenient; speedy*

   It was more expedient to use FedEx than to use the post office.

transient   TRAN zhent
> *passing quickly in time or space*

   Jack Dawson enjoyed his transient lifestyle; with nothing but the clothes
   on his back and the air in his lungs, he was free to travel wherever he
   wanted.

FULL ON

augment   awg MENT
> *to make greater, as in size, extent, or quantity; to supplement*

   The model Angele Franju is rumored to have augmented her studies in
   chemistry with a minor in German literature.

bolster   BOWL ster
> *to hearten, support or prop up*

   The class bolstered Amelia's confidence; she had no idea she already
   knew so much.

burgeon   BER jun
> *to grow and flourish*

   The burgeoning Burgess family required a new house because its old
   one had only one bedroom.

copious   KO pee us
> *plentiful; having a large quantity*

   She took copious notes during class, using up five large notebooks.

distend   dis TEND

  to swell out or expand from internal pressure, as when overly full

  The balloon distended as it was filled with helium, much like Mike's stomach after Mike ate an entire turkey on Thanksgiving.

grandiose   gran dee OHS

  great in scope or intent; grand

  The party was a grandiose affair; hundreds of richly dressed guests danced the night away.

prodigious   pruh DIJ us

  enormous

  Steven Spielberg's prodigious talent has made him the most successful film producer and director of our time.

profundity   pro FUN di tee

  great depth of intellect, feeling, or meaning

  The actor's profundity surprised the director, who had heard that he was a bit of an airhead.

redouble   ree DUB ul

  to make twice as great; to double

  Rita redoubled her efforts to become president of her class by campaigning twice as hard as before.

scintillating   SIN til ay ting

  brilliant

  The writer's scintillating narrative diverted Izabel's attention away from her other guests.

DON'T MAKE WAVES

averse   uh VERS
strongly disinclined

Ava proved so averse to homework that she would break out in hives at the mere mention of it.

conspicuous   kun SPIK yoo us
easy to notice; obvious (antonym: inconspicuous)

The red tuxedo was conspicuous among all the classic black ones. What was he thinking?

demure   duh MYUR
modest and reserved

Muriel was the most demure girl in the class, always sitting quietly in the back of the room and downplaying any compliments she received.

diffidence   DIF uh dins
timidity or shyness

Lea's diffident nature often prevented her from speaking out in class.

docile   DAHS i ul
submissive to instruction; willing to be taught

The SAT class was so docile that the teacher wondered if she was in the right room.

innocuous   in NAHK yoo us
having no adverse effect; harmless

The plants were as innocuous as they looked; we suffered no ill effects from eating their leaves.

placid   PLAS id
calm or quiet; undisturbed

Lake Placid was the place to go for those in need of a quiet vacation.

quiescent   kwee ES sint
quiet, still, or at rest; inactive

Quinn's quiescent behavior made him an ideal roommate.

DO YOU AGREE?

concord   **KON kord**
    agreement (antonym: discord)
      The class was in concord about the necessity to perform *Hamlet*, rather
      than *King Lear*, in the spring show.

concur   **kun KUR**
    to agree
      The board concurred that the con artist who had stolen their money
      had to be convicted.

dogmatic   **dog MAT ik**
    stubbornly attached to insufficiently proven beliefs
      Avik was dogmatic in his belief that the power lines were giving his dog
      headaches.

fastidious   **fas TID ee us**
    carefully attentive to detail; difficult to please
      Kelly, always so fastidious, dramatically edited our group's report.

intransigence   **in TRAN zi jents**
    refusal to moderate a position or to compromise
      Jeff was so intransigent in his views that it was impossible to have a
      rational debate with him.

jocular   **JOK yoo ler**
    characterized by or given to joking
      Yung-Ji's jocular disposition helped him gain popularity.

meticulous   **muh TIK yoo lus**
    extremely careful and precise
      Since Kelly was so meticulous, we asked her to proofread our group's
      report.

OFFICER FRIENDLY

affable   AF uh bul

easy going; friendly

My mom always said that the key to being affable is the ability to make others laugh.

alacrity   uh LAK ruh tee

promptness in response; cheerful readiness; eagerness

I was so happy when I got the acceptance letter from the University of Alaska that I sprinted home with great alacrity to share the good news.

amiable   AY mee uh bul

friendly; agreeable; good-natured

Mr. Amis was so amiable that he let us call him "Big A."

benign   be NINE

kind and gentle

Uncle Ben is a benign and friendly man who is always willing to help.

sanguine   SAN gwin

cheerfully confident; optimistic

Harold's sanguine temperament kept him cheerful, even through somber times.

NASTY BOYS

belligerent   buh LIH jer int

eager to fight; hostile or aggressive

The prosecutor was reprimanded for his belligerent cross-examination of the witness, who had dissolved into tears.

byzantine   BIZ un teen

extremely complicated or devious

I gave up trying to understand the byzantine tax code and had an accountant file my taxes for me.

cantankerous   kan TANK er us

ill-tempered and quarrelsome; disagreeable

The dog hid under the tank as a result of the cat's cantankerous disposition.

contentious   kun TEN shus

quarrelsome

The contentious debate over science class content is increasingly making the news.

deleterious   dil uh TER ee us

having a harmful effect

It was only once he started his test that Murray realized the deleterious effects of one too many Red Bulls; he couldn't concentrate, and his hands were shaking so much he could barely write.

exacerbate   eg ZA ser bayt

to increase the severity, violence, or bitterness of; aggravate

Alan's procrastination problems were exacerbated by the monkeys who kept throwing bananas at him while he tried to concentrate.

flippant   FLIP ent

disrespectfully humorous or casual

Flap's flippant remarks to the teacher got him sent to the principal's office.

insolent   IN suh lint

insulting in manner or speech

The insolent prime minister stuck her tongue out at the queen.

nefarious   nuh FAYR ee us

flagrantly wicked; vicious

Dorothy's kindness and bravery triumphed over the nefarious antics of the Wicked Witch of the West.

pernicious   per NISH us

extremely or irrevocably harmful; deadly

The fertilizer's pernicious effects were not immediately obvious, but researchers became suspicious when all their petunias died.

rancorous   RANK er us

marked by bitter, deep-seated ill-will

They had such a rancorous relationship that no one could believe that they had ever gotten along.

repugnant   ree PUG nent

arousing disgust or aversion; offensive or repulsive

The pug's behavior at the dog park was repugnant, causing other dogs to avoid him altogether.

tawdry   TAW dree

gaudy and cheap

Connor's tawdry attire embarrassed his snooty host.

EARTH, WIND, AND FIRE

arboreal   ar BOR ee ul

relating to or resembling a tree or trees

The Rocky Mountain National Forest will celebrate its arboreal splendor with an Arbor Day concert.

invocation (n)   in vo KAY shun

a call (usually upon a higher power) for assistance, support, or inspiration

The group invoked the god of war as their protector on the field of battle.

stratify   STRAT i fy

to layer or separate into layers

Jonas studied the stratified bedrock and was able to see which time periods went with which layers.

variegated   VAR ee ih gay tid

having streaks, marks, or patches of a different color or colors; varicolored

The wood's markings were so variegated that Mr. Vargas assumed they had been painted on.

verdant   VUR dent

green with vegetation

The garden was verdant after the rain.

Summary

o   To learn vocabulary for the PSAT, it's best to take things in daily doses.

o   Flash cards are a great way to learn vocabulary; customize yours with funny sentences and mnemonics to help you remember words you have trouble with.

o   For more help with vocabulary, check out the *Word Smart* series of books. They're all focused on the words found most often on standardized tests such as the PSAT.

Part III
Drill Answers and
Explanations

CHAPTER 7

Drill 1 Answers

1. r   Examples: –7, 0, 1, 8

2. d   Examples: .5, 2, 118

3. k   Examples: –.5, –2, –118

4. f   Examples: –4, 0, 10

5. p   Examples: –5, 1, 17

6. a   Examples: *Factors* of 12 are 1, 2, 3, 4, 6, and 12. Factors of 10 are 1, 2, 5, and 10.

7. i   Examples: *Multiples* of 12 include –24, –12, 0, 12, 24, and so on. Multiples of 10 include 20, –10, 0, 10, 20, 30, and so on.

8. o   Examples: 2, 3, 5, 7, 11, and so on. There are no negative *prime numbers*, and 1 is not prime.

9. e   Examples: 3 and 4 are *distinct* numbers. –2 and 2 are also distinct.

10. j   Examples: In the number 274, 2 is the *digit* in the hundreds place, 7 is the digit in the tens place, and 4 is the digit in the ones place.

11. b   Examples: –1, 0, 1, and 2 are *consecutive* numbers. Be careful—sometimes you will be asked for *consecutive even* or *consecutive odd* numbers, in which case you would use just the odds or evens in a consecutive list of numbers.

12. n   Examples: 6 is *divisible* by 2 and 3, but not by 4 or 5.

13. l   Examples: When you divide 26 by 8, you get 3 with a *remainder* of 2 (2 is left over). When you divide 14 by 5, you get 2 with a remainder of 4 (4 is left over).

14. g   Examples: When you add 2 and 3, you get a *sum* of 5. When you add –4 and 1, you get a sum of –3.

15. c   Examples: When you multiply 2 and 3, you get a *product* of 6. When you multiply –4 and 1, you get a product of –4.

16. m   Examples: When you subtract 2 from 3, you get a *difference* of 1. When you subtract –4 from 1, you get a difference of 5.

17. q   Examples: When you divide 2 by 3, you get a quotient of $\frac{2}{3}$. When you divide –4 by 1, you get a quotient of –4.

18. h   Examples: The absolute value of –3 is 3. The absolute value of 41 is 41.

Drill 2 Answers

a   3, 5, 7

b   1, 2, 5, 10

c   2, 5

d   1, 2, 3, 4, 6, 8, 12, 16, 24, 48

e   2, 2, 2, 2, 3

f   6, 12, 18, 24, 30, 36, 42

g   4, 8, 12, 16, 20, 24, 28

h   42

i   5 and 6 or 6 and 5

j   15 and 2 or 2 and 15

1. **C**   51 can be divided evenly by 3 with no remainder.

2. **E**   The thousandths place is the third to the right of the decimal.

3. **C**   27 can be divided by 3 and 9.

4. **C**   The three consecutive integers must be 6, 7, and 8. The least of them is 6.

5. **B**   If the numbers are 2, 4, 6, 8, and 10, then 8 + 10 = 18 and 2 + 4 = 6. The last two numbers are 12 greater than the first two. (Don't forget that the numbers have to be consecutive and even!)

6. **A**   While this problem can be solved by listing multiples of 3 and 14, you end up having to list a lot of multiples to get to the answer! When this happens, you can factor instead. 14 can be factored into 2×7, so any number divisible by 3 and 14 must be divisible by 3, 2, and 7. That means it must be divisible by 6 since $2 \times 3 = 6$. Thus, choice (A) is the correct answer.

Drill 3 Answers

a 3^5

b 3^1

c 3^6

d x^8

e x^4

f x^{12}

3.   **A**   If $3^4 = 9^x$, then $81 = 9^x$. Therefore, $x = 2$. You could also rewrite 3^4 as $3 \times 3 \times 3 \times 3 = 9 \times 9$.

5.   **B**   If $(3x)^3 = 3^{15}$, then by the rules of MADSPM, $3x = 15$, and $x = 5$.

11.   **E**   Let's take the two equations separately, using the rules of MADSPM. If $x^y \times x^6 = x^{54}$, then $y + 6 = 54$, and $y = 48$. If $(x^3)^z = x^9$, then $3z = 9$, and $z = 3$. Now we know that $y = 48$ and $z = 3$, so $y + z = 51$.

Drill 4 Answers

a   36

b   24

c   20

d 16π

e 8π

f   10, 5

g   30

h   22

i   6

j   6

k   −1

17. **D**   Because this is a square, the two sides are equal. Therefore, $2x + 1 = x + 3$. Solve for x, and you get that x must be 2. Therefore, a side equals $x + 3$ or $2x + 1 = 5$, so the area equals 25.

10. **E**   Here are four lines; a and b are parallel, d intersects a and b, and c does not intersect both parallel lines. In statement I, angles 1 and 5 do not have to be equal because a side of angle 1 is line c, which has nothing to do with the parallel lines. Thus, the angles in statement I do not have to be equal, and you can eliminate (B). The angles in statement II have to be equal because angles 2 and 7 are opposite angles (two angles made up of the same two lines) and opposite angles must be equal. Eliminate (A) and (D). The angles in statement III must be equal because angles 3 and 9 are made up of the same line (line d) and one of the parallel lines. In fact, 3, 6, 5, and 9 are all the same "small angle," so eliminate (C). Therefore, statements II and III are true, and the correct answer is (F).

19. **B**   This question involves simultaneous equations, so the trick is to stack and combine them. You're being asked for $x + y$, so even getting the same number of x variables as y variables would be useful. Let's see what happens when we add the equations:

$$x + 2y = 12$$

$$2x + \ y = \ \ 9$$

$$3x + 3y = 21$$

Now all we need to do is divide both sides of the equation by 3 to get the expression we're being asked for, $x + y$, and we end up with the answer, 7.

10. **B**   When we simplify the fractional exponent, we get $\sqrt{x^5} = 8x$. Squaring both sides gives us $x^5 = 64x^2$. We can divide by x^2 on each side to get $x^3 = 64$ (remember your MADSPM rules!). Finally, taking the cube root of both sides gives us $x = 4$.

Drill 5 Answers

33.   Because the triangle is isosceles, with $AB = BC$, we know that angles A and C must have the same measure. So angle A must also be 40 degrees. Angles A and C have a combined measure of 80 degrees, and we need 180 total degrees in the triangle. Therefore, x must measure 100.

34.   If five consecutive integers have a sum of 100, they must be 18, 19, 20, 21, and 22. The next four consecutive integers are 23, 24, 25, and 26. Their sum is 98.

35.   Because $5x^2 = 125$, we know that $x^2 = 25$ and $x = 5$. Therefore, $5x^3 = 5 \times 125 = 625$.

36. Remember your prime factor tree? The prime factors of 140 are 2, 2, 5, and 7, but the *distinct* prime factors are 2, 5, and 7. Add them up and you get 14.

CHAPTER 8

Drill 1 Answers

4. **D** Let's plug in a number for the amount of homework Martha has. Let's say she has 12 pages of work to do. If she does half of this on Tuesday, she does 6 pages, and there are 6 pages left. If, on Wednesday, she does one-third of the remaining 6 pages, that means she does 2 more pages. So she has 4 pages left over from the original 12. What fractional part is left over? $\frac{4}{12}$ or $\frac{1}{3}$.

14. **D** Let's pick numbers for a, b, and c such that $a = \frac{b}{c^2}$. We can pick $4 = \frac{16}{2^2}$. Now the question becomes, what is $\frac{1}{b^2}$ or $\frac{1}{16^2}$? The answer is $\frac{1}{256}$. When you work through all of the answer choices using $a = 4$, $b = 16$, and $c = 2$, which choice says this? Choice (D) does.

12. **A** Let's pick a number for p. How about 2? Now the problem reads $\dfrac{\frac{1}{8}}{2(2)} =$. When you plug $p = 2$ into the answers, (A) turns out to be right.

18. **E** Variables in the answer choices? Absolutely! So let's plug in our own numbers: for x (Jodi's account), plug in \$18 (hey, who said Jodi had to be rich?). With \$18 in her account, $\frac{1}{6}$ for rent is \$3 and the car payment is also \$3. Subtract that from the \$18, and Jodi's got \$12 left in her account. Now we have to plug in for y (the amount Jodi deposits); let's make that \$8, bringing her account balance to \$20. Well, she now purchases a set of knives for \$10 ($\frac{1}{2}$ the amount in her account) and has \$10 left. Go through all of the answer choices, using $x = 18$ and $y = 8$ and see which one gives you \$10. The only one that works is (E).

Drill 2 Answers

8. **C** Let's begin by plugging in the middle number, 3, for x. Does $3^5 = 243$? Yes. So the answer is (C).

14. **D** If we try plugging in (C), $\frac{1}{4}$, for x, the equation becomes $\frac{6}{4} + 4 = 5$, which is false. If we try plugging in (D), $\frac{1}{2}$, for x, the equation becomes $\frac{12}{4} + 2 = 5$, which is true.

15. **B** This is another great example of Plugging In. Let's plug in a number for a. How about 90, just to make the math easy? If $a = 90$, then the other angle inside the triangle must be equal to 60. Therefore, b must be equal to 120. What choice says 120, remembering that $a = 90$? (B) does.

Drill 3 Answers

a　90

b　320

c　6

d　$x = 8$

e　120

f　108

g　10%

h　$\dfrac{2,600}{18,600}$ = approximately 14%

i　40

4.

11. D   60% of 80 translates as $\dfrac{60}{100} \times 80$, which is the same as 48. So the problem now reads: 48 is the same as 40% of what number? We can translate this question as $48 = \dfrac{40}{100}x$. Then we solve for x, which equals 120, which is choice (D).

14. D   50% of the adults = 15, and 80% of the children = 16, so 31 total people went swimming. 31 out of 50 is 62%.

CHAPTER 9

Drill 1 Answers

5. B   The first thing we should do with this problem is factor the quadratics. This turns the equation into $\dfrac{(x+4)(x-2)}{(x-2)(x-5)} = 4$. We can cancel $(x-2)$ in the numerator and the denominator leaving us with $\dfrac{(x+4)}{(x-5)} = 4$. To solve, we can cross-multiply. This gives us $x + 4 = 4x - 20$. Solving for x gives us a value of 8. The answer is choice (E).

10. B   In this problem, all we need to do is follow the directions given. We replace 6 for a and 8 for b. This gives us $\dfrac{6}{2} + 3(8) - 7$ which equals 20. The answer is choice (B).

12. B   Since the problem gives us one of the solutions for x, we can plug it into the quadratic to find the value of k. This gives us $(-3)2 + 8(-3) + k = 0$. The value of k is then 15. If we put k back into the equation, we get $x^2 + 8x + 15 = 0$. We can then factor this quadratic knowing that one of the factors is $(x + 3)$. The other factor must be $(x + 5)$ making the other solution −5. The correct answer is choice (B).

15. E   The first thing we should do with this problem is factor the quadratics. This turns the equation into $\dfrac{(x+4)(x-2)}{(x-2)(x-5)} = 4$. We can cancel $(x-2)$ in the numerator and the denominator leaving us with $\dfrac{(x+4)}{(x-5)} = 4$. To solve, we can cross-multiply. This gives us $x + 4 = 4x - 20$. Solving for x gives us a value of 8. The answer is choice (E).

19. A   The first thing we need to do here is replace a for x in the function and set this equal to 2, as the second part of the problem states. This gives us $a^2 + 7a + 12 = 2$. Now, in order to be able to solve the quadratic, we need to set the equation equal to zero. By subtracting 2 from both sides, we get $a^2 + 7a + 10 = 0$. Now we can factor the quadratic. This gives us $(a + 5)(a + 2) = 0$. Our solutions for a are then −5 and −2. The answer choice that contains one of these solutions is (A).

Drill 2 Answers

13. **C** Using the Third Side Rule, we know that the third side of the triangle must be greater than 4, but less than 10. Since the sum of two of the sides is 10, the perimeter must be between 14 and 20. The only choice that is between these values is (C). Alternatively, we could Plug in the Answers. This could be done by subtracting the sum of the two known sides from the answer choices to find which one has a value between 4 and 10.

8.   **C** Since we know that the area of the rectangle is 48, we can figure out the length of the rectangle using the formula $A = l \times w$. Putting in the numbers we have gives us $48 = 6l$. If we divide both sides by 6, the length BC then is 8. In rectangles, all angles are 90 degrees, so we can also use the Pythagorean Theorem to find the hypotenuse. Since we have a 6 and an 8 as the legs of the right triangle, we can identify this as one of the common triples. This gives us a hypotenuse of 10. Since the hypotenuse runs through the center of the circle, we know then that this is the diameter of the circle. If the diameter is 10, the radius is 5. Using the formula for the area of a circle, $A = \pi r^2$, we get $A = \pi(5)^2$ which equals 25π. The answer then is choice (C).

14. **C** The problem tells us that the triangle is isosceles and we see there is a right angle present in the figure. This tells us that the base angles are 45 degrees each. Since the length of side AB is 5, that means that the length of side BC is 5 as well. Using the relationships for a 45:45:90 right triangle, we can infer than the length of AC is $5\sqrt{2}$. To find the perimeter, we add all three sides together: $5 + 5 + 5\sqrt{2} = 10 + 5\sqrt{2}$. The correct choice is (C).

16. **E** Angle AOB is 60 degrees which is $\frac{1}{6}$ of 360 degrees. Since arc AB is 2π, it is $\frac{1}{6}$ of the total circumference. The circumference then is $6 \times 2\pi$, which comes to 12π. The diameter of the circle is 12, making the radius 6. The area of the circle then is 36, choice (E)π.

18. **D** Since there is no figure given, we should draw one according to the directions. The figure should look like the following:

Given that the area of the circle is 36π, the radius is 6. That means that the diameter is 12. The point where a tangent hits the circle makes a 90 degree angle, so angle OAC is 90 degrees. Now that we have a right triangle, we can use the Pythagorean theorem to find that the length of BC is 13. Adding 5 + 12 + 13 gives us 30.

CHAPTER 10

Drill 1 Answers

1.   *Over* is the preposition, and *the bridge* is the object.

2.   *Beyond* is the preposition, and *the green* is the object.

3.   *With* is the preposition, and *the other reference books* is the object.

4.   *To* is the preposition, and *her* is the object. Be careful—*to* also appears in this sentence in front of the verb *return,* but it's not being used as a preposition. *To return* is the whole verb; if *to* were being used as a preposition, it would be followed by a noun. (A verb like *to peel, to writhe,* or *to expire* is said to be in the *infinitive* form.)

Drill 2 Answers

1.   to

2.   of

3.   for

4.   of

5.   about, for, by

6.   by

7.   over

8.   to

9.   from

10.   No preposition is needed after considered.

Drill 3 Answers

1. **C**   One thing that splits the answer choices is the *were* versus *was*; it's not easy to see because it's in the middle of each choice, but it is there. *Neither* follows the same rules as *either* when connecting two subjects: The second subject determines whether we need a singular or plural verb. *The superintendent* is singular, so *was* is correct, and we can eliminate (A) and (B). Of the remaining answer choices, we can eliminate (D) because it adds in the word *of* unnecessarily, and we can eliminate (E) because when *neither* is used, it should always be followed by *nor*, not *or*. That leaves (C) as our best answer.

2. **D**   As written, the sentence lacks a verb, so it's not a sentence at all, but a fragment. Get rid of (A) and anything else that repeats this error, which rules out choices (B), (C), and (E), so the answer is (D), the only choice that contains a verb.

3. **C**   The word *but* in the underlined portion indicates a change of direction, but that doesn't make sense in the sentence. Eliminate (A). (B) is out because *where* can only refer to a location. (D) has *being*, which nearly always makes a sentence awkward and wordy. Cross it out. (E) doesn't makes sense with the meaning of the sentence and uses a comma incorrectly to connect what should be two separate sentences. Eliminate it. (C) contains no errors and has the right meaning, indicating that the physical recovery was contingent upon the psychological one.

4. **E**   If you don't spot an error right off the bat, look at the answer choices. One main difference is the form of the word *master*. Answer choices (A), (B), and (C) aren't parallel with the verb *to learn*, so we can eliminate those. (D) changes the meaning of the sentence by using *simply* instead of *simple*, so it's gone too. (E), the best answer, keeps the verbs parallel and doesn't create any new errors.

5. **B**   The original sentence is trying to connect two separate sentences with a comma, so (A) is wrong. (C) is constructed in a very confusing way, leaving an *it* at the end that doesn't clearly refer to one noun, so it can be eliminated. In choice (D), the phrase between the commas is a complete sentence, so it needs to be marked off with a semicolon or period instead of a comma. Choice (E) says *when he was Jackie Robinson,* which is nonsense (unless the question is about reincarnation). (B) is straightforward and doesn't introduce new grammatical errors, so it is the best answer.

6. **B**   The *they* in the underlined portion doesn't agree with *A well-organized person*, so (A) is out. (B) doesn't appear to have any new problems and it fixes the pronoun agreement error, so we can keep it. (C), (D), and (E) fix the pronoun agreement error, but are needlessly wordy, so (B) is correct.

7. **E**   The original sentence contains a pronoun agreement problem, because *it* is singular and the *folk songs* it refers to is plural. Get rid of (A). (C) uses the wrong conjunction, as we should have a change in direction, rather than the same direction. (D) changes the intended meaning of the original. (B) and (E) both look all right grammatically, but (B) is passive, so (E) is the right answer because ETS likes the active voice better.

8. **A** The answer choices again provide great places to start if an error isn't immediately apparent. When a sentence uses *not only*, it must be followed with *but also*, so answer choices (C) and (D) are out. One difference in the remaining answer choices is the form of the verb *encourage*. It should be parallel to the verb *enhance*, so (B) can be eliminated. (E) uses *them* to refer to *a child*, which is a mismatch, leaving (A) as the best answer.

21. **A** The verb *was* is singular, but its subject is *CD*, an abbreviation for the phrase "compact disc," which is singular. Thus, we have a subject/verb agreement error in (A).

22. **E** There is no error in the sentence.

23. **E** There is no error in the sentence. Remember, ETS likes to use *none* as a singular pronoun, so *is* agrees.

24. **B** *You* and *I* are objects of the preposition *between*, so they must be in the object case. *I* is subject case, so it is erroneous and (B) is the best answer.

25. **A** The past perfect verb *had looked* doesn't match with the other tenses in the sentence, and there's no reason to use the past perfect since we don't have another action in the past. (A) is the error.

26. **B** *Splendid* is an adjective and it's being used to modify *worked*, a verb. An adverb, such as *splendidly*, would be better. The correct answer is (B).

27. **C** *Abide with* is incorrect; the correct idiom is *abide by*. (C) is the correct answer.

28. **B** *Where* can only be used to describe a location, and an announcement is not a location. *That* would be better, so (B) is the best answer.

29. **C** The present perfect *has cast* is not necessary, because there is no continuous action. The correct form is the simple past *cast,* so the correct answer is (C).

Drill 4 Answers

35. **C** Because there's no event in the past that this sentence comes before, past perfect cannot be correct. Let's eliminate (A). (D) and (E) completely change the meaning of the sentence (and when we get some context from the passage, we can see that this paragraph is a discussion of censorship in the past), so they are gone. (B) leaves out an important word, *an,* which makes the sentence not make sense, so (C) is the best answer.

36. **E** This essay follows a chronological order in its discussion of media censorship, so it would make the most sense to precede it with something that comes before the censorship of the 1950s. Therefore, (E) is the most logical choice.

37.   **C**   Sentence 4 changes direction, because it starts talking about a reaction to the standards described in the first three sentences. This change of topic makes (C) the best answer.

38.   **D**   This question can be done just like a Vocab-in-Context or Sentence Completion question. Reading sentences 5 and 6 for context, we learn that artists were expressing themselves very freely in reaction to earlier codes of censorship, so we can replace *unlikely* with something like *unthinkable*. (D) is the closest answer.

39.   **A**   Remember that there is no "correct as is" unless explicitly stated in the answer choices. (D) and (E) add *being,* which is awkward. (C) includes the pronoun *they,* which is ambiguous because it could refer to either the albums or the warning labels. (B) also doesn't make clear whether it was the albums or the labels that indicated something. (A) is the best choice.

Part IV
The Princeton Review Practice Tests and Explanations

Chapter 12
Practice Test 1

SECTION 1
Time — 25 minutes
24 Questions

Directions: For each question in this section, select the best answer from among the choices given and fill in the corresponding circle on the answer sheet.

Each sentence below has one or two blanks, each blank indicating that something has been omitted. Beneath the sentence are five words or sets of words labeled A through E. Choose the word or set of words that, when inserted in the sentence, best fits the meaning of the sentence as a whole.

Example:

Desiring to ------- his taunting friends, Mitch gave them taffy in hopes it would keep their mouths shut.

(A) eliminate   (B) satisfy   (C) overcome
    (D) ridicule   (E) silence

1. Though many people are willing to ------- saving the environment when speaking in public, they are often not willing to ------- their lifestyles to help protect the earth.

    (A) promote . . maintain
    (B) condone . . justify
    (C) advocate . . alter
    (D) denounce . . adjust
    (E) champion . . substantiate

2. Due to his ------- personality, Prince Klemens von Metternich dominated the Congress of Vienna after the defeat of Napoleon.

    (A) amiable   (B) pleasant   (C) commanding
        (D) duplicitous   (E) sympathetic

3. The floor of the forest is enlivened by ------- hues whenever the lush canopy is ------- by the strong rays of the sun.

    (A) vibrant . . blemished
    (B) muted . . overwhelmed
    (C) threatening . . enveloped
    (D) mellow . . blanketed
    (E) vivid . . pierced

4. The reclusive nature of the iguana helps to explain the longstanding ------- of fruitful investigations of its behavior in the wild.

    (A) constancy   (B) notoriety   (C) necessity
        (D) paucity   (E) probity

5. The aim of the governor's plan was to make more housing available for middle-income families, but unfortunately she only ------- the problem by making such housing even more scarce.

    (A) repealed   (B) exacerbated   (C) abolished
        (D) hoisted   (E) ingratiated

6. Many people consider Dana ------- because of her friendly and honest manner, but she is actually a ------- negotiator.

    (A) trustworthy . . relaxed
    (B) naive . . shrewd
    (C) taciturn . . decisive
    (D) vigilant . . lenient
    (E) eccentric . . secluded

7. When jazz was first introduced to Europe, many musicians were greatly ------- it and tried to ------- its free-form style.

    (A) drawn to . . emulate
    (B) impressed by . . reject
    (C) attracted to . . originate
    (D) opposed to . . adopt
    (E) afraid of . . accept

8. The senator's aide claimed that even though the United States was established by rebellion, it is now inclined to view ------- in other nations with -------.

    (A) reactionaries . . adoration
    (B) misers . . disdain
    (C) insurgents . . animosity
    (D) autocrats . . malevolence
    (E) revolutionaries . . indifference

GO ON TO THE NEXT PAGE

The passages below are followed by questions based on their content; questions following a pair of related passages may also be based on the relationship between the paired passages. Answer the questions on the basis of what is <u>stated</u> or <u>implied</u> in the passage and in any introductory material that may be provided.

Questions 9-10 are based on the following passage.

The Oulipo, short for *Ouvroir de Littérature Potentielle*, is a literary group that was founded in Paris in 1960. It has met for monthly meetings without fail for over forty years.
ine The products of this group are not the novels or short stories
5 that other writing groups churn out. Rather, the business of the Oulipo is to collaboratively produce "constraints," or procedures, usually mathematical in nature, which must be followed in constructing a text. Although it might seem like following rules would limit what is possible to write,
10 these constraints function as a recipe for anyone to produce interesting, if not always sensible, texts. Among Oulipian inventions are many methods of word replacement; ways of restricting certain words or letters of the alphabet; and various methods of combining texts. Following these
15 techniques is not so different from using the centuries-old rules for haikus or sonnets. That poems, novels, and stories are actually created using the Oulipo's methods is almost beside the point. The group considers its product to be the *potential* writing that might be created using its methods.

9. The author brings in the examples of the haiku and the sonnet in order to

   (A) create a rhythmic flow in the text of the passage
   (B) point out that the Oulipo's methods are completely unoriginal
   (C) demonstrate the potential writing produced by Oulipo's "constraints"
   (D) connect a new way of writing with long-practiced traditions
   (E) indicate the international demographic of the Oulipo

10. The use of the phrase "churn out" in sentence 3 implies that the author

   (A) is unenthusiastic about the work of some literature groups
   (B) has little use for the writing methods of the Oulipo
   (C) is placing the narrative in a bucolic setting
   (D) demands tremendous production from her writing group
   (E) is disgusted at the training received at writing schools

Questions 11-12 are based on the following passage.

The Gulf of Tonkin Resolution, passed on August 7, 1964, empowered President Lyndon Johnson to resolve a brewing conflict with the North Vietnamese using whatever means
Line he deemed necessary. Five days prior to Congress's approval
5 of the resolution, the U.S.S. *Maddox*, a naval destroyer, was patrolling the waters in the Gulf of Tonkin near Hon Me, a North Vietnamese island. Three North Vietnamese torpedo boats encountered the U.S.S. *Maddox*, forcing the American vessel to flee. Two days later, the U.S.S. *Maddox* returned
10 to the Gulf of Tonkin accompanied by the U.S.S. *Turner Joy*, another naval destroyer. Suspiciously, that evening the *Turner Joy* picked up three high-speed vessels on its radar, but the Maddox did not. The U.S.S *Turner Joy* sought and attacked these ships. Some have hypothesized that President Johnson,
15 who had been quite vocal about the need for an increased military presence in the area, may have manufactured this crisis, but there is no evidence to support such claims.

11. The structure of the passage could best be described as the presentation of a historical event that is

   (A) elaborated upon and a possible controversy downplayed
   (B) explained, and its repercussions enumerated
   (C) cited, and the character of one participant attacked
   (D) noted, and its cultural significance elaborated upon
   (E) explained, and its validity questioned

12. The argument that President Johnson did not have any inappropriate involvement with the Gulf of Tonkin incident would be best supported by

   (A) a statement from crewmen on the U.S.S. *Maddox* stating that they did not see any high-speed vessels the night of August 4th
   (B) a report stating that many destroyers at that time had difficulty locating and tracking high-speed vessels
   (C) several North Vietnamese soldiers testifying that they were not in the Gulf of Tonkin on the night in question
   (D) a report stating that the U.S.S. *Maddox* had no mechanical problems with its radar
   (E) a poll of Americans stating that the majority believed President Johnson

GO ON TO THE NEXT PAGE

Questions 13-24 are based on the following passages.

The process of changing wild animals into tame ones is known as domestication, an important development in the course of human cultural history. Two reasons for the domestication of animals are explored here.

Passage 1

The geographer Eduard Hahn (1896), in a series of writings at the turn of the century, posed the basic questions involved in the study of the domestication of cattle. These are the questions still raised today, and they are still answered by culture historians substantially in the way he answered them. Hahn pointed to the exceptional position of cattle among animals that have been domesticated. In the case of some animals, domestication may have come about spontaneously. For example, the ancestor of the dog as well as that of the domestic pig probably, as scavengers, sought out man, and gradually man assumed the leadership in the relationship. One may indeed ask, "Who then initially domesticated whom?" Domestication, again, may have been furthered by instincts which make us cherish our own infants and which are aroused by young mammals of somewhat similar bodily proportions. Piglets and dog pups are nursed by women in some primitive societies. But the domestication of wild cattle cannot be explained as an inadvertent process. Wild cattle presumably did not seek human company, and the initiative must have come from man. Furthermore, man must have had a strong motivation since the wild urus was a powerful, intractable animal of whom it is said in Job (Job 3:9–10): "Will the urus be willing to serve thee, or abide by thy crib? Canst thou span him into a plowing harness or will he harrow the valleys after thee?"

Eduard Hahn has postulated that the motive for capturing and maintaining the urus in the captive state was to have available a supply, for sacrificial purposes, of the animal sacred to the lunar mother goddess worshipped over an immense area of the ancient world. The economic uses of the animal would then have been a by-product of a domestication religious in origin. Why the urus was selected as the animal sacred to the deity is uncertain, but this was probably because its gigantic curved horns resembled the lunar crescent. Studies in prehistoric and early historic religion have shown that the bovine was early regarded as an epiphany of the goddess or her consort and was slain in the ritual reenactment of the myth of her death. This myth involves the notion of the death and resurrection in new life of the deity. Of course, if cattle were domesticated because the horns of the urus resembled the moon's crescent, it is possible that other horned animals such as sheep and goats were also domesticated for their horns. For example, it is possible that an unsuccessful attempt to domesticate crescent-horned gazelles was made for this reason.

Passage 2

Man probably entered into a state of beneficial mutualism with certain animal species because, to put it in very general terms, the animals were already socially and psychologically preadapted to being tamed without loss of reproductive abilities. A second factor was that the human culture milieu had evolved to a state of organization such that the animals could be controlled and maintained, generation after generation, in a condition of dependence. At least to some degree these animals had to be protected from predators and provided with food—the latter perhaps only in time of scarcity. The detailed pattern of the process leading to domestication naturally varied with both the particular species and the human culture that were interacting; certainly the domestication of the wolf to the dog by the Maglemosian hunter-collectors of northwestern Europe was different in detail from the domestication of the hoofed food animals by the post-Natufian cultivators. Unfortunately, we know nothing of the details of either process, partly because of our inability to reconstruct the behavior and cultural environment of the people involved and partly because of our ignorance of the psychology of the various wild animals involved.

With the exception of one of the most recently domesticated mammals, the laboratory rat, we know little enough about the behavior patterns of our common domestic animals, but we know much less about the behavior of their wild progenitors. Furthermore, detailed comparative observations of wild and domestic *Rattus norvegicus* emphasize the tremendous behavioral changes undergone by a species during domestication. Thus, psychological studies on domesticates probably cannot yield the total behavior pattern of the wild ancestors. It was, however, these wild ancestors that man first tamed and reared.

The social enzyme that activated the union of man and beast was undoubtedly the human proclivity, not only of children but of women also, to keep pets, although purposeful capture of young animals by men, to serve as hunting decoys, may well have been another avenue toward domestication.

The psychological factor of "imprinting," explored particularly by Lorenz in a notable series of animal experiments, was undoubtedly a major influence in the domestication of birds with precocial young (chickens, ducks, geese, turkeys, and so on). *Imprinting* refers to the tendency, most pronounced in such precocial birds, to recognize and psychologically to attach themselves to the most frequently seen and heard living thing during an early and short "critical period." Typically this would be the mother, and we have thus an instinctive mechanism for recognition of the parent by an active newborn.

GO ON TO THE NEXT PAGE

13. The author's primary purpose in Passage 1 is to

(A) provide an argument as to why the horns of cattle, sheep, and goats had social significance

(B) explain a religious motivation for the domestication of cattle and other horned animals

(C) detail the anatomical differences between wild animals and their domesticated counterparts

(D) discuss the scavenger nature of wild cattle and how that led them into domestication

(E) examine the domestication of pigs and dogs based on the similarities of their body proportions to man's

14. The quote in line 12, "Who then initially domesticated whom?" refers to

(A) the nursing of piglets and puppies by women in some primitive societies

(B) man's strong motivation to domesticate cattle

(C) the exceptional position of cattle among animals that have been domesticated

(D) the theory that pigs and dogs, as scavengers, sought out man

(E) the controversy inspired by Hahn's cultural history

15. In line 18, the word "inadvert" most nearly means

(A) motivated

(B) accidental

(C) sacrificial

(D) difficult to domesticate

(E) intractable

16. The myth discussed in lines 34-39 revolves around

(A) the gigantic curved horns of the urus

(B) the economic uses of early cattle

(C) the cow as an incarnation of the moon goddess

(D) ritual sacrifice of gazelles

(E) prehistoric reenactments of the creation of the moon

GO ON TO THE NEXT PAGE

17. The author of Passage 2 uses the term "beneficial mutualism" in lines 45 to characterize

   (A) a harmony of needs between man and some species that leads to the domestication of those species
   (B) the domestication experiments with the musk ox
   (C) a process opposed to imprinting as a means for offspring to recognize their mother
   (D) the reproductive abilities of tamed species
   (E) man's protection from predators and provision of food for animals that have been domesticated

18. The author of Passage 2 compares the domestication of the wolf by Maglemosian hunter-collectors to the domestication of hoofed food animals by post-Natufian cultivators in order to

   (A) reconstruct the behavior and cultural environment in which domestication occurred
   (B) show how ignorant we are of the psychology of wild animals and the peoples who domesticated them
   (C) suggest that the process of domestication varied with the species but not with the human culture
   (D) support the notion that the process of domestication is dependent upon both the species and the human culture
   (E) imply that the process of domestication was a process independent of both the species and the human culture

19. The studies mentioned in Passage 2 with regard to *Rattus norvegicus* revealed

   (A) the behavior patterns of wild progenitors of hoofed animals
   (B) psychological insights into the laboratory rat
   (C) how man first tamed and reared wild animals
   (D) that observing a domestic animal can lead to an understanding of its wild counterpart
   (E) dramatic differences in behavior between wild and domesticated rats

20. Lorenz's experiments with birds and imprinting are used by the author to support the contention that

   (A) imprinting is the method by which young birds recognize and attach themselves to a parent
   (B) hunting decoys may have been an avenue of domestication for some species
   (C) chickens, ducks, geese, and turkeys are birds that have precocial young
   (D) imprinting was a major influence in the domestication of birds
   (E) the mother is the parent to which most young attach themselves

GO ON TO THE NEXT PAGE

21. The authors of the two passages would most likely agree that

(A) the human proclivity to keep pets is the single most important factor in domestication

(B) domestication of some species, such as the wolf-dog, occurred because both man and the species benefited from the arrangement

(C) a combination of imprinting and religious mythology shaped the process by which cattle were domesticated

(D) the purposeful capture of young animals for use in religious ceremonies was a critical stage in the domestication of cattle

(E) women felt sorry for the young animals used as hunting decoys and turned them into pets

22. Which of the following statements best characterizes the main difference between the two passages?

(A) The first focuses on religious motivations for the domestication of cattle, but does not exclude other factors for the domestication of other species, whereas the second covers a variety of motivations for domestication, yet does not rule out religion.

(B) The first presents the hypothesis that religious motivations were responsible for domestication of many species, while the second argues that religious motivations were totally absent in the process of domesticating birds.

(C) The first explores in detail how the scavenger nature of dogs and pigs led to their domestication, and the second argues against that proposition, offering a hypothesis for dog and pig domestication based on a desire for pets and social enzymes.

(D) The first suggests that only horned animals had religious significance, but the second focuses on the use of hoofed animals for food.

(E) The second implicitly criticizes the first for ignoring the importance of psychological insights into wild animal behavior that can be gleaned from studying laboratory rats and birds with precocial young.

23. The authors of both passages would be LEAST likely to agree with which of the following statements?

(A) The bison, a large herbivore with crescent-shaped horns, was probably domesticated initially for religious reasons and then for economic reasons (food and products derived from the animal).

(B) The cat, a scavenger with body proportions similar to humans, probably insinuated itself into human culture, which was able to adapt and accept the animal for the advantages it gave in terms of rodent control.

(C) Reptiles have not been domesticated since they are not scavengers, not a valued food source, lack body proportions similar to humans, and are a species that does not imprint.

(D) The urus is an example of a hoofed and horned food animal that may have been originally domesticated for religious purposes (such as a supply for sacrifice), but whose economic importance led to its continued role and domestication in human society.

(E) *Rattus norvegicus* is an example of a scavenger with body proportions similar to humans, which was probably domesticated through the purposeful capture of the young to use as hunting decoys.

24. The "social enzyme" noted in Passage 2 is most closely associated with which of the following quotations from Passage 1?

(A) ". . . the exceptional position of cattle among animals that have been domesticated"

(B) "Will the urus be willing to serve thee?"

(C) "Piglets and dog pups are nursed by women in some primitive societies."

(D) ". . . the motive for capturing and maintaining the urus . . . was to have available a supply, for sacrificial purposes . . ."

(E) ". . . the ancestor of the dog as well as that of the domestic pig probably, as scavengers, sought out man . . ."

STOP
If you finish before time is called, you may check your work on this section only.
Do not turn to any other section in the test.

SECTION 2
Time — 25 minutes
20 Questions

Directions: For this section, solve each problem and decide which is the best of the choices given. Fill in the corresponding circle on the answer sheet. You may use any available space for scratchwork.

Reference Information

$A = \pi r^2$ $A = lw$
$C = 2\pi r$ $A = \frac{1}{2}bh$ $V = lwh$ $V = \pi r^2 h$ $c^2 = a^2 + b^2$ Special Right Triangles

The number of degrees of arc in a circle is 360.

The sum of the measures in degrees of the angles of a triangle is 180.

---

1. If $12b - 4 = 0$, then $b =$

(A) 4

(B) 3

(C) 0

(D) $\frac{1}{3}$

(E) $\frac{1}{4}$

Handwritten work:
$12b = 4$
$b = \frac{4}{12} = \frac{1}{3}$

---

2. If an oil tank contains 60 gallons of fuel and is $\frac{5}{12}$ full, how many gallons does the tank hold when full?

(A) 72
(B) 84
(C) 128
(D) 144
(E) 720

Handwritten work:
12
$\times 12$
24
12
144

12
$5\overline{)60}$
5
10

GO ON TO THE NEXT PAGE

3. If the area of rectangle *ABDE* is 16 square inches, and *C* is the midpoint of $\overline{BD}$, what is the area, in square inches, of $\triangle ACE$?

   (A) 2
   (B) 4
   (C) 6
   (D) 8
   (E) 16

5. In $\triangle ABC$ above, what is the value of *x* ?

   (A) 18
   (B) 23
   (C) 32
   (D) 38
   (E) 42

$$90 + x + (3x - 2) = 180$$
$$x + 3x - 2 = 90$$
$$4x - 2 = 90$$
$$4x = 88 \qquad 4x = 92$$
$$x = 23$$

4. An integer that is a multiple of 32 must also be a multiple of which of the following integers?

   (A) 11
   (B) 9
   (C) 8
   (D) 5
   (E) 3

6. If *x*, *y*, and *z* are consecutive integers and $x < y < z$, what is the sum of *y* and *z* in terms of *x* ?

   (A) $2x + 6$
   (B) $2x + 4$
   (C) $2x + 3$
   (D) $2x - 2$
   (E) $2x - 1$

GO ON TO THE NEXT PAGE

7. If $(2^a)^b = 64$, then $ab =$

(A) 2
(B) 3
(C) 4
(D) 5
(E) 6

(handwritten work)
$$2 \cdot 2 \frac{2}{4} \cdot 2 \cdot \frac{2 \cdot 2 \cdot 2}{4}$$
$$\begin{array}{r} 2 \\ \times \ 64 \\ \hline 6.4 \end{array}$$

8. $6\sqrt{18} + 4\sqrt{72} - \left(\sqrt{8} + 10\sqrt{32}\right) =$

(A) −1
(B) 0
(C) 1
(D) $2\sqrt{2}$
(E) $6\sqrt{2}$

(handwritten work)
$$18\sqrt{2} + 24\sqrt{2} - \left(2\sqrt{2} + 40\sqrt{2}\right)$$
$$18\sqrt{2} + 24\sqrt{2} - 42\sqrt{2}$$
$$-24\sqrt{2} + 24\sqrt{2}$$

$$\begin{array}{r} 42 \\ -18 \\ \hline 24 \end{array}$$

$(a, 8)$ $(b, 8)$

9. In the 6-sided regular polygon above, how many diagonals can be drawn that have negative slope?

(A) 0
(B) 1
(C) 2
(D) 3
(E) 4

10. If a certain number is 3 more than 7 times itself, what is the number?

(A) −3

(B) $-\dfrac{3}{2}$

(C) $-\dfrac{1}{2}$

(D) $-\dfrac{3}{8}$

(E) $\dfrac{1}{2}$

(handwritten work)
$$x = 7x + 3$$
$$x - 7x = 3$$
$$-6x = 3$$
$$6x = -3$$
$$x = -\frac{3}{6} = -\frac{1}{2}$$

GO ON TO THE NEXT PAGE

11. Which of the following is equivalent to
$-12 \le 3b + 3 \le 18$?

(A) $-5 \le b \le 5$
(B) $-4 \le b \le 6$
(C) $-5 \le b \le 6$
(D) $3 \le b \le 5$
(E) $5 \le b \le 5$

12. If x is an odd integer divisible by 3, which of the
following must be divisible by 4 ?

(A) $x + 1$
(B) $x + 2$
(C) $x + 3$
(D) $2x$
(E) $2x - 2$

13. If $\overline{AC} \cong \overline{BC}$ in the figure above, what is the perimeter of
$\triangle ABC$?

(A) 14
(B) 15
(C) 16
(D) 18
(E) $10 + 3\sqrt{3}$

$$4^2 + 3^2 = x^2$$
$$16 + 9 = x^2$$
$$25 = x^2$$
$$x = 5$$

5, 11, 29, . . .

14. If the nth term in the sequence above is defined by
$2 + 3^n$, what is the sum of the 5th and 7th terms?

(A) 40
(B) 245
(C) 2,189
(D) 2,434
(E) 2,920

$$2 + 3^5 = 245$$
$$2 + 3^7 = 2189$$

GO ON TO THE NEXT PAGE

15. A bottle containing c ounces of juice can be emptied to fill g identical glasses. How many such bottles would be needed to fill n of these glasses with juice?

    (A) $\dfrac{gn}{c}$

    (B) $\dfrac{cn}{g}$

    (C) $\dfrac{g}{n}$

    (D) $\dfrac{n}{g}$

    (E) $\dfrac{c}{n}$

$$A = \{-1,\ 0,\ 1,\ 2\}$$
$$B = \{0,\ 1,\ 2,\ 3\}$$
$$C = \text{Intersection of } A \text{ and } B$$
$$D = \text{Union of } A \text{ and } B$$

16. Sets A, B, C, and D are shown above. A set is said to be "interior" if, for any two numbers x and y in the set, xy is also in the set. Which of the following is an interior set?

    (A) A
    (B) B
    (C) C
    (D) D
    (E) A union C

17. A large cubical block of cheese measures 8 inches on each edge. If a small rectangular solid measuring 4 inches by 2 inches by 2 inches is cut out and thrown away, the volume of the remaining block of cheese is what fraction of its original volume?

    (A) $\dfrac{1}{32}$

    (B) $\dfrac{3}{4}$

    (C) $\dfrac{7}{8}$

    (D) $\dfrac{15}{16}$

    (E) $\dfrac{31}{32}$

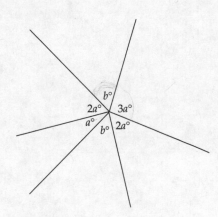

Note: Figure not drawn to scale.

18. In the figure above, what is the value of b in terms of a ?

    (A) $90 + 2a$
    (B) $180 - 4a$
    (C) $180 - 8a$
    (D) $360 - 8a$
    (E) $360 - 12a$

GO ON TO THE NEXT PAGE

19. If x and y are integers and $y = 4x$, which of the following could be the average (arithmetic mean) of x and y ?

(A) −36
(B) −35
(C) 4
(D) 12
(E) 28

20. If y is directly proportional to the square of x, and $x = 3$ when $y = 18$, then when $y = 2$, $x =$

(A) $\dfrac{1}{3}$

(B) 1

(C) 3

(D) 9

(E) 81

x^2y

$y = x^2$ 18

$18 = 3^2$

$2 =$

$8a + 2b = 360.$
$2b = 360 - 8a$
$b = 180 - 4a$

STOP

If you finish before time is called, you may check your work on this section only.
Do not turn to any other section in the test.

SECTION 3
Time — 25 minutes
24 Questions

Directions: For each question in this section, select the best answer from among the choices given and fill in the corresponding circle on the answer sheet.

Each sentence below has one or two blanks, each blank indicating that something has been omitted. Beneath the sentence are five words or sets of words labeled A through E. Choose the word or set of words that, when inserted in the sentence, best fits the meaning of the sentence as a whole.

Example:

Hoping to ------- the dispute, negotiators proposed a compromise that they felt would be ------- to both labor and management.

(A) enforce . . useful
(B) end . . divisive
(C) overcome . . unattractive
(D) extend . . satisfactory
(E) resolve . .acceptable

25. While its unique eating habits make the mountain gorilla a fascinating subject for observation, its small population and its shyness serve to ------- many potential studies.

(A) inspire   (B) release   (C) fortify
(D) hinder   (E) extenuate

26. Originally designed as work clothes for miners, jeans are now worn by all segments of society, their appeal ------- by their comfort and affordability.

(A) overwhelmed   (B) corroded   (C) broadened
(D) lessened   (E) complicated

27. While many consumer electronics are ------- in a very short time by newer technologies, it will be many years before the home computer becomes -------.

(A) supplanted . . obsolete
(B) popularized . . uncommon
(C) noticeable . . forgotten
(D) discovered . . disparaged
(E) replaced . . remembered

28. Although many believed that the problems of the community were -------, the members of the governing council refused to give up and devised several ------- solutions.

(A) insoluble . . ingenious
(B) intractable . . inconsequential
(C) exorbitant . . promising
(D) irrelevant . . lofty
(E) obscure . . meager

29. So ------- were the voters of Winesburg that, despite the blizzard, 2,500 of the 3,200 residents made their way to the voting sites.

(A) endemic   (B) relenting   (C) ephemeral
(D) resolute   (E) erratic

GO ON TO THE NEXT PAGE

The passages below are followed by questions based on their content; questions following a pair of related passages may also be based on the relationship between the paired passages. Answer the questions on the basis of what is <u>stated</u> or <u>implied</u> in the passage and in any introductory material that may be provided.

Questions 30-33 are based on the following passages.

Passage 1

It is often said that history is written by the winners, and for good reason. Contrary to the revisionist teachings of some "new historicists," history is not by nature an
ne interpretive discipline. Facts are facts are facts, after all. New
5 interpretations of Woodrow Wilson's isolationist policies do not change the fact that the United States entered World War I later than its European counterparts, or that the United States was instrumental in winning that particular war. Trying to rewrite our understanding of U.S. policy does a grave
10 disservice to the facts of history.

Passage 2

History is by nature a discipline of interpretation. The bigger issue is the bias of the interpreter. Much of a historian's job is related to distinguishing relevant information from extraneous material. For too long, the contributions of racial
15 minorities, women, and other groups have been deemed inessential to an understanding of history. Recognizing the vital role of African American soldiers in a segregated military or the factory work of women in World War II will give us a more complete picture of America, both in the past
20 and in the present.

30. On what point would the authors of both passages agree?

(A) History is based on irrefutable facts.
(B) Revisionist history is antithetical to historical analysis.
(C) Historical analysis requires a basis of factual information.
(D) Military victories are the most important part of history.
(E) Interpretation is essential to an understanding of history.

31. Unlike Passage 2, Passage 1 contains

(A) vocabulary specific to the discipline of history
(B) references to historical events
(C) an international perspective
(D) a partisan judgment
(E) a reference to historical bias

32. The conflict between the passages can be most accurately described as that between the importance of

(A) military history and social history
(B) domestic history and international history
(C) objectivity and subjectivity
(D) fact-based analysis and limited interpretation
(E) bias and accuracy

33. The author of Passage 2 is most concerned that

(A) the segregationist policies of the American military were wrong
(B) history cannot be accurately analyzed
(C) historians cannot be trusted
(D) factual analysis is impossible
(E) traditional historical analysis ignores minority groups

GO ON TO THE NEXT PAGE

Questions 34-39 are based on the following passage.

The following excerpt is from an essay by a leading scientist and professor of paleontology. In it he describes how an experience in one field—choral music—led to a revelation about himself.

Thirty years ago, on April 30, 1958, to be exact, I sat with 250 students facing one of the most formidable men of our generation—Peter J. Wilhousky, director of music in the New

Line York City Schools and conductor of the New York All-City
5 High School Chorus. As the warm, and primarily parental, applause receded at the concert's end, Wilhousky returned to the podium of Carnegie Hall, gestured for silence, and raised his baton to conduct the traditional encore, "Madame Jeanette." Halfway through, he turned and, without missing
10 a beat (to invoke a cliché in its appropriate, literal sense), smiled to acknowledge the chorus alumni who stood at their seats or surrounded the podium, singing with their current counterparts. These former members seemed so ancient to me—though none had passed forty, for the chorus itself was
15 by then only twenty years old—and their solidarity moved me to a rare fit of tears at a time when teenage boys did not cry in public.

"Madame Jeanette" is a dangerous little piece, for it ventures so near the edge of cloying sentimentality. It tells the
20 tale, in close four-part a cappella harmony, of a French widow who sits at her door by day and her window by night. There she thinks only of her husband, killed so many years before on the battlefield of St. Pierre, and dreams of the day when they will be reunited at the cemetery of Père Lachaise. With
25 250 teenagers and sloppy conducting, "Madame Jeanette" becomes a maudlin and embarrassing tearfest. Wilhousky, ever the perfectionist, ever the rationalist, somehow steered to the right side of musicality, and ended each concert with integrity and control.

30 "Madame Jeanette" was our symbol of continuity. For a very insecure boy, singing second bass on the brink of manhood, "Madame Jeanette" offered another wonderful solace. It ends, for the basses, on a low D-flat, just about as far down the scale as any composer would dare ask a singer
35 to venture. Yes, I knew even then that low did not mean masculine, or capable, or mature, or virile, but that fundament resonated with hope and possibility, even in pianissimo.

We lived, thirty years ago, in an age of readier obedience, but I still marvel at the discipline that Wilhousky could
40 maintain with his mixture of awe (inspired) and terror (promulgated). He forged our group of Blacks from Harlem, Jews from Queens, and Italians from Staten Island into a responsive singing machine. He worked, in part, through intimidation by public ridicule. One day, he stopped the
45 rehearsal and pointed to the tenor section, saying: "You, third row, fourth seat, stand up. You're singing flat. Ten years ago, Julius La Rosa sat in the same seat—and sang flat. And he's still singing flat." (Memory is a curious trickster. La Rosa, in a recent *New Yorker* profile, states that Wilhousky praised
50 him in the same forum for singing so true to pitch. But I know

what I heard. Or is the joke on me?) Each year, he cashiered a member or two for talking and giggling—in public, and with no hope of mercy or reinstatement.

But Peter Wilhousky had another side that inspired us
55 all and conveyed the most important lesson of intellectual life. He was one of the finest choral conductors in America, yet he chose to spend every Saturday morning with high school kids. His only rule, tacit but persuasive, proclaimed: "No compromises." We could sing, with proper training and
60 practice, as well as any group in America; nothing else would be tolerated or even conceptualized. Anything less would not be worth doing at all. I had encountered friendliness, grace, kindness, animation, clarity, and dedication among my teachers, but I had never even considered the notion that
65 unqualified excellence could emerge from anything touched or made by students. The idea, however, is infectious. As I worked with Wilhousky, I slowly personalized the dream that excellence in one activity might be extended to become the pattern, or at least the goal, of an actual life.

34. The author's main purpose in writing the passage is to

(A) urge students to participate in music
(B) worship a gifted individual
(C) analyze a particular piece of music
(D) relate an incident from his childhood
(E) trace the development of a particular attitude

35. The author describes "Madame Jeanette" as a "dangerous little piece" (line 18) because

(A) it can appear trite and melodramatic when performed under less than ideal conditions
(B) it contains seditious material
(C) it has a profoundly moving effect on most audiences
(D) it evokes harrowing images of death and violence
(E) it is a technically difficult piece for most choirs to perform

GO ON TO THE NEXT PAGE

36. It can be inferred from the third paragraph that performing "Madame Jeanette" filled the author with a feeling of

    (A) masculinity
    (B) insecurity
    (C) optimism
    (D) melancholy
    (E) embarrassment

37. In the context of the passage, the term "readier" (line 38) most nearly means

    (A) more prepared
    (B) more willing
    (C) more complete
    (D) more clever
    (E) more punctual

38. The authors includes the anecdote of the student in the "third row, fourth seat" (lines 45-46) in order to

    (A) provide an example of how Wilhousky maintained discipline in the chorus
    (B) suggest that Wilhousky had lied about Julius La Rosa
    (C) show how cruel and arbitrary Wilhousky could be at times
    (D) illustrate how unreliable the human memory can be
    (E) imply that Wilhousky liked to trick his students into obeying him

39. The passage suggests that Wilhousky inspired the author to

    (A) strive for excellence in all of his endeavors
    (B) pursue a career in music
    (C) devote himself to helping high school students
    (D) attend future performances of the chorus as an alumnus
    (E) never resort to compromising with anyone

GO ON TO THE NEXT PAGE

Questions 40-48 are based on the following passage.

The following passage discusses the differing paths of China and India after World War II and offers explanations for the disparity.

The Japanese surrender aboard the U.S.S. *Missouri* ignited a series of events which radically changed the shape and destiny of Eastern and Southern Asia. Within two years,
Line India had gained independence from Britain. Within four,
5 Mao Tse Deng's communists had established the People's Republic of China. At the end of the twentieth century, China and India were the two largest nations in the world. Both were nuclear powers, both were still ruled by the regimes which had founded them and both had embarked on daring reform
10 programs in order to modernize their economies. This is where the similarities end. While China experienced wild success in industrializing, in India, for both political and economic reasons, the process stagnated.

Politically, China was successful because its political
15 system was conducive to the high levels of centralized control required for the scale of development that it was attempting. Economically, China was successful because it was patient. It expanded its economy slowly, only entering new sectors when it had the resources to be successful in them. For example,
20 China only attempted to develop high-tech manufacturing after its initial reforms had taken effect.

What made India so different? Like China, India was established after World War II as an independent country. However, unlike China, the new government was
25 a parliamentary democracy. This factor is essential to understanding why seemingly similar reforms had radically different effects.

India's reforms were quite different from China's in result if not in shape. After its independence from Britain in 1947,
30 India established large State Owned Enterprises (SOE's) that were given generous protections by the government to promote growth. India operated for years under policies that attempted to foster domestic manufacturing of formerly imported goods. Unfortunately, these policies resulted in
35 consumers paying a higher price for and receiving a lower quality of goods than they had previously. SOEs were given protections under the assumption that being free from competition, they could improve their products, increase their business experience, and make their operations more efficient.
40 Unfortunately, India, unlike rigidly communist China, had no way of truly enforcing these policies. China could quash any dissent with few repercussions for government. India's parliament, however, had to seek reelection. This proved a disincentive for "rocking the boat" too much. While everyone
45 wanted more efficient businesses, no one wanted to tell the voters back home that jobs would be lost to cut costs.

So what went wrong in India? China was able to successfully reform because it acted in stages and acted fully. India never actually changed the system enough to
50 promote development. Its politicians remained too dependent upon reelection to make sweeping reforms. Its financial sector

was not developed enough to foster growth independent of the government. Its political system remained in question; even today assassination remains a popular way to voice dissenting
55 opinions. In order for India to industrialize fully and develop a level of economic depth comparable to China's, it must reevaluate its priorities and set truly national goals. Given its democratic system, India's task is harder than China's was, but it is not so hard as to be impossible.

40. It can be inferred from the passage that prior to World War II India and China were

(A) both behind other countries in modernizing their economic systems
(B) the two largest nations in the world
(C) the victims of continual bloody and destructive political revolutions
(D) competitors in various economic and martial arenas
(E) concerned with setting truly national goals

41. Which of the following facts, if true, would most call into question the author's claims about the reasons for China's relative success?

(A) The Chinese government had the resources to enter the high-tech market a decade before it actually did.
(B) India had been a British colony while China had remained nominally sovereign.
(C) Many far-flung provinces felt free to ignore the mandates of China's central government.
(D) China also used a version of SOEs in order to encourage national manufacturing rather than foreign imports.
(E) India actually has more natural resources per capita than does China.

42. The author would be most likely to agree with which of the following statements about parliamentary democracies?

(A) They are highly preferable to forms of rule such as communism.
(B) They must be abolished if a country is to flourish economically.
(C) They tend to make reform difficult because leaders must worry about the approval of their constituents.
(D) They were the best possible option for Eastern and Southern Asian countries after World War II.
(E) They can be risky because they encourage countries to make economic moves for which they are not fully ready.

GO ON TO THE NEXT PAGE

43. SOEs were put into place in India for all of the following reasons EXCEPT

   (A) to discourage foreign manufacturing
   (B) to increase business experience
   (C) to cultivate domestic manufacturing
   (D) to improve the quality of products
   (E) to increase efficiency in manufacturing

44. As used in line 42, "repercussions" most closely means

   (A) returning
   (B) loud noises
   (C) labors
   (D) consequences
   (E) new laws

45. The line "So what went wrong in India?" (line 47) serves as

   (A) a request for information
   (B) a move to summation
   (C) a shift in focus
   (D) an unanswerable complaint
   (E) a flippant rejoinder

46. Suppose that India, rather than trying to move directly into free trade, had implemented reform in stages. The author would most likely argue that

   (A) India would certainly have been more successful than it is today
   (B) the process would have fostered revolution, which would have been disastrous considering India's nuclear capabilities
   (C) such a move would lead to a reevaluation of priorities and national goals
   (D) changing the shape of the reforms would certainly lead to different results
   (E) there might need to be a simultaneous centralization of governmental power to achieve positive results

47. According to the passage, in order to be economically successful, India must

   (A) abolish its democratic system and move to totalitarian communism
   (B) promote the use of SOEs
   (C) vote out current leaders and elect new ones who are willing to "rock the boat"
   (D) let go of old beliefs and offer reforms aimed at changing the priorities of the country as a whole
   (E) cut jobs in order to reduce costs

48. The author's attitude toward China can best be described as

   (A) awed reverence
   (B) measured admiration
   (C) guarded dislike
   (D) disdainful pity
   (E) politic respect

STOP

If you finish before time is called, you may check your work on this section only.

Do not turn to any other section in the test.

SECTION 4
Time — 25 minutes
18 Questions

Directions: For this section, solve each problem and decide which is the best of the choices given. Fill in the corresponding circle on the answer sheet. You may use any available space for scratchwork.

21. What is the value of z if $3z + 4z + 7z = -42$?

    (A) 3

    (B) $\dfrac{1}{3}$

    (C) $-\dfrac{1}{3}$

    (D) −3

    (E) −588

$14z = -42$

$z =$

22. If 10 pecks are equivalent to 2.5 bushels, then 4 bushels are equivalent to how many pecks?

    (A) 1
    (B) 4
    (C) 10
    (D) 12.5
    (E) 16

$10p = 2.5b$

$p = 0.25b$

GO ON TO THE NEXT PAGE

23. What is the y-intercept of the line with equation $2x + 3y = 12$?

(A) 4

(B) 3

(C) 2

(D) $\dfrac{1}{4}$

(E) $-\dfrac{2}{3}$

24. For $x \neq 0$, $\dfrac{a}{x^2} + \dfrac{7}{x} =$

(A) $\dfrac{a + 7x}{x}$

(B) $\dfrac{a + 7x}{x^2}$

(C) $\dfrac{a + 7}{x^2 + x}$

(D) $\dfrac{a + 7}{x^2}$

(E) $\dfrac{a + 7}{x^2}$

25. If $y = 6x + 3$ and $y = cx + 3$ are the equations of perpendicular lines, then what is the value of c ?

A) -6

(B) $-\dfrac{1}{6}$

(C) $\dfrac{1}{6}$

(D) $\dfrac{1}{3}$

(E) 6

26. The positive difference between -5 and p is the same as the positive difference between -1 and 2.5. Which of the following could be the value of p ?

(A) -8.5

(B) -6.5

(C) -2.5

(D) 6.5

(E) 8.5

GO ON TO THE NEXT PAGE

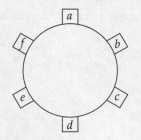

27. If $f(x) = x^{-\frac{2}{3}}$, what is the value of $\dfrac{f(8)}{f(3)}$?

(A) $\dfrac{3}{4}$

(B) $\dfrac{4}{\sqrt[3]{9}}$

(C) $\dfrac{8}{3}$

(D) $\sqrt{\dfrac{512}{27}}$

(E) $\dfrac{\sqrt[3]{9}}{4}$

28. The figure above represents a circular amusement park ride with 6 seats, labeled a through f. If two students are to sit next to each other, leaving the other seats empty, how many such arrangements of the two students are possible?

(A) 3
(B) 6
(C) 10
(D) 12
(E) 30

GO ON TO THE NEXT PAGE

Directions for Student-Produced Response Questions

Each of the remaining 10 questions requires you to solve the problem and enter your answer by marking the ovals in the special grid, as shown in the examples below. You may use any available space for scratch work.

Answer: $\frac{7}{12}$

Write answer in boxes.

Fraction line

Grid in result.

Answer: 2.5

Decimal point

Note: You may start your answers in any column, space permitting. Columns not needed should be left blank.

• Mark no more than one circle in any column.

• Because the answer sheet will be machine-scored, **you will receive credit only if the circles are filled in correctly.**

• Although not required, it is suggested that you write your answer in the boxes at the top of the columns to help you fill in the circles accurately.

• Some problems may have more than one correct answer. In such cases, grid only one answer.

• No question has a negative answer.

• **Mixed numbers** such as $3\frac{1}{2}$ must be gridded as

3.5 or 7/2. (If [3 1 / 2] is gridded, it will be

interpreted as $\frac{31}{2}$, not $3\frac{1}{2}$.)

• **Decimal Answers:** If you obtain a decimal answer with more digits than the grid can accommodate, it may be either rounded or truncated, but it must fill the entire grid. For example, if you obtain an answer such as 0.6666..., you should record your result as .666 or .667. **A less accurate value such as .66 or .67 will be scored as incorrect.**

Acceptable ways to grid $\frac{2}{3}$ are:

29. What is the value of $\bigl|-10\bigr| - \bigl|3\bigr|$?

30. If 20 percent of n is 36, what is 0.2 percent of n ?

GO ON TO THE NEXT PAGE

31. In $\triangle RST$, $\overline{RS} \cong \overline{ST}$. If the measure of $\angle S$ is 20°, then what is the degree measure of $\angle T$?

_____

32. If all of the angles in the figure above are right angles, what is its perimeter?

33. If $x - 8 = 5y$ and $x = 23$, then what is the value of $x - y$?

_____

34. What is the product of all the positive integer factors of 20 ?

GO ON TO THE NEXT PAGE

35. Marcia can type 18 pages per hour, and David can type 14 pages per hour. If they work together, how many <u>minutes</u> will it take them to type 24 pages?

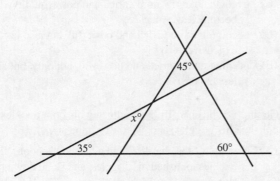

Note: Figure not drawn to scale.

36. What is the value of x in the figure above?

37. If $f(x) = x^2 - x + 4$, a is non-negative, and $f(a) = 10$, then what is the value of a ?

38. A box contains only large marbles and small marbles. There are twice as many large marbles as small marbles in the box. The large marbles are all either blue or red, and there are 5 times as many large blue marbles as large red marbles. If one marble is drawn from the box at random, what is the probability that it will be a large blue marble?

STOP
If you finish before time is called, you may check your work on this section only.
Do not turn to any other section in the test.

SECTION 5
Time — 30 minutes
39 Questions

Directions: For each question in this section, select the best answer from among the choices given and fill in the corresponding circle on the answer sheet.

The following sentences test correctness and effectiveness of expression. Part of each sentence or the entire sentence is underlined; beneath each sentence are five ways of phrasing the underlined material. Choice A repeats the original phrasing; the other four choices are different. If you think the original phrasing produces a better sentence than any of the alternatives, select choice A; if not, select one of the other choices.

In making your selection, follow the requirements of standard written English; that is, pay attention to grammar, choice of words, sentence construction, and punctuation. Your selection should result in the most effective sentence—clear and precise, without awkwardness or ambiguity.

EXAMPLE:

Bobby Flay baked his first cake <u>and he was thirteen years old then</u>.
(A) and he was thirteen years old then
(B) when he was thirteen
(C) at age thirteen years old
(D) upon the reaching of thirteen years
(E) at the time when he was thirteen

Ⓐ ● Ⓒ Ⓓ Ⓔ

1. After visiting their friends in Paris, my parents told me that <u>in France they sometimes</u> do not wear bathing suits on the beach.

   (A) in France they sometimes
   (B) in France some people
   (C) some people, who are French,
   (D) in France there are some who
   (E) in France, men and women

2. Today's computers <u>are becoming not only more varied and powerful, but also less expensive</u>.

   (A) are becoming not only more varied and powerful, but also less expensive
   (B) not only are becoming more varied and powerful, they cost less
   (C) become not only more varied and powerful, they become less expensive
   (D) becoming more varied and powerful, but also less expensive
   (E) become more varied and powerful, not only, but also less expensive

3. <u>Getting off the chairlift, Neil adjusted his boot buckles, polished his goggles, and skied down the slope.</u>

   (A) Getting off the chairlift, Neil adjusted his boot buckles, polished his goggles, and skied down the slope.
   (B) He got off the chairlift, Neil adjusted his boot buckles, polished his goggles, and skied down the slope.
   (C) After getting off the chairlift, Neil adjusted his boot buckles, polished his goggles, and then he went skiing down the slope.
   (D) Neil, after getting off the chairlift, adjusted his boot buckles, polished his goggles, and was skiing down the slope.
   (E) After he got off the chairlift, Neil adjusted his boot buckles, polished his goggles, and skied down the slope.

4. Since they have been told not to do so in their school books, students often hesitate to write in their personal books; yet, circling an unknown word or underlining an important phrase <u>is critically when one wishes to learn something</u>.

   (A) is critically when one wishes to learn something
   (B) is critically being as one might wish to learn something
   (C) is critical when one wishes to learn something
   (D) is critical when you want to learn that something has been
   (E) can only be seen as critical when one wishes to learn something

GO ON TO THE NEXT PAGE →

5. One of Humphrey Bogart's earlier movies, Samuel Spade is a detective trying to solve the mystery of his partner's death in *The Maltese Falcon*.

(A) One of Humphrey Bogart's earlier movies, Samuel Spade is a detective trying to solve the mystery of his partner's death in *The Maltese Falcon*.

(B) One of Humphrey Bogart's earlier movies, *The Maltese Falcon* is a movie in that Samuel Spade, detective, tries to solve the mystery of his partner's death.

(C) One of Humphrey Bogart's earlier movies, *The Maltese Falcon* is a mystery in which Samuel Spade tries to solve his partner's death.

(D) In *The Maltese Falcon*, one of Humphrey Bogart's earlier movies, Samuel Spade is a detective trying to solve the mystery of his partner's death.

(E) In *The Maltese Falcon*, one of Humphrey Bogart's roles is that of Samuel Spade, a detective trying to solve the mystery of his partner's death, and it was also one of his earlier movies.

6. While Boudin's own paintings have never been held in the highest regard, he is seen as having played a critical role in the education of Impressionist painter Monet.

(A) While Boudin's own paintings have never been held in the highest regard, he is seen as having played a critical role in the education of Impressionist painter Monet.

(B) While Boudin's own paintings were never regarded highly, Monet is seen as having been one of his most educated students.

(C) It is seen that Boudin's critical role in educating the Impressionist painter Monet was held in higher regard than his paintings.

(D) Since Boudin's own paintings have never been held in that high regard, he has been seen as having played a critical role in the education of Impressionist painter Monet.

(E) Since Boudin's own paintings, which were never held in that high regard, were seen as having played a critical role in the education of Impressionist painter Monet.

7. Although everyone was forewarned about the upcoming exam, yet only three students out of the entire class passed it.

(A) yet only three students out of the entire class
(B) only three students out of the entire class
(C) only three students, which was out of the entire class,
(D) yet only three students that were forewarned out of the entire class
(E) but only three students out of the entire class

8. The committee chairpersons agreed to return to their respective committees and they would discuss the proposals made by the executive board.

(A) to return to their respective committees and they would discuss
(B) upon return to their respective committees, thereby discussing
(C) to return to her respective committees and discuss
(D) to return to their respective committees discussing
(E) to return to their respective committees and discuss

9. The clog has come back into fashion recently, yet few people know that originally it was called the sabot, made by hollowing a single piece of wood, and was worn by peasants in Europe.

(A) it was called the sabot, made by hollowing a single piece of wood, and was worn by peasants in Europe
(B) it was called the sabot, making it by hollowing a single piece of wood, and worn by peasants in Europe
(C) it was called the sabot, made by hollowing a single piece of wood, and worn by peasants in Europe
(D) it was called the sabot, making it by hollowing a single piece of wood, and was worn by peasants in Europe
(E) it was called the sabot, and the peasants made it by hollowing a single piece of wood, and wore it in Europe

10. Many say that, after inventing an explosive more powerful than any then known, Alfred Nobel instituted the Nobel Peace Prize to atone for his "accomplishment" and relieve his conscience.

(A) after inventing an explosive more powerful than any then known
(B) after inventing an explosive that was more powerful than any that were then known
(C) after he invented an explosive more powerful than he or any others had then known
(D) after he invented an explosive, it being more powerful than any then known
(E) after inventing an explosive more powerful then any than known

GO ON TO THE NEXT PAGE

11. For many a brilliant actor, <u>being free to interpret their character as they wish</u> is more important than being well paid.

   (A) being free to interpret their character as they wish

   (B) being free to interpret his or her character as they wish

   (C) being free to interpret their character as they wishes

   (D) being free to interpret his or her character as he or she wishes

   (E) being free to interpret his or her character as he or she wish

12. On Sunday afternoons, Omar and his family enjoy playing Monopoly with the neighbors, <u>and they always win</u>.

   (A) and they always win

   (B) even though they always win

   (C) even though the neighbors always win

   (D) and the neighbors, they always win

   (E) it being that the neighbors always win

13. Known for graduating from college despite being blind and deaf, <u>the fact that Helen Keller spent over six decades fighting for socialist causes is often left out of accounts of her life</u>.

   (A) the fact that Helen Keller spent over six decades fighting for socialist causes is often left out of accounts of her life

   (B) accounts of Helen Keller's life often leave out that she spent over six decades fighting for socialist causes

   (C) many people are unaware that Helen Keller spent over six decades fighting for socialist causes, as this fact is often left out of accounts of her life

   (D) six decades were spent by Helen Keller fighting for socialist causes, though this fact is often left out of accounts of her life

   (E) Helen Keller spent over six decades fighting for socialist causes, a fact often left out of accounts of her life

14. After getting her driver's license, Jenny used her father's car <u>as often as possible, and her father said to put less miles on it</u> by walking to school and work.

   (A) as often as possible, and her father said to put less miles on it

   (B) as often as possible; eventually her father told her to put fewer miles on it

   (C) as often as possible, but then eventually her father told her to be putting fewer miles on it

   (D) as often as possible; eventually her father told her to put less miles on it

   (E) as often as possible, and her father said to be putting less miles on it

15. The French classical composer, <u>Maurice Ravel, has enlisted as an ambulance driver</u> during World War I.

   (A) Maurice Ravel, has enlisted as an ambulance driver

   (B) Maurice Ravel, was to be enlisted as an ambulance driver

   (C) Maurice Ravel, was enlisting as an ambulance driver

   (D) Maurice Ravel, enlisting to be an ambulance driver

   (E) Maurice Ravel, enlisted as an ambulance driver

16. <u>The art of carving totem poles with fantastic animal figures were practiced by Pacific Northwest Native American tribes</u>.

   (A) The art of carving totem poles with fantastic animal figures were practiced by Pacific Northwest Native American tribes.

   (B) The art of carving totem poles with fantastic animal figures was practiced by Pacific Northwest Native American tribes.

   (C) The art of carving totem poles with fantastic animal figures were being practiced by Pacific Northwest Native American tribes.

   (D) Pacific Northwest Native American tribes were practicing the art of carving totem poles with fantastic animal figures.

   (E) Pacific Northwest Native American tribes practiced the art of carving totem poles with fantastic animal figures.

GO ON TO THE NEXT PAGE

17. The bristlecone pine, regarded to be one of the varieties of longest living trees, is native to the American West.

(A) The bristlecone pine, regarded to be one of the varieties of longest living trees, is native to the American West.

(B) The bristlecone pine, regarded to be one of the varieties of longest living trees, are native to the American West.

(C) The bristlecone pine, regarded as one of the varieties of longest living trees, are native to the American West.

(D) The bristlecone pine, regarded as one of the longest-lived varieties of trees, is native to the American West.

(E) The bristlecone pine, regarded as being one of the varieties of longest living trees, is native to the American West.

18. Scholars of popular culture have found that the mainstream music of one decade often originates from the most obscure underground music of the previous decade.

(A) the mainstream music of one decade often originates from the most obscure

(B) the mainstream music of one decade often originates from the more obscure

(C) the mainstream music of one decade often originates in the most obscure

(D) the mainstream music of one decade often originates with the more obscure

(E) the mainstream music of one decade often originates with the more obscure

19. P. T. Barnum catered to the taste of the public with such circus acts as Major Tom Thumb and Jumbo the elephant.

(A) P. T. Barnum catered to the taste of the public

(B) P. T. Barnum catering to the taste of the public

(C) P. T. Barnum catering for the taste of the public

(D) P. T. Barnum catered for the taste of the public

(E) P. T. Barnum, having catered to the taste of the public,

20. In the early 1900's, Enrico Caruso was America's finest operatic tenor, more recently opera fans have enjoyed the talents of Plácido Domingo and José Carreras.

(A) In the early 1900s, Enrico Caruso was America's finest operatic tenor, more recently opera fans have enjoyed the talents of Plácido Domingo and José Carreras.

(B) In the early 1900s, Enrico Caruso was America's finest operatic tenor; more recently, opera fans have enjoyed the talents of Plácido Domingo and José Carreras.

(C) In the early 1900s, Enrico Caruso was America's finest operatic tenor: more recently, opera fans have enjoyed the talents of Plácido Domingo and José Carreras.

(D) In the early 1900s, Enrico Caruso was America's finest operatic tenor; but more recently, opera fans have enjoyed the talents of Plácido Domingo and José Carreras.

(E) In the early 1900s, Enrico Caruso was America's finest operatic tenor, however, more recently, opera fans have enjoyed the talents of Plácido Domingo and José Carreras.

GO ON TO THE NEXT PAGE

The following sentences test your ability to recognize grammar and usage errors. Each sentence contains either a single error or no error at all. No sentence contains more than one error. The error, if there is one, is underlined and lettered. If the sentence contains an error, select the one underlined part that must be changed to make the sentence correct. If the sentence is correct, select choice E. In choosing answers, follow the requirements of standard written English.

EXAMPLE:

The other players and her significantly improved
　　A　　　　　　　　B　　C

the game plan created by the coaches. No error
　　　　　　　　　D　　　　　　　　　　E

Ⓐ ● Ⓒ Ⓓ Ⓔ

21. Revered as one of the world's most versatile genius-
　　A
es, Leonardo da Vinci excelled in every endeavor he attempted
　　　　　　　　　　　　　B
and serving as a prototype for the Renaissance man. No error
　　C　　　　　　D　　　　　　　　　　　　　　E

22. The twins wanted to be a member of the team, but the
　　　　　　　　　　　A　　　　　　　B
captain had already made her selections. No error
　　　　C　　　　　　D　　　　　E

23. Of the nominees for the Nobel Prize in Literature this
　　A　　　　　　B
year, few are as qualified as the English novelist Anthony
　　　C　　　　D
Powell. No error
　　　E

24. The recent production of Arthur Miller's A View from
　　　　　　　　　　A
the Bridge exemplifies the strength of this unsung
masterpiece and demonstrates that the work has been
　　　　　　　B　　　　　　　　　　C
ignored unjust. No error
　　　D　　　E

25. Yoga is more than simply a series of stretches and poses;
　　　　　　A　　　　　　　　B
it is a means of centering oneself spiritually and focus in
　　　　　　　　　　　　　　　　　　　　　C
such a way as to put one's life in order. No error
　　　　D　　　　　　　　　　　　E

26. Prior to the Industrial Revolution, children and parents
　　A
spend a great deal of time working together to meet the
　B　　　　　C
needs of the family. No error
　　　D　　　　E

27. Neither the president nor the CEO of the three sister
　　　　　　　　　　A
companies was able to determine why the last quarter's
　　　　　B
financial reports were so inconsistent with previous years.
　　　　　　C　　　　　　　　　　　D
No error
E

GO ON TO THE NEXT PAGE

28. If one is interested in learning more about Jacob
$$\underset{A}{\underline{}}$$
Lawrence, you should visit the Metropolitan Museum of
$$\underset{B}{\underline{}}$$
Art when next his work is exhibited. No error
$$\underset{C}{\underline{}}\quad\underset{D}{\underline{}}\quad\underset{E}{\underline{}}$$

29. Despite the dangerous road conditions
$$\underset{A}{\underline{}}$$
after the blizzard, the company insisted on its employees
$$\underset{B}{\underline{}}\quad\underset{C}{\underline{}}\;\underset{D}{\underline{}}$$
be on time. No error
$$\underset{E}{\underline{}}$$

30. While in training, each member of the team were required
$$\underset{A}{\underline{}}$$
to focus exclusively on the tasks associated

with her position, and therefore had little sense of the
$$\underset{B}{\underline{}}\;\underset{C}{\underline{}}$$
functioning of the team as a whole. No error
$$\underset{D}{\underline{}}\quad\underset{E}{\underline{}}$$

31. The gift that Karen and Mary ultimately purchased for

her mother was much less expensive than the gift they
$$\underset{A}{\underline{}}\quad\underset{B}{\underline{}}\quad\underset{C}{\underline{}}$$
originally intended to purchase. No error
$$\underset{D}{\underline{}}\quad\underset{E}{\underline{}}$$

32. Deciding to follow his conscience and not give in to the
$$\underset{A}{\underline{}}$$
pressure to conform, the local worker was a vocal
$$\underset{B}{\underline{}}\quad\underset{C}{\underline{}}$$
critic toward the regional vice president. No error
$$\underset{D}{\underline{}}\quad\underset{E}{\underline{}}$$

33. Many scholars agree that there has been no greater
$$\underset{A}{\underline{}}\qquad\underset{B}{\underline{}}$$
contributor to the advancement of architecture in the
$$\underset{C}{\underline{}}$$
twentieth century than that of Frank Lloyd Wright.
$$\underset{D}{\underline{}}$$
No error
$$\underset{E}{\underline{}}$$

34. Constructing a fence ought not to be seen as an
$$\underset{A}{\underline{}}$$
insurmountable task; rather, it should be viewed as a
$$\underset{B}{\underline{}}$$
challenge that can be accomplished by a
$$\underset{C}{\underline{}}$$
combination of perseverance and patience. No error
$$\underset{D}{\underline{}}\quad\underset{E}{\underline{}}$$

GO ON TO THE NEXT PAGE

Directions: The following passage is an early draft of an essay. Some parts of the passage need to be rewritten.

Read the passage and select the best answers for the questions that follow. Some questions are about particular sentences or parts of sentences and ask you to improve sentence structure or word choice. Other questions ask you to consider organization and development. In choosing answers, follow the requirements of standard written English.

Questions 35-39 are based on the following passage.

(1) Our town needs to make more of an effort to make its museums accessible to children. (2) Raised with frequent exposure to sculpture and paintings, it is much more likely that young people will mature into artists and patrons of the arts.

(3) It is often quite easy to accomplish a great deal simply. (4) Placed slightly lower on the walls, paintings become more visible to children. (5) But extensive programs to encourage children to appreciate art are often not a necessity. (6) Children have a natural enjoyment of art. (7) A museum is an excellent place for a child. (8) We must only understand that these young museum patrons can not help acting like them. (9) Children should not be asked to be silent, or spend long periods of time in front of any one piece. (10) If necessary, museums should set up special "children's times" during which young people may roam through the building, enjoying the artwork in their own way. (11) A wonderful learning experience! (12) Children can have a great time, and at the same time gain an appreciation of art. (13) Precautions could be taken to make sure that no damage was done.

(14) This is necessary because places like museums must be available for everyone. (15) These changes cannot happen overnight, but if we volunteered and were helping to make these changes in our town's museums, we can realize the goal of making them accessible to people of all ages.

35. Which version of the underlined portion of sentence 8 (reproduced below) provides the most clarity?

    We must only understand that these young museum patrons can not help acting like them.

    (A) (as it is now)
    (B) like it
    (C) as if they were
    (D) like what they are
    (E) like children

36. After sentence 13, the writer's point would have been strengthened most by the inclusion of

    (A) a description of possible damage
    (B) an explanation of the precautions to be taken
    (C) a historic precedent
    (D) an extension of her argument to include other institutions
    (E) an explanation of the mission of a museum

37. Which of the following represents the best version of sentence 4 (reproduced below) ?

    Placed slightly lower on the walls, paintings become more visible to children.

    (A) (As it is now)
    (B) Placing them slightly lower on the walls, the paintings become more visible to the children.
    (C) For example, placing paintings slightly lower on the walls makes them more visible to children.
    (D) For example, when placed slightly lower on the walls, children can see the paintings better.
    (E) Placed paintings that are lower on the walls are more visible to children.

GO ON TO THE NEXT PAGE

38. Which of the following is the best way to revise sentences 10 and 11 (reproduced below)?

If necessary, museums should set up special "children's times" during which young people may roam through the building, enjoying the artwork in their own way. A wonderful learning experience!

(A) To avoid disrupting everyone else, create "children's times" in the museum, during which children could roam throughout the building, enjoying the artwork in their own way and a wonderful learning experience.

(B) Museums should set up "children's times." This would be a wonderful learning experience. Children could roam through the museum. Children could enjoy the artwork in their own way.

(C) If necessary, museums should set up a wonderful learning experience called "children's times." During it, young people could roam throughout the building, enjoying the artwork in their own way.

(D) To enjoy artwork in their own way, children should be given the freedom to roam throughout the building. This would be a wonderful learning experience, and it could be called "children's times."

(E) To avoid disrupting other museum-goers, museums should set up special "children's times." During these times, children would be allowed to roam throughout the building and enjoy the artwork in their own way. What a wonderful learning experience!

39. In context, sentence 14 could be made more precise by changing the phrase "This is" to which of the following?

(A) That is
(B) These changes are
(C) The reasons for these changes is that they are
(D) It is
(E) These changes, as mentioned above, are also

STOP

If you finish before time is called, you may check your work on this section only.
Do not turn to any other section in the test.

PRACTICE TEST 1 ANSWERS

Section 1	Section 2	Section 3	Section 4	Section 5	
1. C	1. D	25. D	21. D	1. B	31. A
2. C	2. D	26. C	22. E	2. A	32. D
3. E	3. D	27. A	23. A	3. E	33. D
4. D	4. C	28. A	24. B	4. C	34. E
5. B	5. B	29. D	25. B	5. D	35. E
6. B	6. C	30. C	26. A	6. A	36. B
7. A	7. E	31. A	27. E	7. B	37. C
8. C	8. B	32. C	28. D	8. E	38. E
9. D	9. D	33. E	29. 7	9. C	39. B
10. A	10. C	34. E	30. .36	10. A	
11. A	11. A	35. A	31. 80	11. D	
12. B	12. E	36. C	32. 14	12. C	
13. B	13. C	37. B	33. 20	13. E	
14. D	14. D	38. A	34. 8,000	14. B	
15. B	15. D	39. A	35. 45	15. E	
16. C	16. C	40. A	36. 40	16. E	
17. A	17. E	41. C	37. 3	17. D	
18. D	18. B	42. C		18. C	
19. E	19. B	43. A	38. $\dfrac{5}{9}$	19. A	
20. D	20. B	44. D	or	20. B	
21. B		45. B		21. C	
22. A		46. E	.555	22. A	
23. E		47. D	or	23. E	
24. C		48. B	.556	24. D	
				25. C	
				26. B	
				27. D	
				28. B	
				29. C	
				30. A	

You will find a detailed explanation for each question beginning on page 302.

SCORING YOUR PRACTICE PSAT

Critical Reading

After you have checked your answers against the answer key, you can calculate your score. For the two Critical Reading sections (Sections 1 and 3), add up the number of correct answers and the number of incorrect answers. Enter these numbers on the worksheet on the next page. Multiply the number of incorrect answers by .25 and subtract this result from the number of correct answers. Then round this to the nearest whole number. This is your Critical Reading "raw score." Next, use the conversion table to convert your raw score to a scaled score.

Math

Figuring your Math score is a bit trickier, because some of the questions have 5 answer choices (for these, the incorrect answer deduction is .25), and some are Grid-Ins (which have no deduction for wrong answers).

First, check your answers to all of the problem-solving questions on Sections 2 and 4. For Section 2 and questions 21–28 of Section 4, put the number of correct answers and the number of incorrect answers into the worksheet on the next page. Multiply the number of incorrect answers by .25 and subtract this total from the number of correct answers. For questions 29–38 of Section 4, the Grid-In questions, simply put in the number of correct answers. Now, add up the totals for both types of math questions to give you your total Math raw score. Then you can use the conversion table to find your scaled score.

Writing Skills

The Writing Skills section should be scored just like the Critical Reading sections. Add up the number of correct answers and the number of incorrect answers from Section 5, and enter these numbers on the worksheet on the next page. Multiply the number of incorrect answers by .25 and subtract this result from the number of correct answers. Then round this to the nearest whole number. This is your Writing Skills raw score. Next, use the conversion table to convert your raw scores to scaled scores.

WORKSHEET FOR CALCULATING YOUR SCORE

Critical Reading

	Correct	Incorrect	
A. Sections 1 and 3	_____	– (.25 × _____) =	[A]
B. Total rounded Critical Reading raw score			[B]

Math

	Correct	Incorrect	
C. Section 2 and Section 4—Problem Solving	_____	– (.25 × _____) =	[C]
D. Section 4—Grid-Ins	_____	=	[D]
E. Total unrounded Math raw score (C + D)			[E]
F. Total rounded Math raw score			[F]

Writing Skills

Section 5	_____ – (.25 × _____) =	[ ]
Total rounded Writing Skills raw score		[ ]

SCORE CONVERSION TABLE

Math Raw Score	Math Scaled Score	Critical Reading Raw Score	Critical Reading Scaled Score	Writing Skills Raw Score	Writing Skills Scaled Score
0	26	0	25	0	29
1	29	1	27	1	30
2	30	2	29	2	31
3	32	3	30	3	32
4	34	4	32	4	33
5	35	5	33	5	35
6	36	6	34	6	36
7	38	7	36	7	37
8	39	8	37	8	39
9	40	9	38	9	40
10	41	10	39	10	41
11	42	11	40	11	43
12	43	12	41	12	44
13	44	13	42	13	45
14	45	14	43	14	46
15	46	15	44	15	48
16	47	16	45	16	49
17	48	17	46	17	50
18	50	18	47	18	51
19	51	19	48	19	52
20	52	20	49	20	54
21	53	21	50	21	55
22	54	22	51	22	56
23	55	23	52	23	57
24	57	24	53	24	59
25	58	25	54	25	60
26	59	26	54	26	62
27	60	27	55	27	63
28	61	28	56	28	65
29	62	29	57	29	66
30	64	30	58	30	68
31	65	31	59	31	69
32	66	32	60	32	71
33	68	33	61	33	73
34	70	34	62	34	74
35	72	35	62	35	76
36	74	36	63	36	77
37	77	37	64	37	78
38	80	38	66	38	80
		39	67	39	80
		40	68		
		41	69		
		42	71		
		43	72		
		44	74		
		45	76		
		46	78		
		47	80		
		48	80		

Chapter 13
Practice Test 1:
Answers and
Explanations

Section 1

1. **C** It's probably easier to start with the second blank on this question. The clue *protect the earth* indicates that we can fill in the blank with something like *change*. That eliminates answer choices (A), (B), and (E). The trigger *though* tells us that the first part of the sentence goes in a different direction than the second (which tells us that people are not willing to change), so we can write down something like *promote*. That eliminates answer choice (D), so only (C) is left.

2. **C** All we know about Prince Klemens von Metternich is that he *dominated* the Congress of Vienna, so he probably had a *dominating* personality. Only answer choice (C) comes close.

3. **E** The first blank has the clues *enlivened* and *by the strong rays of the sun,* so *lively* would be a good word to write down. (B), (C), and (D), therefore, can go. The second blank is talking about the canopy, which typically covers the forest floor; if the forest floor now has sun shining on it, the canopy must have been *broken through.* (E) is much closer than (A).

4. **D** If the iguana is *reclusive,* then fruitful investigations are probably hard to get. So *rarity* would be a good word to fill in the blank. Answer choice (D) is closest.

5. **B** The governor wanted *more housing,* but she ended up making housing *even more scarce.* That means she *worsened* the problem. The only answer choice that means *worsened* is (B).

6. **B** The clues *friendly and honest manner* tell us we can replace the first blank with *friendly and honest,* so we can eliminate (C), (D), and (E). We have a trigger, *but,* which tells us the second part of the sentence goes in the opposite direction, so we can write down *not friendly and honest* for the second blank. The closest answer is (B).

7. **A** Because we don't have clues for each blank here, we should go by the relationship between the blanks. The blanks here have a relationship of similarity; either the musicians loved it and wanted to promote it, or they hated it and wanted to get rid of it. So we would write down *same.* (A) has a relationship of similarity, so we can keep it. (B), (D), and (E) are going in opposite directions, and (C) has no relationship, so we can eliminate those.

8. **C** The first blank can be replaced with something like *rebellion,* based on the clue *rebellion* in the sentence. That eliminates (B) and (D). We can see now in the answer choices that the first words in each pair are actually people, but that doesn't matter—following the technique, we're still right on track. The triggers *even though* and *now* tell us that the second blank is going to have a negative word in it; the United States now views rebels as *bad.* That eliminates (A), which has a positive word, and (E), which has a neutral word, leaving only (C).

9. **D** Answer choice (D) is correct because the passage states that the *centuries-old rules* are *not so different* from Oulipo techniques. (B) is extreme, (C) can be eliminated as the group has been meeting only since 1960, and neither (A) nor (E) is supported by evidence from the passage.

10. **A** Answer choice (A) is correct because *churn out* indicates quantity instead of quality. (B) is incorrect because the phrase is not a reference to Oulipo. There is no evidence for (C) or (D) in the passage, and (E) is extreme—ETS isn't going to include a passage by an author who is "disgusted."

11. **A** Answer choice (E) is too ambitious, as no historical event is really explained in the passage. Cultural significance is not mentioned, so we can eliminate answer choice (D). There is no explanation to support (B), and President Johnson's character is not attacked, as (C) says. As for (A), there is in fact a possible controversy downplayed: The contention that President Johnson manufactured the Gulf of Tonkin crisis is waved away in the last sentence. So (A) is a good fit.

12. **B** The argument would be strengthened by a report explaining the discrepancy between the two destroyers. Which answer choice says this? (C) and (E) are not relevant to the scope of the passage. (A) and (D) don't resolve the discrepancies between the two destroyers, so they actually weaken the argument. But (B) makes the argument stronger by explaining how it could be that the U.S.S. *Maddox* did not pick up the other ships on its radar. Be careful when dealing with weaken/strengthen questions, as the opposite answer to what you're looking for will generally be in the answer choices.

13. **B** This is a primary purpose question, so we want an answer choice that describes what the author was trying to accomplish in Passage 1. (C) is clearly outside the scope of the passage. (D) confuses cattle with pigs and dogs as to which species are scavengers. (A) and (E) are too narrow. (B) is a nice summary of the argument at the end of the passage, so it's the best choice.

14. **D** Here we have a line reference question, so go back to the quote and read above and below it. The quote refers to the interactive nature of the domestication of species such as pigs and dogs. Thus, (B), (C), and (E) are not correct. (A) refers to the same general notion, but it is too narrow, leaving us with answer choice (D).

15. **B** This is a Vocab-in-Context question. We want to come up with our own word based on the context of the passage. We might come up with something like *unplanned*. (A), (C), (D), and (E) are all distracters based on the language of the passage. (B) is the closest thing to our word.

16. **C** Another line reference question, so go back to the passage and read about 5 lines above and 5 lines below. The myth is described as the life and death of the moon goddess. (A) misses the focus, so it's out. (B) is out of context. Gazelles are mentioned later, as an afterthought, so (D) is incorrect. (E) is a distracter that garbles the words of the paragraph. (C) is the best option.

17. **A** The passage indicates that the animals were susceptible to domestication, and the human culture was evolved enough to control the animal. The correct answer needs to reflect both elements. (D) and (E) focus on one side or the other. (B) is out of context. (C) is not even in the ballpark. Knowing the vocabulary helps a lot: We're looking for an answer choice that reflects a *mutually beneficial* relationship. (A), with its mention of "harmony," fits the bill.

18. **D** This is a lead word question. Look for the word *Maglemosian* and you'll find it in line 63. Then read 5 lines up and 5 lines down to find the answer. The author is emphasizing that we don't really know what happened, but domestication clearly differed with respect to both species and human culture. Since the author gives no details, (A) is clearly not the answer. While (B) is probably true, it's not the answer to the question. (C) is out, as the point of mentioning both cultures was to indicate that culture is important. (E) is gone for basically the same reason; culture and species are important. Only (D) says this.

19. **E** This is a Lead Word question. Go find where the passage talks about *Rattus norvegicus* and see what the studies revealed. The passage states that "the tremendous behavioral changes undergone by a species during domestication…cannot yield the total behavior pattern of the wild ancestors." Only (E) reflects that statement. (A) is a distracter based on confusion about what *Rattus norvegicus* is. (B) is a distracter based on the language of the passage, but the passage doesn't say that psychological insights were learned. (C) and (D) are the direct opposites of the implication of the paragraph.

20. **D** Another Lead Word question, so go hunt down where the passage talks about Lorenz's imprinting experiments. Looks like the fourth paragraph tells us that imprinting helped domesticate birds. (A), (B), (C), and (E) are all true, but none answer the question. The question is, "What is the author saying about the role of imprinting in domestication?" (D) answers that question.

21. **B** Here we need to pick an answer that is consistent with the views of both authors. (A) has extreme language: *the single most important factor*, so cross it out. Imprinting applies mainly to birds and not to mammals, so (C) is incorrect. (D) is wrong because capturing animals for ceremonies is a possible stage, not a critical stage. (E) presents what we perhaps would like to think, but it is neither stated nor implied in the passage.

22. **A** The difference in the two passages is really one of emphasis, based in part on the species discussed. The two are closest in terms of dogs and pigs, but neither rules out what the other describes about the domestication of various species. (B) is incorrect since Passage 1 deals mainly with the religious significance of cattle, not other species. (C) is incorrect since Passage 1 treats dogs and pigs in passing; cattle are the focus of Passage 1. (D) is too narrow a construction of both passages. (E) is incorrect because Passage 1 doesn't deal with studying lab rats and birds. (A) is our best choice.

23. **E** Here we need an answer choice that shows a difference between the authors' views or something that states an idea they both reject. (A), (B), (C), and (D) combine ideas from each passage that the authors would agree on. (E) garbles the hypotheses: Lab rats weren't used as hunting decoys!

24. **C** The "social enzyme" has to do with the "proclivity…to keep pets." Neither passage notes the roles of cattle as "pets," so (A), (B), and (D) are incorrect. The scavenger behavior has to do with dogs and pigs seeking out man, not man keeping them as pets, so (E) is incorrect.

Section 2

1. **D** To solve for b, our first move should be to move the 4 to the other side of the equation by adding 4 to both sides. This will give us $12b = 4$. Now we divide each side by 12, and get $b = \dfrac{1}{3}$.

2. **D** Before doing any math on this problem, we should ballpark and eliminate answers we know are wrong. The question tells us that 60 gallons represents $\dfrac{5}{12}$ of the full tank—or a little less than half. So the full tank will need to be a little more than twice 60 gallons, or something a little larger than 120. This makes choices (A), (B), and (E) unreasonable, so let's eliminate those choices. The answer has to be either (C) or (D). To figure out which, let's try plugging in the answer choices. Is $\dfrac{5}{12}$ of 128 equal to 60? Nope, that's equal to 10.67. So let's try choice (D). Is $\dfrac{5}{12}$ of 144 equal to 60? Yes, so (D) is the answer.

3. **D** To make this problem easier, let's plug in some numbers for the sides of this rectangle. We can pick whichever numbers we want, as long as they make the area equal to 16. So let's assume that the rectangle has dimensions 8 and 2. This makes the base of the triangle 8 and the height 2, so the area of the triangle will be $\dfrac{1}{2} \times 8 \times 2$ or 8. (Even if we made the dimensions of the rectangle 16 and 1, we'd still get the same answer!) You may also know the rule that a triangle inscribed in a rectangle will have exactly half the area of that rectangle; but even without knowing the rule, by plugging in some values we can figure it out.

4. **C** The first multiple of 32 is 32, so the correct choice must divide evenly into 32. In other words, 32 must be a multiple of the correct choice. Is 32 a multiple of 11? No; nor is it a multiple of 9, 5, or 3. So we can eliminate (A), (B), (D), and (E).

5. **B** This looks like a good opportunity to Plug In the Answers. If we plug in (C), 32, we find that angle A is 32, angle B is 94, and angle C is 90—which adds to way more than 180, the number of degrees in any triangle. This eliminates (C), (D), and (E). When we try (B), 23, we get a triangle whose angles measure 23, 67, and 90. Perfect!

6. **C** Since we've got variables in the answer choices, we should plug in. We can plug in whatever consecutive numbers we want for x, y, and z, provided that we obey the rule that $x < y < z$. Let's choose 2 for x, 3 for y, and 4 for z, since those are easy numbers. The question then asks: What is the sum of y and z? Using our numbers, the answer will be $3 + 4$, which makes 7. Now the question is: Which of the answer choices gives 7, using our value of 2 for x? Answer choice (C) gives $2(2) + 3$, which equals 7.

7. **E** This question looks nasty, but if we remember our MADSPM rules, it won't be too bad. Whenever we raise an exponent to another exponent, it is the same as multiplying the exponents together. So $(2^a)^b$ is the same thing as $2^{a \times b}$. Using a calculator we can figure out that $64 = 2^6$, so $a \times b$ must be equal to 6.

8. **B** Let's remember our rules for adding and subtracting roots: We can only add or subtract if the number under the radical sign is the same. So first, we have to simplify the expressions. $6\sqrt{18}$ can be rewritten as $6\sqrt{9 \times 2}$. Since we have a perfect square under the radical sign, we can square root it and pull it out, giving us $6 \times 3\sqrt{2}$, or $18\sqrt{2}$.

    $4\sqrt{72}$ equals $4\sqrt{36 \times 2}$, which becomes $4 \times 6\sqrt{2}$ or $24\sqrt{2}$.

    $\sqrt{8}$ equals $\sqrt{4 \times 2}$, which equals $2\sqrt{2}$.

    $10\sqrt{32}$ equals $10\sqrt{16 \times 2}$, which equals $10 \times 4\sqrt{2}$, which becomes $40\sqrt{2}$.

    So finally we have $18\sqrt{2} + 24\sqrt{2} - (2\sqrt{2} + 40\sqrt{2})$. Now all of our roots have been simplified to something $\sqrt{2}$, so we can add and subtract normally. Starting inside the parentheses, $2\sqrt{2} + 40\sqrt{2} = 42\sqrt{2}$. $18\sqrt{2} + 24\sqrt{2} - 42\sqrt{2} = 0$. Of course, you can also just do this problem on your calculator.

9. **D** A line with negative slope is one that you can draw going down and to the right from any starting point. Lines $\overline{AE}$ and $\overline{BD}$ won't count, since they have no slope. The only ones we can draw are $\overline{AC}$, $\overline{FD}$, and $\overline{AD}$.

    Don't be thrown off by the coordinates given for points A and B—they're just there to assure you that segments AB and DE actually are parallel to the x-axis.

10. **C** You can Plug In the Answers here, but in this case translation is a little bit easier: Once we have $x = 3 + 7x$, we can subtract $7x$ from both sides to leave us with $-6x = 3$. Divide both sides by -6 and we find that x is equal to 3 divided by -6, which equates to choice (C).

11. **A** Like many problems on the PSAT, this question will be difficult if we try to do it all at once. Instead, let's break it down into bite-sized pieces. Let's start with just part of the inequality, $-12 \le 3b + 3$. Remember that we can solve inequalities just like equations—provided that if we multiply or divide by a negative value, we swap the direction of the inequality sign. To solve this part of the inequality, though, we just need to subtract 3 from each side (giving us $-15 \le 3b$) and then divide each side by 3, which leaves us with $-5 \le b$. Now we can eliminate several choices that we know won't work: (B), (D), and (E) don't have -5 in them. Now let's take the other part of the inequality: $-3b + 3 \le 18$. If we subtract 3 from each side and then divide by 3, we get $b \le 5$. Now we can cross off (C), and we're left with (A).

12. **E** Let's start by plugging in a number for x. We need an odd integer divisible by 3, so let's pick $x = 9$. The question asks us which of the following must be divisible by 4. (A) says $x + 1$, or 10, which is not divisible by 4. (B) says $x + 2$, or 11, which is also not divisible by 4. This allows us to eliminate

(A) and (B). (C) says $x + 3$, or 12, which is divisible by 4, so we should leave (C) in. (D) says 18, which is not divisible by 4, so we can eliminate this choice too. (E) says 16, which can be divided by 4, so we should leave it in. Now we're down to (C) and (E). Let's pick another number for x and keep working. How about $x = 15$? In this case, (C) gives us 18, which is not divisible by 4. This knocks off (C), so the answer must be (E).

13. **C** To find the perimeter, we need to find the lengths of each of the sides of this triangle. Side AB is fairly easy, since we can just count the points: from $(0, 4)$ to $(6, 4)$ is a length of 6. However, finding sides $\overline{AC}$ and $\overline{BC}$ is a little more difficult. The problem tells us that $\overline{AC} \cong \overline{BC}$, so we know that point C must be on the x-axis right in between points A and B—which places it at coordinate $(3, 0)$.

Now to find the length of $\overline{AC}$, we can look at the triangle formed by A, C, and the origin. This triangle has a base of 3, since point C is at $(3, 0)$, and a height of 4, since point A is at $(0, 4)$. This makes a right triangle with sides 3 and 4, so side $\overline{AC}$ must be equal to 5. We can do the same thing to solve for side $\overline{BC}$. So we know that the sides of this triangle are 6, 5, and 5 for a total perimeter of 16.

14. **D** Let's plug 5 and 7 in for n to find the 5th and 7th terms. The 5th term is $2 + 3^5 = 2 + 243 = 245$. The 7th term is $2 + 3^7 = 2 + 2{,}187 = 2{,}189$. The sum of the 5th and 7th terms is $245 + 2{,}189 = 2{,}434$.

15. **D** Since we have variables in the answer choices, we should plug in on this problem. To make the math work easily, let's pick 5 for c, 10 for g, and 20 for n. If 1 bottle containing 5 ounces will fill 10 glasses, then how many bottles will be needed to fill 20 glasses? Two bottles. So now 2 is our target answer. Using 5 for c, 10 for g, and 20 for n, (A) equals 40, which is too large. (B) gives 10, which is also too large. (C) gives .5, which is too small. (D) gives 2, which is our target, but let's remember to do POE completely and check the remaining answer choice. (E) gives .25, which is too small.

16. **C** First, let's figure out sets C and D. Set C is the intersection of sets A and B, so its elements are the elements that are in both sets: 0, 1, and 2. Set D is the union of A and B, so we figure out its elements by taking all the distinct elements from each set: -1, 0, 1, 2, and 3. So $C = \{0, 1, 2\}$ and $D = \{-1, 0, 1, 2, 3\}$. Now we can work through the answer choices and eliminate any that don't fit the description of an "interior" set. In answer choice (A), if we multiply -1 by 2, we would get a product of -2. -2 is not in set A, so we can eliminate (A). In (B), we can multiply 2 and 3 for a product of 6, which isn't in set B, so (B) can be eliminated too. (D) also has a 2 and 3 but no 6, so we can eliminate it. In (E), the union of A and C is $\{-1, 0, 1, 2\}$. Since -1 and 2 give a product of -2 and there is no -2 in the set, (E) is also not correct.

17. **E** This question is testing volume. The volume of the original block of cheese is $8 \times 8 \times 8$, or 512. The piece that we cut out measures $4 \times 2 \times 2$, so its volume is 16. If we take away 16 from 512, so we get 496. The fractional part that remains will be $\dfrac{496}{512}$, or $\dfrac{31}{32}$.

18. **B** This figure is not drawn to scale, so we won't be able to trust our eyes on this one. We can, however, still plug in, since we have variables in the answer choices. Let's plug in 30 for a and see what happens. If we make $a = 30$, then we will have values for four of our angles: angle a (30), angle $2a$ (60), angle $3a$ (90), and the other angle that measures $2a$ (60). This makes a total of 240 degrees out of 360. This means that the other angles, b and b, must add up to 120. So b must be equal to 60. The question asks us for the measure of b, so 60 is our answer. Now we just see which choice (remembering that $a = 30$) gives 60. This shows us that (B) is the answer.

19. **B** If we're averaging two numbers x and y, then this average will always be half of the sum of these numbers. Let's try some values for x and y and see what kind of numbers we get. Since $y = 4x$, if $x = 5$ then $y = 20$, and their sum is 25. If $x = 6$ then $y = 24$, and their sum is 30. If $x = 7$ then $y = 28$, and their sum is 35. It looks like the sum of x and y will always be a multiple of 5. Now let's look at the choices we have, starting with (C). If the average of x and y is 4, then their sum will be 8. But we know that the sum of x and y will always be a multiple of 5, so (C) can't be right. Likewise for answer choices (D) and (E): If the average is 12, the sum of x and y will be 24; if their average is 28, their sum would have to be 56. So neither of these could be right. The only answer choice that would give us a sum of x and y as a multiple of 5 is choice (B).

20. **B** To solve direct proportion questions, just set up a proportion. In this case, $\dfrac{y_1}{\left(x_1\right)^2} = \dfrac{y_2}{\left(x_2\right)^2}$ becomes $\dfrac{18}{\left(3\right)^2} = \dfrac{2}{\left(x_2\right)^2}$. Cross-multiplying and solving gives you $x2 = 1$.

Section 3

25. **D** The sentence mentions *small population* and *shyness,* which are both factors that would *hurt* studies, so *hurt* is a good word to fill in the blank. Only (D) comes close to the same definition.

26. **C** *All segments of society* provides a good clue to tell us that something like *increased* or *made popular* would be a good replacement for the blank, making (C) the best answer choice.

27. **A** It looks like we can start with the first blank easily enough: What happens to old technology when new technology comes along? It gets *replaced*, which allows us to eliminate (B), (C), and (D). A trigger helps us nail down the second blank: *While many* consumer electronics are replaced, apparently the home computer is an exception, and it will be many years before it becomes...*useless*, maybe? That allows us to eliminate (E). (A) still works, so pick (A).

28. **A** Let's work on the first blank. We have the clue *refused to give up* and the trigger word *although* which means that a good word for the first blank would be something like *insurmountable*. That eliminates (C), (D), and (E). For the second blank, we know that we're looking for something positive, perhaps *good* or *clever*. That eliminates (B), so (A) is correct.

29. **D** Wow, if 2,500 out of 3,200 residents made their way through a blizzard to vote, they must have been pretty *determined*. (D) has the closest definition.

30. **C** Answer choice (C) is correct; both passages mention the importance of facts or relevant information. (A) and (B) are incorrect; only Passage 1 supports those answers. (D) is extreme. (E) is wrong because only the author of Passage 2 would agree with the answer.

31. **A** Answer choice (A) is correct; Passage 1 mentions *new historicist*, revisionism. (B) is wrong because both passages mention historical events. (C) is incorrect because both passages are focused on U.S. history, and both mention one of the world wars. (D) is wrong because both passages are partisan—one toward conservative historical analysis, one toward revisionist history. (E) is never mentioned.

32. **C** Answer choice (C) is correct; Passage 1 claims that *facts are facts*, while Passage 2 admits the possibility of bias. (A) is wrong because both passages mention military history. (B) is wrong because both deal with U.S. history. (D) is wrong because Passage 2 deals with bias, not limited interpretation. (E) is wrong because both passages believe that their approach to history is the most accurate one.

33. **E** Answer choice (E) is correct; the second passage is concerned that historians overlook the contributions of minority groups. (A) is too narrow. (B) and (D) are extreme. (C) is extreme and offensive.

34. **E** The author's main purpose in writing the passage, as can be seen in the last paragraph, is to show how his experiences with the choir affected his approach to other areas of his life. While (C) and (D) occur in the passage, neither adequately summarizes the entire passage. In (B), *worship* is too strong. (A) is never mentioned in the passage. Therefore, (E) is the best answer.

35. **A** Here's a line reference question, so let's go back to the passage and read enough to get the context. In describing "Madame Jeanette," the author uses terms such as *cloying sentimentality*, and states that, when performed by teenagers under the guidance of *sloppy conducting*, it becomes *maudlin* and an *embarrassing tearfest*. (B) and (D) are never mentioned in the passage. (C) is incorrect because the piece becomes compelling and poignant only under the guidance of a director of Wilhousky's caliber. While (E) might look tempting, the reader is never told that the piece is technically difficult for most choirs, and we are never told that this is a reason for it to be considered "dangerous." Therefore, (A) is the best answer.

36. **C** In lines 32–33, the author states that performing the piece was a *wonderful solace* for an insecure boy of his age, and later in the paragraph he refers to its ability to fill him with a sense of *hope and possibility*. This makes (C) the best answer.

37. **B** Here's a Vocab-in-Context question, so let's come up with our own word. The author states in line 42 that he *still marvels* at the level of obedience Wilhousky was able to command, which implies that children at that time were quite obedient to begin with. So perhaps *more common* will work. While (A), (C), (D), and (E) could be considered plausible definitions of the word *ready*, only (B) is close to our word. Thus, it is the best answer.

38. **A** This question asks us why the author included a particular detail. The author introduces the anecdote of the boy in the third row immediately after discussing how Wilhousky instilled discipline "through intimidation by public ridicule," and the boy's story serves as an example of this. (B) is incorrect because the author himself confesses that he is uncertain about what was really said, so we can't be sure that Wilhousky was really lying. This also eliminates (E), since we can't be sure that he's really trying to *trick* his students. (D) is incorrect because while the author does mention the human memory, this is not the purpose of the anecdote. While the author suggests that Wilhousky was a disciplinarian, it's hard to find evidence in the passage that the author would go so far as to call him *cruel*, which eliminates (C). Therefore, (A) is the best answer.

39. **A** In the last paragraph, the author states that, as a result of working with Wilhousky, the author "slowly personalized the dream that excellence in one activity might be extended to become the pattern, or at least the goal, of an actual life." (B), (C), (D), and (E) are never mentioned. Therefore, (A) is the best answer.

40. **A** We're being asked to infer something here, so we need something that stays close to the passage, even if it's not literally mentioned. The passage states that China and India both "embarked on daring reform programs in order to modernize their economies," making (A) a solid inference. (B) describes the situation at the end of the twentieth century, not before World War II. There is nothing in the passage to support (C) or (D). (E) is what the author says India must do now to gain economic success.

41. **C** The author argues that "China was successful because its political system was conducive to the high levels of centralized control"; (C) would most hurt this claim. (A) would support the argument that China was economically patient. (B) and (E) are both irrelevant to the author's arguments about politics and economics. India's SOEs were ineffective, but the fact that China also had them would not hurt the author's argument about why China was more successful, making (D) incorrect.

42. **C** The author states that the fact that India had a parliamentary democracy made all the difference in terms of the effects of its reforms and then goes on to discuss how Indian leaders were hampered by their fear of *rocking the boat* and losing the ability to get elected, making (C) the best answer. (A) and (D) both take a far more positive stance toward parliamentary democracies than the author does. (B) is too extreme. (E) is not supported by the passage; parliamentary democracies and economic patience are not discussed in conjunction with each other.

43. **A** This is a weird question with an EXCEPT for us to deal with. We need to find which answer choices have support and which don't. The odd one out will be our answer. India wanted to decrease the country's dependence on *formerly imported goods*, not to discourage foreign manufacturing in and of itself. Thus, (A) is the only answer not supported by the passage. (B), (C), (D) and (E) can all be found in the fourth paragraph.

44. **D** Vocab-in-Context. From the context, it is clear that "repercussions" are negative effects; the author contrasts India's leaders, who would have to get reelected, to those in China, making (D) the credited answer. (A) and (B) attempt to trick the readers with words that remind one of the original word. The sentence does not go into how much work would be involved, making (C) incorrect. The sentence does not suggest that India would need to change laws to quash rebellion, making (E) incorrect.

45. **B** The final paragraph serves to reiterate India's difficulties in modernizing and point to a future path, making (B) the correct answer. The author offers answers about what happened to India, so (A) and (D) are not correct. The final paragraph follows the tone and direction of the rest of the passage, making (C) incorrect. (E) is not a possible answer; there is nothing lighthearted about the passage.

46. **E** This is a weird, hypothetical question. We need the answer most consistent with the author's argument. The author asserts that India would have needed both development in stages and the capability to enforce changes fully, making (E) the credited answer. (A) and (D) are drawing too strong a conclusion since they deal with only half of the equation. There is nothing in the passage to support (B). (C) is not correct; it is what the author insists India must do now to foster success.

47. **D** The passage states that India "must reevaluate its priorities and set truly national goals," as in (D). (A) is not correct; the passage argues for changes within India's democratic system. SOEs were one of the reasons India did not succeed, so (B) is incorrect. While the passage argues that India's leaders are ineffective because they will not rock the boat, voting them out, as in (C), is not suggested as a solution. (E) is not correct: The fact that no one is willing to cut jobs is simply offered as one of the current problems with India's system.

48. **B** This is a tone question, so we need to focus on how the author talked about China. Throughout the passage, the author emphasizes China's strengths, making (B) the credited answer. (A) is too extreme. (C) and (D) both suggest a negative attitude toward China not found in the passage. (E) indicates that the author's admiration for China is because of the need to keep a good relations with the country; the passage does not support this reading.

Section 4

21. **D** We can add the like terms to find $14z = -42$. Divide by 14 to find $z = -3$.

22. **E** This question is asking us to compare pecks and bushels, so let's make a proportion: $\dfrac{10 \text{ pecks}}{2.5 \text{ bushels}} = \dfrac{x \text{ pecks}}{4 \text{ bushels}}$. Then we can cross-multiply and solve for x, which results in $x = 16$.

23. **A** The slope-intercept form of the equation of a line is $y = mx + b$, where m is the slope, and b is the y-intercept. So we would manipulate this equation to solve for y. Subtracting $2x$ from both sides of the equation and then dividing both sides by 3 gives us $y = -\dfrac{2}{3}x + 4$, so the y-intercept is 4.

24. **B** We've got variables in the answer choices, so let's plug in. Try $a = 3$ and $x = 2$. The expression turns into $\dfrac{3}{4} + \dfrac{7}{2}$, which equals $\dfrac{17}{4}$, our target number. Now we can replace a with 3 and x with 2 in the answers to see which hits our target. Only (B) does.

25. **B** The slope-intercept form of the equation of a line is $y = mx + b$, where m is the slope and b is the y-intercept. So the slope of the line given by the first equation is 6. To find the slope of a perpendicular line, we would take the negative reciprocal. So $c = -\dfrac{1}{6}$.

26. **A** Positive difference just means the absolute value of the difference. So for $|{-1} - 2.5|$, the difference is 3.5. Plug in the answer choices to find the one with the difference of 3.5:

$$|(-5) - (-8.5)| = 3.5$$

27. **E** Negative exponents mean to take the reciprocal of the positive exponent. For example, $y^{-2} = \dfrac{1}{y^2}$, and $2^{-3} = \dfrac{1}{2^3}$. For fractional exponents, the denominator tells us what root of the number to take and the numerator acts as a normal exponent. So, $f(x)$ is $\dfrac{1}{\sqrt[3]{x^2}}$. First, let's find $f(8)$: $\dfrac{1}{\sqrt[3]{8^2}} = \dfrac{1}{\sqrt[3]{64}} = \dfrac{1}{4}$. Next, let's find $f(3)$: $\dfrac{1}{\sqrt[3]{3^2}} = \dfrac{1}{\sqrt[3]{9}}$. Put these values in for $\dfrac{f(8)}{f(3)}$. So, $\dfrac{\frac{1}{4}}{\frac{1}{\sqrt[3]{9}}} = \dfrac{1}{4} \div \dfrac{1}{\sqrt[3]{9}} = \dfrac{1}{4} \times \sqrt[3]{9} = \dfrac{\sqrt[3]{9}}{4}$. Remember to look at the answer choices so you don't keep trying to simplify when there's no need to.

28. **D** The first student has 6 choices of where to sit. For each place the first student sits, the second student has 2 choices of where to sit—only on either side of the first student. (So, if the first student sits in seat b, the second student can sit in seat a or seat c.) Thus, the total number of possible arrangements is $6 \times 2 = 12$.

29. **7** The vertical bars around a number mean absolute value, which tells us to find the distance on the number line between that number and zero. To find the absolute value of a negative number, simply remove the negative sign. The absolute value of $|{-10}|$ is 10, and the absolute value of $|3|$ is 3. So, $10 - 3 = 7$.

30. **.36** Let's start with the first part of the question. Twenty percent of n is 36. If we translate this into math, it becomes $\dfrac{20}{100} n = 36$. Now we can solve for n by reducing $\dfrac{20}{100}$ to $\dfrac{1}{5}$ and by multiplying each side by 5. $\dfrac{1}{5} n = 36$, so $n = 36 \times 5$. This gives us $n = 180$. Now we translate the other part and plug in 180 for n. What is .2 percent of 180 becomes: $x = \dfrac{.2}{100} \times 180$. Now we solve for x, and get $x = .36$.

31. **80** When we draw it, we see that triangle *RST* is isosceles, with angle *R* equal to angle *T*. Since there are 180 degrees in a triangle, and we are told that angle *S* is 20 degrees, angles *R* and *T* must add up to 160 degrees. Since *R* has the same measure as *T*, each is 80 degrees.

32. **14** While we don't know the exact lengths of the bottom or right side of the figure, we don't need to know them. We know that the edges unknown horizontal edges must have a total length of 3, and the unknown vertical edges must have a total length of 4.

Therefore, we know that the total perimeter of the object is 4 + 3 + 4 + 3 = 14. You can also simply make up values for the missing side lengths, so long as the horizontal ones add up to 3 and the vertical ones add up to 4.

33. **20** Since the problem tells us the value of *x*, which is 23, we can put this into the equation and solve for *y*. 23 − 8 = 5*y*, so we know that 15 = 5*y* and 3 = *y*.

Now we know the value of *y*. However, on this problem, let's not forget that we're not just solving for *y*; we're solving for *x* − *y*. So the correct answer is 23 − 3, or 20.

34. **8,000** Let's start by finding all of the positive integer factors of 20. We can factor 20 into 1 × 20, 2 × 10, and 4 × 5. The question asks for the product of these numbers, which will be 1 × 20 × 2 × 10 × 4 × 5, or 8,000.

35. **45** If Marcia types 18 pages per hour, and David can type 14 pages per hour, then together they will be able to type 18 + 14, or 32 pages per hour. To see what fraction of an hour it will take them to type 24 pages, we can set up a proportion:

$$\frac{32\ pages}{1\ hour} = \frac{24\ pages}{x\ hours}$$

If we solve for *x*, we can see that they can type 24 pages in .75 of an hour. But that isn't our answer! The question asks for the answer in minutes. Three-quarters of an hour is equal to 45 minutes, so the answer is 45.

36.   40   When it's difficult to tell where to start on a geometry question, it's best to just start filling in what you know. Since we know that the angles in a triangle always add up to 180, we can figure out the third angle of the triangle with angles 45 and 60. The sum of these angles is 105, so the third angle must measure 75. This means that the angle next to it on the line must also measure 105. Now in the triangle on the left, we have angles 105 and 35. Together these angles make 140, so we know that the third angle (marked with an x) is equal to 40.

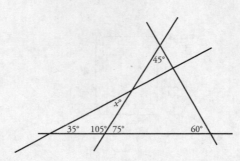

37.   3   Since the problem tells us that $f(a) = 10$, and that $f(x) = x^2 - x + 4$, we can say plug a into the function for x so $f(a) = a^2 - a + 4$, and $10 = a^2 - a + 4$. Now we need to factor to solve for a. If we subtract 10 from both sides of the equation, we get $a^2 - a - 6 = 0$ which we can factor as $(a - 3)(a + 2) = 0$. The value of a could be 3 or −2, but since the question tells us that a is non-negative, the value of x must be 3.

38. $\dfrac{5}{9}$ or .555 or .556

When the problem asks for relationships between numbers (read: fractions, percents, ratios, probabilities) but doesn't give any actual numbers, it's time for us to plug in! Let's start with the large blue and large red marbles and work our way out: Say there are 2 large red marbles and 10 large blue marbles. That means there are 12 large marbles, so there must be 6 small marbles, giving us a total of 18 marbles. Therefore, the probability of picking a large blue marble out of the whole box is $\dfrac{10}{18}$ which won't fit in the grid, so we can reduce it to $\dfrac{5}{9}$ or divide it out to get .555 or .556.

Section 5

1.   B   *They* is an ambiguous pronoun—does it refer to the French, the friends, or the parents (yuck)? (B) is the only answer that fixes the pronoun problem without changing the meaning of the sentence.

2. **A** The sentence is correct as written. It's a little awkward, but none of the answers improves the sentence.

3. **E** Neil couldn't possibly have done all of those things at the same time. (C), (D), and (E) fix that problem, but only (E) fixes it in a way that doesn't introduce parallelism errors.

4. **C** *Critically* is an adverb, but the sentence needs an adjective to modify *circling* and *underlining*. (Yes, they look like verbs, but they are the subjects of the second part of the sentence, so we treat them like nouns.) (A) and (B) are gone, then, and (E) adds way too many redundant words, so we can eliminate it, too. The first difference between (C) and (D) is *one* versus *you*. *One* stays in the same voice as the other subjects in the sentence, and *you* does not. (D) also has some extra words on the end, so it's out anyway, and (C) is correct.

5. **D** The sentence has a misplaced modifier; Samuel Spade is not a movie. (And you don't have to be a film buff to know that—even the sentence says that Samuel Spade is a detective and the movie is *The Maltese Falcon*.) So (A) can be eliminated, and so can (E), which doesn't fix the misplaced modifier. (B) mentions that *The Maltese Falcon* is a movie twice, so it's redundant, and also the phrase "Samuel Spade, detective" is awkward. (C), like (B), is missing a comma after *The Maltese Falcon*. (D) fixes the misplaced modifier problem without adding new errors, so it is the best answer.

6. **A** The sentence is correct as written.

7. **B** The sentence has a redundant conjunction; *yet* is unnecessary because there is already an *although* at the beginning. So we can eliminate (A), as well as (D) and (E), which don't solve the problem. (B) and (C) say the same thing, but (B) is short and sweet while (C) is awkward and wordy, so (B) is correct.

8. **E** The pronoun *they* in the underlined portion is ambiguous—we don't know whether it refers to the chairpersons or the committees—so (A) is gone. (B) unnecessarily introduces *thereby*, and both (B) and (D) change the verb form, so we can eliminate them. (C) replaces *their* with *her*, which does not agree with the subject, *chairpersons*. Only (E) fixes the error without creating new ones.

9. **C** The verbs in the underlined portion are not parallel, so (A) can be eliminated. (B) and (D) don't fix the parallelism problem. (E) changes the meaning slightly, so (C) is our best answer.

10. **A** The sentence is correct as written.

11. **D** The word *actor* is singular, so *their character* is wrong; *his or her character* is correct. Eliminate (A) and (C). For the same reason, *as they wish* is wrong, so eliminate (B), and *as he or she wish* has an agreement error that you can spot without even referring back to the rest of the sentence, so eliminate (E). That leaves (D).

12. **C** *They* is an ambiguous pronoun; we don't know whether it refers to *Omar and his family* or *neighbors*. (B) repeats the problem. (D) fixes the ambiguity but is redundant, and (E) adds awkwardness by adding *being* unnecessarily.

13.	E	This one is easier than it might look. Who was known for graduating from college despite being blind and deaf? Helen Keller was: not *the fact*, not *accounts*, not *many people*, and not *six decades*. Eliminate (A), (B), (C), and (D). Only (E) fixes the error, so you can stop there.

14.	B	Miles can be counted, so the comparison word *less* is incorrect; therefore, we can eliminate (A), (D), and (E). The *to be putting* in (C) is awkward, which typically happens when an *–ing* verb is added, so (B) is the best answer.

15.	E	The verb *has enlisted* is in present perfect tense, but the action happened in the past and does not continue to the present. Only (E) has the correct verb tense.

16.	E	(A) and (C) both have the verb *were*, which doesn't agree with the subject, *art*. (B) is passive, and (D) has the progressive tense *were practicing*, which changes the meaning. (E) is in active voice with no grammatical errors.

17.	D	There is a clear split between the answer choices, so we can use that to determine the first thing being tested. (A) and (B) have *regarded to be*, and (C), (D), and (E) have *regarded as*. Which idiom is correct? *Regarded as* is correct, so we can eliminate (A) and (B). Now let's look for differences in the remaining answer choices. (C) has the plural verb *are*, while (D) and (E) have the singular verb *is*. Since the subject *the bristlecone pine*, *is* is correct we can eliminate (C). (E) adds an unnecessary *being*, making the answer choice awkward and wordy, so (D) is the best answer.

18.	C	The correct idiom here is *originates in*, not *originates from* or *originates with*. The only choice with the correct form is (C).

19.	A	The sentence is correct as written.

20.	B	The sentence uses a comma to connect two independent clauses. We need a period, a semicolon, or a conjunction here, so we can eliminate (A). (C) joins the clauses with incorrect punctuation, as a colon should introduce an example or examples of what came before it. (D) is incorrect because we don't want a semicolon *and* a conjunction. (E) adds a *however*, which should come only after a semicolon. Only (B) joins the independent clauses correctly, with a semicolon.

21.	C	The verb *serving* is not parallel to *attempted*. *Served* would be correct.

22.	A	*A member* doesn't agree with *twins*. *Members* would be correct.

23.	E	The sentence is correct as written.

24.	D	*Unjust* is an adjective, yet it is modifying the verb *ignored*. The adverb *unjustly* would be correct.

25.	C	The verb *focus* is not parallel to *centering*. *Focusing* would be correct.

26.	B	The verb *spend* is in the wrong tense in the context of the sentence. *Spent*, which is in past tense, would be correct.

27. D *Previous years* is being compared to *last quarter's financial reports,* creating an incorrect comparison. *Previous years' reports* or *those of previous years* would be correct.

28. B The pronoun *you* is being used to replace *one,* which is in a different form. *One* would be correct.

29. C *Insisted on* is an incorrect idiom. *Insisted that* would be correct.

30. A *Were* is paired up with the singular pronoun *each,* but a singular verb is needed. *Was* would be correct.

31. A The possessive pronoun *her* doesn't agree with the subject that it's replacing, *Karen and Mary. Their* would be correct.

32. D *Critic toward* is an incorrect idiom. *Critic of* would be correct.

33. D *That of* is being compared to *contributor,* which is an apples-and-oranges comparison. Leaving out *that of* entirely would be correct.

34. E The sentence is correct as written.

35. E The answer choice that provides the most clarity would be the one that identifies who *them* is. (E) is the only answer choice that does that.

36. B (B) is the answer choice that is most relevant to the passage; all the other answer choices are too far out of scope.

37. C (C) and (D) provide the best transition from sentence 3 with the addition of *for example,* but (D) and (A) have misplaced modifiers—are the children going to be placed on the walls? (E) is passive and (B) is very awkward. Therefore, (C) is the best answer.

38. E Though most of (A) flows well with no errors, it has a missing verb at the end that makes it incorrect. (B) has no transitions between each short, choppy sentence, so there is no logical flow. (C) and (D) change the meaning of the sentence. Only (E) keeps the meaning, has a good flow, and doesn't introduce new errors.

39. B A good replacement for *This is* would agree with (and make clear) what's being referred to. (A), (C), and (D) do not do that. (E) introduces the redundant *as mentioned above,* so (B) is the best answer.

Chapter 14
Practice Test 2

SECTION 1
Time — 25 minutes
24 Questions

Directions: For each question in this section, select the best answer from among the choices given and fill in the corresponding circle on the answer sheet.

Each sentence below has one or two blanks, each blank indicating that something has been omitted. Beneath the sentence are five words or sets of words labeled A through E. Choose the word or set of words that, when inserted in the sentence, best fits the meaning of the sentence as a whole.

Example:

Desiring to ------- his taunting friends, Mitch gave them taffy in hopes it would keep their mouths shut.

(A) eliminate   (B) satisfy   (C) overcome
   (D) ridicule   (E) silence

1. Unlike her award-winning first book, Roberta's new volume can only be considered a ------- effort.

    (A) significant   (B) mediocre   (C) whimsical
       (D) feasible   (E) laudable

2. Most animals respond to ------- with excessive violence; in contrast, some remain ------- when facing serious physical danger.

    (A) kindness . . calm
    (B) peril . . aggressive
    (C) sympathy . . impassive
    (D) neutrality . . belligerent
    (E) threats . . placid

3. Unfortunately, many of Aristotle's works are ------ to us, since they were ------- along with the ancient library at Alexandria.

    (A) unknown . . promoted
    (B) lost . . destroyed
    (C) meaningless . . investigated
    (D) important . . chastised
    (E) clear . . suppressed

4. Engineers attribute the building's ------- during the earthquake, which destroyed more rigid structures, to the surprising ------- of its steel girders.

    (A) obliteration . . strength
    (B) damage . . weakness
    (C) survival . . inadequacy
    (D) endurance . . suppleness
    (E) devastation . . inflexibility

5. Prior to the discovery of one intact ancient burial site in Central America, it had been thought that all of the Mayan tombs had been ------- by thieves.

    (A) levitated   (B) exacerbated   (C) inculpated
       (D) delayed   (E) desecrated

6. Although the first viewers of *Waiting for Godot* jeered and called the play -------, later audiences came to recognize the ------- of the piece, and it soon became one of the classics of world theater.

    (A) abominable . . impenetrability
    (B) complicated . . fickleness
    (C) lenient . . unpleasantness
    (D) melancholy . . exultation
    (E) preposterous . . subtlety

7. In his later works, Langston Hughes's discussions of ethnic issues in America became increasingly -------, as he relied less on veiled criticism and more on direct confrontation.

    (A) concrete   (B) coherent   (C) forthright
       (D) confused   (E) delineated

8. Few would call the company president ------- ; in fact, he would often ------- the ideas of his subordinates, alleging that they were his own.

    (A) xenophobic . . exemplify
    (B) original . . expropriate
    (C) innovative . . inculcate
    (D) duplicitous . . arrogate
    (E) egregious . . steal

GO ON TO THE NEXT PAGE

The passages below are followed by questions based on their content; questions following a pair of related passages may also be based on the relationship between the paired passages. Answer the questions on the basis of what is <u>stated</u> or <u>implied</u> in the passage and in any introductory material that may be provided.

Questions 9-12 are based on the following passages.

Passage 1

Medicine as a discipline is focused on the concept of "complete benevolence": that is, the purpose of medicine is to heal patients. This idea has been espoused by doctors and other medical professionals since time immemorial. The
5 Hippocratic Oath—conceived by doctors in ancient Greece and still used today—reinforces this idea: according to the oath, the first job of a medical worker is to "do no harm" to the patient. Complete benevolence is the highest moral standard of science and should be the focus of every doctor's
10 practice and decision-making ability.

Passage 2

Patient care is a large part of medicine; this fact cannot be denied. However, medicine is a science, and as such its primary goal is a quest for knowledge. Without the use of human subjects in laboratory experiments, doctors would still
15 be using leeches to cure their patients. The use of humans as well as lab animals to further science has led to the development of vaccines, cures for common aliments, and the introduction of revolutionary drug therapies. Doctors are healers, but care for their patients should never interfere with
20 the process of scientific discovery.

9. The difference between the two passages' views on the purposes of medicine can best be described as the difference between an emphasis on

(A) research on human subjects and research on animal subjects
(B) subjective care and objective care
(C) sympathy and practicality
(D) patients' rights and doctors' rights
(E) patient care and science

10. Which of the following would the author of Passage 1 most likely claim in order to weaken the author of Passage 2's assertion that scientific discovery is paramount in medicine?

(A) Scientific discovery is impossible without practical tests.
(B) Biology may be a research-based science, but medicine is applied knowledge.
(C) More patients die under the care of surgeons than under family doctors.
(D) Humans use scientific discovery to destroy life as well as preserve it.
(E) Preliminary research often reaches inaccurate conclusions.

11. The author of Passage 1 refers to the Hippocratic Oath in order to

(A) support the claim that patient care has been a primary concern of doctors for millennia
(B) highlight changes in ancient Greek medicine and modern medicine
(C) disprove the usefulness of modern laboratory experiments
(D) allude to a higher standard of medicine than the one currently used
(E) differentiate between medicine and research

12. On which of the following points would the authors of both passages most likely agree?

(A) Patient care and scientific discovery are sometimes incompatible.
(B) Patients are essential to the practice of medicine.
(C) Patient care and research can coexist for the good of the patient.
(D) Medicine is a science of discovery.
(E) Medicine has always valued patients over everything else.

GO ON TO THE NEXT PAGE

Questions 13-24 are based on the following passages.

The following passages both concern ecological conservation. Passage 1 discusses the Serengeti, one of the last remaining African nature preserves, while Passage 2 discusses a specific conservation study there.

Passage 1

There is no other plain in the world comparable to the Serengeti. Wild animals still graze in obscure corners of the African continent from Cape Town to Chad, but as
Line civilization moves in, the animals are quickly crowded out; in
5 Botswana, for example, the northwest corner was said to hold abundant game up until 1973, but now the diamond industry is preparing to drill wells for its mines and the Okovanggo Basin, which sustained the game, may be drained out. Every major civilization has eventually destroyed its wildlife, and
10 civilization is fast overtaking Africa.

The Serengeti remains the great anachronism, its survival maintained through an odd, almost mystical series of countervailing conditions that have thus far managed to tip a fragile balance slightly to the side of the animals: population
15 increases vs. drought and famine; cattle proliferation vs. pestilence and disease; land pressure for cultivation vs. tourist income; scientific research vs. the vagaries of nature.

The Serengeti's agonies are local and for the most part unrealized by the rest of the world; its importance as a
20 cultural resource for the world community, however, is unchallenged. Scientists see it as a sort of an ecological paradise regained, however briefly, and not only for its importance as the last gathering place for the rich diversity of African wildlife but as well for the light it may shed on the
25 larger question of man's survival.

"The Serengeti is basic to the concerns of conservation," says William Conway, director of the Bronx Zoo. "If animals can live there, so can man; if not, man cannot. It is the case of what is often referred to as the canary simile—the miners in
30 Wales took canaries into the pits to serve as an early-warning system; when the foul air killed the canaries, the miners knew it was time to get out. There are practical aspects to all this. The production of the Salk vaccine required the destruction of 600,000 wild monkeys over a three-year period.
35 Between the United States and Japan, science is currently using them up at the rate of 100,000 a year." Peter Jackson, director of information at the World Wildlife Fund, says, "All our domestic crops and animals have been bred from wild stock, and especially among plants it is the genetic resources
40 available in the wild which have helped to produce new wild yields." Conway asks, "Do we save animals for themselves or for ourselves? Will man set aside for tomorrow something he can use today? It hasn't happened yet. Does man truly want wildlife on Earth, and is he willing to make the sacrifices
45 necessary to keep it here?"

Passage 2

Of all his projects, John Owen's decision to establish a scientific observation in the midst of the Serengeti Plain was his most inspired. In 1961, the wildebeest appeared to be overgrazing the grasslands of the Serengeti. Owen felt he
50 ought to find out if this was so; and if it was, what should be done about it. Soon, in characteristic fashion, he virtually backed the new government into the establishment of an observatory station.

In order to answer Owen's early question of whether the
55 wildebeest were overgrazing the Serengeti, the scientists first had to establish the relationship of the wildebeest to their food supply. In 1958, the Michael Grzimek Laboratory had counted 99,000 wildebeest. In 1963, Lee and Martha Talbot counted 240,000. By 1969, there would be more
60 than half a million. It appeared that, in fact, the wildebeest were not overgrazing the Serengeti; by the mid-1960s some of the reason for this would become clear. There was a severe drought in 1960-1961 that had since ended. However, although the grasses feeding the wildebeest within the park
65 had become thick and healthy, the land surrounding the Serengeti, which fed cattle, was overgrazed. Inexplicably, as the cattle outside the park were starving, the wildebeest inside were flourishing.

The fact that the wildebeest population was increasing
70 is significant. More important, however, is the fact that a principal regulating mechanism tended to keep their numbers below levels that would have damaged their habitat. In other words, even though the high rainfall throughout the 1960s produced more food for more animals, there were
75 never too many animals for the grass that was there. Thus, the wildebeest population was regulated by a symmetrical relationship between the wildebeests' birth and death rates, the number of animals adjusted by the death rate—starvation as a form of control even in a time of abundance.

80 What had now become apparent to the scientists of the Research Institute was that the grasslands of the Serengeti formed a self-sustaining ecological system. Everything, they found, was interdependent—fire, rain, soil, grass, the host of animals. Each living thing depended on the other, each
85 flourished because of the other. The Serengeti, with its extraordinary residents, was at a stage, still undisturbed, of an evolutionary process that had been going on for hundreds of thousands of years.

GO ON TO THE NEXT PAGE

13. Passage 1 implies which one of the following about the northwest corner of Botswana?

   (A) All of its wildlife will be destroyed through increasing encroachment by civilization.
   (B) After 1973, it was no longer home to as much wildlife as it had previously been.
   (C) Its problems are local concerns and have no effect on the world ecology.
   (D) The world must study its ecological destruction in order to prevent similar tragedies.
   (E) The Okovanggo Basin was drained to make room for diamond mines.

14. The author of Passage 1 believes that we should study the problems of the Serengeti plain because

   (A) many other regions of the world share similar concerns
   (B) of the disappearance of certain types of wildlife
   (C) the natural balance may be now tipping toward mankind
   (D) the results of this study may assist humanity in its quest for survival
   (E) of increasing development in the region

15. The author of Passage 1 quotes Conway (lines 26-36) in order to

   (A) point out the distinction between survival and conservation drawn in the previous paragraph
   (B) show why current conservation methods have failed to achieve the desired results
   (C) provide further support for the claim that conservation assists humans as well as animals
   (D) discuss conservation methods from earlier centuries
   (E) support the position that the Serengeti is no longer an interesting subject of study

16. The word "yields" (line 41) most nearly means

   (A) reservations
   (B) claims
   (C) output
   (D) traffic
   (E) difficulties

GO ON TO THE NEXT PAGE

17. The examples of the miners in Wales and the Salk vaccine (lines 29-34) provide support for which one of the following claims?

   (A) Animals may in some cases be able to help humans live longer and happier lives.
   (B) Wherever people can live, animals can live there also.
   (C) The natural competition between animals and humans in the wild is detrimental to humans.
   (D) Animals that cannot be tamed are of no use to humans.
   (E) Advances in medical science will be impossible without the continued use of animals for scientific experimentation.

18. The author of Passage 2 mentions that prior to John Owen

   (A) there had been no attempt made to study the Serengeti
   (B) the national government was reluctant to support any scientific research
   (C) there had been some investigation of the wildlife on the Serengeti
   (D) the Serengeti was a natural habitat virtually unknown to humans
   (E) other scientists had unsuccessfully attempted to enlist governmental support for their studies

19. The author of Passage 2 discusses the three studies that counted the number of wildebeest (lines 57-60) in order to

   (A) show that many scientists were working on the same problem of wildebeest populations
   (B) support the claim that the Serengeti was not being overgrazed
   (C) discuss the effects of a severe drought on animal populations
   (D) demonstrate the importance of cattle in the Serengeti ecosystem
   (E) show the dramatic climatic changes that occurred during the 1960s

20. The phrase "principal regulating mechanism" in line 71 refers to

   (A) the natural limit placed on population growth by the food supply
   (B) the way in which the wildebeest were harmful to the environment
   (C) the difference between wildlife on the Serengeti and wildlife just outside the Serengeti
   (D) the effect of humanity's attempts to control disease in wildlife
   (E) the interaction of different types of wildlife in the Serengeti

21. According to the author of Passage 2, the primary conclusion of the Research Institute was that

(A) the wildebeest was an isolated and unique case of wildlife population growth

(B) humans were in danger of disturbing the ecological balance on the Serengeti

(C) the Serengeti was a good example of a breakdown in a natural food chain

(D) the Serengeti was a complex ecosystem with each member closely linked to the rest of the structure

(E) the evolution of life on the Serengeti was coming to an end

22. For which of the following claims made in Passage 1 does Passage 2 provide the strongest evidence?

(A) "Between the United States and Japan, science is currently using them [wild monkeys] up at the rate of 100,000 a year." (lines 35-36)

(B) "Scientists see it as sort of an ecological paradise regained . . . for the light it may shed on the larger question of man's survival." (lines 21-25)

(C) "Every major civilization has eventually destroyed its wildlife, and civilization is fast overtaking Africa." (lines 8-10)

(D) "'All our domestic crops and animals have been bred from wild stock . . .'" (lines 37-39)

(E) "The Serengeti remains the great anachronism, its survival maintained through an odd, almost mystical series of countervailing conditions that have thus far managed to tip a fragile balance slightly to the side of the animals." (lines 11-14)

23. The author of Passage 1 would most likely argue that if the Serengeti continues to develop according to recent trends, it will probably

(A) eventually no longer be able to support wildlife

(B) remain relatively stable for the foreseeable future

(C) push back against the encroachment of civilization and regain lost territory

(D) rapidly evolve new species of plants and animals that are better adapted to coexisting with civilization

(E) be destroyed by researchers

24. Both authors would agree that the success of the Serengeti in maintaining its ecosystem is due in part to

(A) a variety of different counterbalancing elements, both natural and artificial

(B) humanity's lack of interest in the development of the plain

(C) conservation efforts focusing on maintaining the fragile ecosystem

(D) the fear of animals that keeps most people away from the Serengeti

(E) the success of certain species in fully utilizing the abundant natural resources

STOP

If you finish before time is called, you may check your work on this section only.
Do not turn to any other section in the test.

SECTION 2
Time — 25 minutes
20 Questions

Directions: For this section, solve each problem and decide which is the best of the choices given. Fill in the corresponding circle on the answer sheet. You may use any available space for scratchwork.

Notes

1. The use of a calculator is permitted.

2. All numbers used are real numbers.

3. Figures that accompany problems in this test are intended to provide information useful in solving the problems. They are drawn as accurately as possible EXCEPT when it is stated in a specific problem that the figure is not drawn to scale. All figures lie in a plane unless other wise indicated.

4. Unless otherwise specified, the domain of any function f is assumed to be the set of all real numbers x for which $f(x)$ is a real number.

Reference Information

$A = \pi r^2$ $A = lw$ $A = \frac{1}{2}bh$ $V = lwh$ $V = \pi r^2 h$ $c^2 = a^2 + b^2$
$C = 2\pi r$

Special Right Triangles

The number of degrees of arc in a circle is 360.

The sum of the measures in degrees of the angles of a triangle is 180.

1. If each of the 12 small squares in the figure above has a side of length 2, what is the perimeter of rectangle *WXYZ*?

(A) 28
(B) 32
(C) 36
(D) 46
(E) 56

2. If z is an even integer, which of the following must be an odd integer?

(A) $3z$
(B) $3z - 1$
(C) $2z$
(D) $2z - 2$
(E) $z + 2$

GO ON TO THE NEXT PAGE

3. If 16 feet of a 96-foot-tall tree are below ground, approximately what percent of the tree is above ground?

   (A) 16.6%
   (B) 20%
   (C) 25%
   (D) 33.3%
   (E) 83.3%

4. The number of holiday cookies sold at a certain bakery in the month of December varies directly with the day of the month. If 24 holiday cookies are sold on the 4th day of December, how many holiday cookies are sold on the 20th day of December?

   (A) 72
   (B) 108
   (C) 120
   (D) 144
   (E) 176

5. If $x = \dfrac{5n}{20}$, what is the value of n in terms of x?

   (A) $\dfrac{x}{40}$

   (B) $4x$

   (C) $40x$

   (D) $100x$

   (E) $200x$

6. If $f(x) = 4x^2 + 3x + 8$, then $f(x) - 4 =$

   (A) $x^2 + 3x - 4$
   (B) $x^2 - x - 8$
   (C) $2x^2 + x + 8$
   (D) $4x^2 - x + 4$
   (E) $4x^2 + 3x + 4$

GO ON TO THE NEXT PAGE

7. Eighty students went on a class trip. If there were 14 more boys than girls on the trip, how many girls went on the trip?

(A) 66
(B) 47
(C) 40
(D) 33
(E) 26

8. If the area of one face of a cube is 36, what is the volume of the cube?

(A) 18
(B) 36
(C) 64
(D) 72
(E) 216

Bake Sale Results

Item	Number Sold
Cupcakes	33
Cookies	68
Small cakes	w
Large cakes	z
Doughnuts	24

9. At a bake sale, a total of 260 items were sold, as shown in the table above. If four times as many small cakes as large cakes were sold, what is the value of z ?

(A) 22
(B) 27
(C) 32
(D) 39
(E) 135

10. For which of the following lists is the average (arithmetic mean) less than the median?

(A) 1, 2, 6, 7, 8
(B) 2, 4, 6, 8, 11
(C) 4, 4, 6, 8, 8
(D) 4, 5, 6, 7, 8
(E) 4, 5, 6, 11, 12

GO ON TO THE NEXT PAGE

11. During a sale, for every three shirts purchased at regular price, a customer can buy a fourth at 50% off. If the regular price of a shirt is $4.50, and a customer spent $31.50 on shirts, how many shirts did the customer purchase?

    (A) 5
    (B) 6
    (C) 7
    (D) 8
    (E) 9

13. If the value of x is at most 10 less than twice the amount by which z is greater than y, which of the following expresses x in terms of y and z ?

    (A) $x \leq 2(z - y - 10)$
    (B) $x \leq 2(z - y) - 10$
    (C) $x \leq 10 - 2(z - y)$
    (D) $x \geq 10 - 2(z - y)$
    (E) $x \geq 2(z - y) - 10$

12. If $\dfrac{x^2 - x - 12}{2x^2 - 10x + 8} = \dfrac{5}{2}$, what is the value of x ?

    (A) $\dfrac{1}{2}$

    (B) 2

    (C) $\dfrac{5}{2}$

    (D) 3

    (E) 5

14. Which of the following is the product of two consecutive multiples of 3 ?

    (A) 240
    (B) 255
    (C) 270
    (D) 285
    (E) 300

GO ON TO THE NEXT PAGE

15. What are the coordinates of the midpoint of the line segment with endpoints (6, –3) and (6, 9) ?

(A) (3, 3)
(B) (3, 6)
(C) (6, 1)
(D) (6, 3)
(E) (6, 6)

16. The ratio of a to b is 4 : 7 and the ratio of c to d is 2 : 5. Which of the following is equivalent to the ratio of bc to ad ?

(A) $\dfrac{8}{35}$

(B) $\dfrac{7}{10}$

(C) $\dfrac{1}{2}$

(D) 2

(E) $4\dfrac{3}{8}$

17. A student took five tests. He scored an average (arithmetic mean) of 80 on the first three tests and an average of 90 on the other two. Which of the following must be true?

I. The student scored more than 85 on at least one test.
II. The average (arithmetic mean) score for all five tests is less than 85.
III. The student scored less than 80 on at least two tests.

(A) I only
(B) II only
(C) I and II
(D) II and III
(E) I and III

18. The figure above shows two semicircles inscribed in a square. If the square has a side of length 10, what is the area of the shaded region?

(A) $50 - 75\pi$

(B) $50 - 25\pi$

(C) $100 - 25\pi$

(D) $\dfrac{100 - 25\pi}{2}$

(E) $\dfrac{100 - 75\pi}{2}$

GO ON TO THE NEXT PAGE

19. If x is a positive integer such that $\dfrac{x}{4}$ is an odd integer and $\dfrac{x}{3}$ is an even integer, which of the following statements must be true?

   I. $\dfrac{x}{4} - \dfrac{x}{3}$ is odd.

   II. x is odd.

   III. $\left(\dfrac{x}{3}\right)^2$ is even.

(A) I only
(B) II only
(C) I and II
(D) I and III
(E) I, II, and III

20. A circle and a triangle have equal areas. If one base of the triangle has length 9, and the altitude to that base has length 8, what is the radius of the circle?

(A) 6

(B) 6π

(C) $\dfrac{6}{\sqrt{\pi}}$

(D) $\sqrt{72\pi}$

(E) 72

STOP
**If you finish before time is called, you may check your work on this section only.
Do not turn to any other section in the test.**

SECTION 3
Time — 25 minutes
24 Questions

Directions: For each question in this section, select the best answer from among the choices given and fill in the corresponding circle on the answer sheet.

Each sentence below has one or two blanks, each blank indicating that something has been omitted. Beneath the sentence are five words or sets of words labeled A through E. Choose the word or set of words that, when inserted in the sentence, best fits the meaning of the sentence as a whole.

Example:

Desiring to ------- his taunting friends, Mitch gave them taffy in hopes it would keep their mouths shut.

(A) eliminate   (B) satisfy   (C) overcome
    (D) ridicule   (E) silence

Ⓐ Ⓑ Ⓒ Ⓓ ●

25. Though he is usually very ------- at such occasions, John was surprisingly quiet at his engagement party.

    (A) reserved   (B) outgoing   (C) successful
        (D) irreverent   (E) vague

26. Although a few critics loved Isabel's new play, it never achieved the ------- success necessary for a long run in the theaters.

    (A) intellectual   (B) eccentric   (C) persuasive
        (D) dignified   (E) popular

27. Despite their very ------- cultural and religious backgrounds, the leaders of the civil rights march were able to put their differences behind them and fight for a ------- goal.

    (A) diverse . . common
    (B) different . . poetic
    (C) similar . . joint
    (D) indifferent . . unified
    (E) incompatible . . remote

28. The ------- water made it extremely difficult for the divers to search for the sunken treasure, as they could see no more than a few feet in front of their faces.

    (A) transparent   (B) murky   (C) malodorous
        (D) turgid   (E) noxious

29. She was a very ------- student; she checked every reference in her papers and always used the correct form in her footnotes.

    (A) prodigious   (B) supercilious   (C) punctilious
        (D) acute   (E) inspirational

GO ON TO THE NEXT PAGE

The passages below are followed by questions based on their content; questions following a pair of related passages may also be based on the relationship between the paired passages. Answer the questions on the basis of what is <u>stated</u> or <u>implied</u> in the passage and in any introductory material that may be provided.

Questions 30-31 are based on the following passage.

Elizabeth Cady Stanton, along with her more famous colleague Susan B. Anthony, was one of the architects of the Women's Suffrage Movement. An avid diarist, she frequently
ine recorded events in her journal. Of her historic first meeting
5 with Miss Anthony in May 1851, she wrote these words: "How well I remember the day! . . . There she stood, with her good earnest face and genial smile, dressed in gray delaine, hat and all the same color, relieved with pale blue ribbons, the perfection of neatness and sobriety. I liked her thoroughly,
10 and why I did not at once invite her home with me to dinner I do not know . . ."

30. Stanton writes "How well I remember the day!" primarily to emphasize

  (A) the vividness with which she can recall this significant meeting
  (B) the beauty of the fall afternoon in her small town
  (C) the fact that Susan B. Anthony later claimed to have no recollection of their first meeting
  (D) the excitement she felt in meeting a famous person like Susan B. Anthony
  (E) the paramount importance this meeting had in furthering the suffrage movement

31. The author uses the word "relieved" in line 8 to mean

  (A) pleased
  (B) calmed
  (C) contrasted
  (D) replaced
  (E) reassured

Questions 32-33 are based on the following passage.

Studies have shown that male scientists tend to formulate their most influential theories while they are still fairly young. Albert Einstein, for instance, published his breakthrough
Line work on relativity at the tender age of 26. One recent theory
5 explains this phenomenon by contending that young male scientists, like young criminals, are subconsciously motivated by the desire to attract a mate. Most male criminals commit crimes in their late twenties and early thirties; most male scientists make the greatest impact in their respective fields
10 during the same period in their lives. After these scientists have found mates, according to this theory, their predilection for pursuing momentous scientific discoveries declines. In a similar vein, the severity and frequency of illegal activity among male criminals generally diminishes after they marry.
15 Both types of men have already attained the ultimate goal: a spouse.

32. In context, the word "predilection" in line 11 most nearly means

  (A) natural curiosity
  (B) strong dislike
  (C) intellectual ability
  (D) financial compensation
  (E) underlying preference

33. The primary argument of the "recent theory" in line 4 is that

  (A) young male scientists are essentially criminals
  (B) the main goal of momentous scientific discoveries is for the scientist to attract a mate
  (C) criminals commit crimes in their late twenties in order to attract a mate
  (D) people should make great discoveries if they seek a mate
  (E) the actions of one group of individuals are analogous to those of another in that the unconscious purpose of each is the same

GO ON TO THE NEXT PAGE

Questions 34-39 are based on the following passage.

The passage below is a short story written in 1982 that focuses on the reliability of an individual's perceptions of the outside world. The author investigates the psychology of several characters as they respond to a situation in their town.

One night a terrible screaming sounded through the city.
It sounded so loudly and piercingly that there was not a soul
who did not hear it. Yet when people turned to one another in
fear and were about to remark "Did you hear it, that terrible
5 screaming?" they changed their minds, thinking: "Perhaps it
was my imagination, perhaps I have been working too hard
or letting my thoughts get the upper hand" (one must never
work too hard or be dominated by one's thoughts); "perhaps if
I confess that I heard this terrible screaming others will label
10 me insane, I shall be hidden behind locked doors and sit for
the remaining years of my life in a small corner, gazing at the
senseless writing on the wall."

Therefore no one confessed to having heard the
screaming. Work and play, love and death, continued as
15 usual. Yet the screaming persisted. It sounded day and night
in the ears of the people of the city, yet all remained silent
concerning it, and talked of other things. Until one day a
stranger arrived from a foreign shore. As soon as he arrived
in the city he gave a start of horror and exclaimed to the
20 Head of the Welcoming Committee, "What was that? Why, it
has not yet ceased! What is it, that terrible screaming? How
can you possibly live with it? Does it continue night and
day? Oh, what sympathy I have for you in this otherwise fair
untroubled city!"

25 The Head of the Welcoming Committee was at a loss. On
the one hand the stranger was a Distinguished person whom
it would be impolite to contradict; on the other hand, it would
be equally unwise for the Head of the Welcoming Committee
to acknowledge the terrible screaming. He decided to risk
30 being thought impolite.

"I hear nothing unusual," he said lightly, trying to suggest
that perhaps his thoughts had been elsewhere, and at the same
time trying to convey his undivided attention to the concern
of the Distinguished Stranger. His task was difficult. The
35 packaging of words with varied intentions is like writing
a letter to someone in a foreign land and addressing it to
oneself; it never reaches its destination.

The Distinguished Stranger looked confused. "You hear
no terrible screaming?"

40 The Head of the Welcoming Committee turned to his
assistant. "Do you perhaps hear some unusual sound?"

The Assistant who had been disturbed by the screaming
and had decided that very day to speak out, to refuse to ignore
it, now became afraid that perhaps he would lose his job if he
45 mentioned it. He shook his head.

"I hear nothing unusual," he replied firmly.

The Distinguished Stranger looked embarrassed. "Perhaps
it is my imagination," he said apologetically. "It is just as well
that I have come for a holiday to your beautiful city. I have
50 been working very hard lately."

Then aware once again of the terrible screaming he
covered his ears with his hands.

"I fear I am unwell," he said. "I apologize if I am unable to
attend the banquet, in honor of my arrival."

55 "We understand completely," said the Head of the
Welcoming Committee.

So there was no banquet. The Distinguished Stranger
consulted a specialist who admitted him to a private rest
home where he could recover from his disturbed state of mind
60 and the persistence in his ears of the terrible screaming.

The specialist finished examining the Distinguished
Stranger. He washed his hands with a slab of hard soap, took
off his white coat, and was preparing to go home to his wife
when he thought suddenly, "Suppose the screaming does
65 exist?"

He dismissed the thought. The Rest Home was full, and
the fees were high. He enjoyed the comforts of civilization.
Yet supposing, just supposing, that all the patients united
against him, that all the people of the city began to
70 acknowledge the terrible screaming? What would be the
result? Would there be a complete panic? Was there really
safety in numbers where ideas were concerned?

He stopped thinking about the terrible screaming. He
climbed into his Jaguar and drove home.

75 The Head of the Welcoming Committee, disappointed
because he could not attend another banquet, yet relieved
because he would not be forced to justify another item of
public expenditure, also went home to his wife. They dined
on a boiled egg, bread and butter and a cup of tea, for they
80 both approved of simple living.

Then they went to the bedroom, switched out the light and
enjoyed the illusion of uncomplicated dreams.

And outside in the city the terrible screaming continued
its separate existence, unacknowledged. For you see its name
85 was silence. Silence had found its voice.

34. What is the purpose of the parenthetical statement in lines
7-8 ?

(A) It signals that the narrator disapproves of the
informal tone of the people's thoughts.

(B) It offers advice directly to the reader of the story.

(C) It suggests that people tend to rationalize decisions
that might be questionable.

(D) It indicates that the people in the story are suffering
from schizophrenia.

(E) It emphasizes how surprising the people found the
scream.

GO ON TO THE NEXT PAGE

35. With which of the following statements would the author most likely agree?

(A) Trust the perceptions of those around you rather than obsessing about your own ideas.

(B) It is important to fall in with the beliefs of others.

(C) Insanity always spreads most quickly at night.

(D) People should never agree with the sensory perceptions of those surrounding them.

(E) The fear of speaking out allows evil to be perpetuated.

36. As used in line 19, the word "start" most nearly means

(A) sympathetic stare

(B) quick beginning

(C) sudden jump

(D) pleased surprise

(E) endless scream

37. It can be inferred from the passage that the author believes that the "packaging of words with varied intentions" (line 35)

(A) guarantees the reception of those words

(B) needs to be translated for those from other countries

(C) always conveys several different meanings according to the listener

(D) should be used by dignitaries dealing with foreign visitors

(E) is inherently unlikely to convey the ideas behind the words, regardless of what those ideas are

38. According to the passage, one reason the Rest Home specialist dismisses the thought that the screaming might exist is that

(A) the status quo affords him a lifestyle replete with material possessions

(B) acknowledging the screaming would certainly lead to complete panic

(C) if the screaming were real, the Rest Home would have to begin admitting more patients

(D) such a conclusion would go against his professional training

(E) he cannot accept that a foreigner such as the Distinguished Stranger might be right

39. This story can best be described as

(A) a fable about how fears of job security lead to cowardice

(B) an allegory that illustrates the pernicious effects of fear

(C) a metaphor for insanity

(D) a trivialization of the crippling effects of silence

(E) a symbol of the benefits of modernity

GO ON TO THE NEXT PAGE

Questions 40-48 are based on the following passage.

Though slang may appear on the surface to be unworthy of serious study, Mario Pei in his 1954 book All About Language *offers an astute examination of the history of slang and its significance in modern society.*

Dialects are a matter of geography. Slang is nationwide. There are some who think that only poorer and less educated people use slang. This is not necessarily true. A little bit of
Line slang, in fact, is used by practically everybody. Slang is a
5 departure from standard, accepted language, but it may easily turn into standard language if it meets with enough favor. Or it may die out and leave little or no trace.

English is a language very rich in slang, but the mortality among slang words is very high. People who make up our
10 dictionaries usually admit slang expressions on probation. They are either placed in a separate section of the dictionary, or marked "colloquial" or "vulgar" or "slang." If they survive a certain number of years, the label is removed, and they are admitted on a basis of equality with other words. If they
15 disappear from use, they vanish also from the dictionaries.

In a many good cases, slang words and uses can be traced to one individual. Dizzy Dean, of baseball fame, is responsible for "goodasterous" as the opposite of "disastrous," and "slud" as the past of "slide." Walter Winchell started
20 the expression "making whoopee," and Shakespeare himself was the first to use, at least in writing, "beat it" and "not so hot." But far more often the creator of the slang expression is unknown.

Slang as we said before is nationwide. The expressions
25 we see would be understood pretty much anywhere in America. Dialect is local, as where sections of the Midwest use "mango" in the sense of "green pepper." Two other items that call for discussion are cant and jargon. Jargon is a form of speech current in a given class or profession and
30 hardly understood on the outside. Cant, the language of the underworld, is a variety of jargon. A French poet of the fifteenth century, François Villon, used in many of his poems a type of Paris underworld cant that cannot be understood today. American and British cant has been mysterious in the
35 past, but today large segments of it are known, having been spread by detective stories, and many of its expressions have become general slang and even regular language. "Sawbuck" for "$10" and "grand" for "$1,000" are generally understood and even used, though they are not the best language in the
40 world. Other cant expressions that have acquired a measure of respectability are "take the rap," "take for a ride," "throw the book at," "blow one's top," "frisk," and "gat." But there are many others not so well known, like "quizmaster" for "District Attorney."
45 There are jargons of the various professions and trades, even jargons of the sexes and age-levels. Bankers, lawyers, and doctors will talk among themselves in specialized languages that people on the outside have difficulty following. So do scientists, technicians, teachers, and
50 scholars in every field. But it is not only the intellectual

professions that have jargons; it is also the manual trades and occupations. From them, too, many words have come into the general language. Shipboard terminology is very extensive and complicated, as you know if you have read stories about
55 ships, particularly the old sailing vessels. When you speak of "knowing the ropes," "keeping on an even keel," "keeping a weather eye open," "giving plenty of leeway," you are using sailors' expressions that have become general. But there are many more such expressions that have not entered the general
60 language and that you have to look up in the dictionary if you want to understand all the details of a sea story.

There is a jargon for the military, railroad workers, rodeo people, truck drivers, and soda fountain attendants. In short, there is no occupation that doesn't have its own special
65 terminology that baffles outsiders. Though linguists might condemn the investigation of slang as unworthy of legitimate study, there is certainly the possibility that its widespread use might cause some of it to become part of the standard language sooner than they think.

40. In line 1, the phrase "Slang is nationwide" refers to the view that
    (A) the use of slang is not restricted to a particular group of people
    (B) slang is considered equivalent to standard English
    (C) dictionary writers often accept slang on a trial basis
    (D) the controversy over slang's popularity is not just a local problem, but also a national concern
    (E) jargon is something that both professional and nonprofessional people have in common

41. In line 8, the word "rich" most nearly means
    (A) wealthy
    (B) abundant
    (C) entertaining
    (D) seasoned
    (E) productive

GO ON TO THE NEXT PAGE

42. In the third paragraph, the author refers to Dizzy Dean and Shakespeare in order to

   (A) present the reader with some of the more amusing examples of slang
   (B) show how slang became popular both in sports and literature
   (C) illustrate how both men shared similar phrases in their everyday speech
   (D) explain that slang can usually be traced back to a single person
   (E) offer examples of single individuals who were responsible for certain expressions

43. It can be inferred that "cant," as mentioned in line 30, was most popularly used by

   (A) criminals
   (B) French aristocracy
   (C) Midwestern farmers
   (D) bankers and doctors
   (E) the military

44. It can be inferred from the passage that François Villon provides an example of

   (A) how slang adds a unique quality to any piece of literature
   (B) why certain slang expressions seem to enter into standard, accepted language
   (C) how some expressions pass out of use over time
   (D) how slang can make the difference in a writer's career
   (E) why the French underworld during the fifteenth century was able to thrive for so long

45. The author describes certain examples of cant as "not the best language in the world" in lines 39-40 so as to

   (A) convey his opposition to the popular belief that cant has become one of the most accepted dialects
   (B) describe the overwhelming popularity that cant seems to possess
   (C) find a reason that cant is generally understood and even used
   (D) communicate that such speech is not universally regarded as proper
   (E) imply his distaste for the use of cant in society

46. The word "measure" in line 40 most nearly means

   (A) rhythm
   (B) meter
   (C) degree
   (D) melody
   (E) regulation

47. The author mentions "shipboard terminology" in line 53 in order to illustrate

   (A) that slang evolved within manual trades as well as intellectual fields
   (B) the intellectual background that inspired such general terms as "keeping on an even keel"
   (C) the complications that often followed sailors who worked on old sailing vessels
   (D) the distinction between complicated nautical terms and more general terms like "knowing the ropes"
   (E) the importance of understanding phrases like "keeping a weather eye open" in order to become an accomplished sailor

48. The author is primarily concerned with

   (A) defining the importance of jargon in intellectual professions
   (B) explaining the origins of slang and its different variations
   (C) tracing the history of slang
   (D) discussing how certain professions have been affected by the popularity of cant
   (E) describing the effect that a single individual can have on slang

STOP

If you finish before time is called, you may check your work on this section only.
Do not turn to any other section in the test.

SECTION 4
Time — 25 minutes
18 Questions

Directions: For this section, solve each problem and decide which is the best of the choices given. Fill in the corresponding circle on the answer sheet. You may use any available space for scratchwork.

Notes

1. The use of a calculator is permitted.

2. All numbers used are real numbers.

3. Figures that accompany problems in this test are intended to provide information useful in solving the problems. They are drawn as accurately as possible EXCEPT when it is stated in a specific problem that the figure is not drawn to scale. All figures lie in a plane unless other wise indicated.

4. Unless otherwise specified, the domain of any function f is assumed to be the set of all real numbers x for which $f(x)$ is a real number.

Reference Information

$A = \pi r^2$
$C = 2\pi r$

$A = lw$

$A = \frac{1}{2}bh$

$V = lwh$

$V = \pi r^2 h$

$c^2 = a^2 + b^2$

Special Right Triangles

The number of degrees of arc in a circle is 360.

The sum of the measures in degrees of the angles of a triangle is 180.

---

21. A certain computer downloads 4 files of equal size per second. How many files of the same size will it download in 2 <u>minutes</u>?

(A)   6
(B)   8
(C)   120
(D)   240
(E)   480

22. In $\triangle ABC$, $AB = BC = CA$. If $\triangle ABC$ is congruent to $\triangle DEF$ then what is the measure of $\angle D$?

(A)   180°
(B)   150°
(C)   120°
(D)   90°
(E)   60°

GO ON TO THE NEXT PAGE

23. Three roommates share their monthly rent payment in a ratio of 7 : 8 : 10. If the monthly rent is $1,200, then what is the amount of the <u>greatest</u> share?

   (A) $336
   (B) $360
   (C) $384
   (D) $400
   (E) $480

24. If $qs \neq 0$, then $\dfrac{2p}{q} - \dfrac{r}{2s} =$

   (A) $\dfrac{4ps - qr}{2qs}$

   (B) $\dfrac{2p - r}{2qs}$

   (C) $-\dfrac{pr}{qs}$

   (D) $\dfrac{2p - r}{q + 2s}$

   (E) $\dfrac{2p - r}{q - 2s}$

25. If $abcd \neq 0$, $c = ab^{-2}$ and $d = a^{-1}b^4$, what is the value of cd in terms of a and b ?

   (A) $\dfrac{1}{ab^8}$

   (B) $a^8\sqrt{b}$

   (C) b^2

   (D) $\left(\sqrt{a}\right)\left(\sqrt[5]{b}\right)$

   (E) $\dfrac{a}{b}$

26. If $a = 9x^2 + 4$ and $b = 3x + 2$, what is a in terms of b ?

   (A) $b^2 - 4b + 8$
   (B) $b^2 - 4b + 4$
   (C) b^2
   (D) $9b^2 - 36b + 72$
   (E) $9b^2 + 36b + 72$

GO ON TO THE NEXT PAGE

27. In a group of 15 integers, the probability of randomly

selecting an even number is $\dfrac{1}{3}$. Based on this

information, which of the following can be determined?

    I. The probability of selecting
        an odd number

    II. The probability of selecting
        a number that is not the
        mode

    III. The average (arithmetic
        mean) of the greatest and
        least numbers in the group

(A) None
(B) I only
(C) II only
(D) III only
(E) I and II only

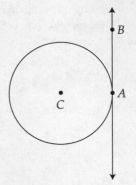

Note: Figure not drawn to scale.

28. In the figure above, the circle with center C is tangent
to $\overrightarrow{AB}$ at point A. If $AB = 12$ and the length of segment
$\overline{BC}$ (not drawn) is 13, what is the area of the circle with
center C ?

(A) 10π
(B) 25π
(C) 144π
(D) 169π
(E) 313π

GO ON TO THE NEXT PAGE

Directions for Student-Produced Response Questions

Each of the remaining 10 questions requires you to solve the problem and enter your answer by marking the ovals in the special grid, as shown in the examples below. You may use any available space for scratch work.

Answer: $\frac{7}{12}$

Write answer in boxes. ← Fraction line

Grid in result.

Answer: 2.5

← Decimal point

Note: You may start your answers in any column, space permitting. Columns not needed should be left blank.

- Mark no more than one circle in any column.
- Because the answer sheet will be machine-scored, **you will receive credit only if the circles are filled in correctly.**
- Although not required, it is suggested that you write your answer in the boxes at the top of the columns to help you fill in the circles accurately.
- Some problems may have more than one correct answer. In such cases, grid only one answer.
- No question has a negative answer.
- **Mixed numbers** such as $3\frac{1}{2}$ must be gridded as 3.5 or 7/2. (If ☐ is gridded, it will be interpreted as $\frac{31}{2}$, not $3\frac{1}{2}$.)

- **Decimal Answers:** If you obtain a decimal answer with more digits than the grid can accommodate, it may be either rounded or truncated, but it must fill the entire grid. For example, if you obtain an answer such as 0.6666..., you should record your result as .666 or .667. **A less accurate value such as .66 or .67 will be scored as incorrect.**

Acceptable ways to grid $\frac{2}{3}$ are:

29. In the figure above, what is the value of $x + y$?

30. If x is a negative integer and $|x| < 3$, what is one possible value of $|x|$?

GO ON TO THE NEXT PAGE →

5, 11, 29, 83, . . .

31. Two numbers have the property that their sum is equal to their product. If one of these numbers is 4, what is the other number?

33. In the sequence above, the nth term can be expressed as $2 + 3^n$. What is the value of the 8th term?

32. If $\frac{1}{2}a$, $\frac{1}{2}a$, and a are the degree measures of a triangle, what is the value of a ?

34. What is the greatest of 4 consecutive integers whose sum is 414 ?

35. What is the area of a square with a diagonal of length $3\sqrt{2}$?

36. If n is a prime number greater than 3, then $6n$ has exactly how many positive integer divisors?

37. If $x + y = 5$ and $x^2 - y^2 = 16$, what is the value of $x - y$?

38. Sally, Abdul, and Juanita have volunteered to stuff a certain number of envelopes for a local charity. Working by herself, Sally could stuff all the envelopes in exactly 3 hours. Working by himself, Abdul could stuff all the envelopes in exactly 4 hours. Working by herself, Juanita could stuff all the envelopes in exactly 6 hours. If Sally, Abdul, and Juanita work together at these rates to stuff all the envelopes, what fraction of the envelopes will be stuffed by Juanita?

STOP
**If you finish before time is called, you may check your work on this section only.
Do not turn to any other section in the test.**

SECTION 5
Time — 30 minutes
39 Questions

Directions: For each question in this section, select the best answer from among the choices given and fill in the corresponding circle on the answer sheet.

The following sentences test correctness and effectiveness of expression. Part of each sentence or the entire sentence is underlined; beneath each sentence are five ways of phrasing the underlined material. Choice A repeats the original phrasing; the other four choices are different. If you think the original phrasing produces a better sentence than any of the alternatives, select choice A; if not, select one of the other choices.

In making your selection, follow the requirements of standard written English; that is, pay attention to grammar, choice of words, sentence construction, and punctuation. Your selection should result in the most effective sentence—clear and precise, without awkwardness or ambiguity.

EXAMPLE:

Bobby Flay baked his first cake <u>and he was thirteen years old then</u>.
(A) and he was thirteen years old then
(B) when he was thirteen
(C) at age thirteen years old
(D) upon the reaching of thirteen years
(E) at the time when he was thirteen

Ⓐ ● Ⓒ Ⓓ Ⓔ

1. A large predatory snake, <u>the muscular body of a boa constrictor</u> can reach over 10 feet in length.

    (A) the muscular body of a boa constrictor
    (B) a boa constrictor whose muscular body
    (C) a boa constrictor's muscular body
    (D) the boa constrictor has a muscular body that
    (E) as well as having a muscular body, the boa constrictor

2. The audience's response was better than Martin could possibly have <u>expected, having received</u> a standing ovation and great cheers from the crowd.

    (A) expected, having received
    (B) expected; and so he was receiving
    (C) expected; he received
    (D) expected: including the reception of
    (E) expected, he was receiving

3. Watering your plant too often is as unhealthy <u>than if you do not water it</u> often enough.

    (A) than if you do not water it
    (B) as not watering it
    (C) as if one were not to water it
    (D) than not watering
    (E) as for not watering it

4. Not only did the ancient Egyptians know about the North Pole, <u>but they also knew in precisely which direction it lay</u>.

    (A) but they also knew in precisely which direction it lay
    (B) but they had also known in precisely which direction it lay
    (C) also knowing its precise direction
    (D) also precisely knowing its direction
    (E) but knowing its precise direction as well

5. <u>The Luna space probes were the first to enter solar orbit and photograph the far side of the moon, in 1959 they were launched.</u>

    (A) The Luna space probes were the first to enter solar orbit and photograph the far side of the moon, in 1959 they were launched.
    (B) Launched in 1959, the Luna space probes were the first to enter solar orbit and photograph the far side of the moon.
    (C) In 1959, the first solar orbit and photograph of the far side of the moon was taking place when the Luna space probes were launched.
    (D) The launching of the Luna space probes was in 1959, the solar orbit was entered and the far side of the moon was photographed.
    (E) The first solar orbit was when the Luna space probes were launched in 1959, and the first photograph of the far side of the moon was taken as well.

GO ON TO THE NEXT PAGE ⟩

6. Perhaps the best-known of all southern American writers, <u>William Faulkner's famous books include</u> *The Sound and the Fury* and *As I Lay Dying*.

  (A) William Faulkner's famous books include

  (B) William Faulkner's books are famous for including

  (C) William Faulkner has included among his famous books

  (D) William Faulkner is famous for such books as

  (E) William Faulkner is famous for including such books as

7. When the coach of the basketball team spoke, <u>new uniforms for all the players were implied, but it was not promised by him</u>.

  (A) new uniforms for all the players were implied, but it was not promised by him

  (B) new uniforms for all the players were implied, but he did not actually promise it

  (C) new uniforms for all the players were implied by him and not actually promised

  (D) he implied new uniforms for all the players, but they were not actually promised by him

  (E) he implied, but did not actually promise, that he would get new uniforms for all the players

8. When Michelle was younger, she was hired by a local furniture store to watch the store in the mornings <u>as well as cleaning the windows</u>.

  (A) as well as cleaning the windows

  (B) and she also cleaned the windows

  (C) as well as to clean the windows

  (D) the cleaning of windows also being done by her

  (E) together with cleaning the windows

9. Jason was nervous about the race he had to run, <u>this</u> nervousness gave him the energy to run even faster than he had expected.

  (A) this

  (B) furthermore

  (C) but this

  (D) for which

  (E) that

10. <u>The earliest design for a helicopter drawn by Leonardo da Vinci</u>, the Italian artist and inventor, more than four hundred years ago.

  (A) The earliest design for a helicopter drawn by Leonardo da Vinci

  (B) Among the earliest designs for a helicopter by Leonardo da Vinci

  (C) Leonardo da Vinci drew the earliest design for a helicopter

  (D) Leonardo da Vinci, creator of one of the earliest design for a helicopter

  (E) The earliest design for a helicopter was drawn by Leonardo da Vinci

GO ON TO THE NEXT PAGE ➡

11. After reading Mary Shelley's masterpiece *Frankenstein*, <u>I couldn't hardly believe</u> that she was only nineteen when she wrote it.

(A) I couldn't hardly believe
(B) I could hardly not believe
(C) I could not hardly believe
(D) I could hardly believe
(E) I could hardly be believing

12. Both Caleb and Joy seem <u>like they are intending to become doctors</u>.

(A) like they are intending to become doctors
(B) like they are intending to become a doctor
(C) to be intending to become doctors
(D) to be intending on becoming doctors
(E) like their intent is of becoming a doctor

13. Hydrogen, <u>in combination with oxygen</u>, forms the molecule we call water.

(A) in combination with oxygen
(B) in its combining with oxygen
(C) in the combination of it and oxygen
(D) having combined itself with oxygen
(E) with oxygen in combination

14. Neither a broken leg nor an upset stomach <u>has prevented Jason to play</u> the flute in this year's concert.

(A) has prevented Jason to play
(B) have stopped Jason playing
(C) have prevented Jason from playing
(D) has prevented Jason from playing
(E) have stopped Jason in his playing

15. Zora Neale Hurston, author of *Their Eyes Were Watching God*, <u>is considered as one of the finest writers in</u> the Harlem Renaissance.

(A) is considered as one of the finest writers in
(B) is considered one of the finest writers of
(C) is considered to be one of the finest writers among
(D) considered as one of the finest writers of
(E) is the consideration of one of the finest writers of

GO ON TO THE NEXT PAGE

16. Since Jonas Salk and Albert Sabin created protective vaccines, <u>Americans are no longer concerned with the spread of polio</u>.

   (A) Americans are no longer concerned with the spread of polio

   (B) Americans are no longer concerned with spreading polio

   (C) Americans have no longer been concerned about the spread of polio

   (D) Americans are no longer concerned about the spreading polio

   (E) Americans are no longer concerned in the spreading of polio

17. The Brothers Grimm collected, <u>wrote, and published a book of fairy tales, they also wrote the first comprehensive German dictionary</u>.

   (A) wrote, and published a book of fairy tales, they also wrote the first comprehensive German dictionary

   (B) wrote, and published a book of fairy tales; but were also writing the first comprehensive German dictionary

   (C) wrote, and published both a book of fairy tales and the first comprehensive German dictionary

   (D) wrote and published a book of fairy tales; and the first comprehensive German dictionary

   (E) wrote and published a book of fairy tales, they were also writing the first comprehensive German dictionary

18. The age-old practice of <u>extracting syrup from maple trees provides a natural source of sugar that has been done for many years</u>.

   (A) extracting syrup from maple trees provides a natural source of sugar that has been done for many years

   (B) extracting syrup from maple trees provides a natural source of sugar, and it has been done for many years throughout history

   (C) extracting syrup from maple trees provides a natural source of sugar

   (D) extracting syrup from maple trees, providing a natural source of sugar

   (E) extracting syrup from maple trees providing a natural source of sugar has been done over time for many years

19. <u>If all citizens would take a more proactive stance on environmental issues,</u> Americans could look forward to a future of cleaner air and water.

   (A) If all citizens would take a more proactive stance on environmental issues,

   (B) Were all citizens to take a more proactive stance on environmental issues,

   (C) Were all citizens taking a more proactive stance on environmental issues,

   (D) If all citizens would be taking a more proactive stance on environmental issues,

   (E) If all citizens would have taken a more proactive stance on environmental issues,

20. Children attending Camp Northwoods need to <u>bring a stamp for the letters they will write home to their parents</u>.

   (A) bring a stamp for the letters they will write home to their parents

   (B) bring a stamp for the letters he or she will write home to their parents

   (C) bring stamps for the letters he or she will write home to their parents

   (D) bring stamps for the letter they will write home to their parents

   (E) bring stamps for the letters they will write home to their parents

GO ON TO THE NEXT PAGE

The following sentences test your ability to recognize grammar and usage errors. Each sentence contains either a single error or no error at all. No sentence contains more than one error. The error, if there is one, is underlined and lettered. If the sentence contains an error, select the one underlined part that must be changed to make the sentence correct. If the sentence is correct, select choice E. In choosing answers, follow the requirements of standard written English.

EXAMPLE:

The other players and her significantly improved
   A   B   C

the game plan created by the coaches. No error
               D   E

Ⓐ ● Ⓒ Ⓓ Ⓔ

21. The actors were exhausted, but each was able to
              A   B

remember all the complicated lines on opening night.
       C   D

No error
  E

22. Mary Anne was indebted with her mother for all the hard
                       A   B

work her mother had done in preparation for the party.
    C   D

No error
  E

23. One way to determine the accuracy of reference books
        A

is to check the credentials of its editorial board. No error
 B   C   D   E

24. It is more convenient to reply to email at one's own
      A   B   C

convenience than answering the phone every time it rings.
                D

No error
  E

25. The works of Stephen King are similar to Peter Straub, a
                 A   B

fact that is not surprising since the two men are friends
                 C

and have even collaborated on two novels. No error
       D   E

26. In flight, a flock of geese encounters scarcely no wind
                     A   B

resistance because of the "v" formation it employs.
      C   D

No error
  E

27. Vital to any analysis of the causes of the Russian
                A

Revolution are an understanding of the many alliances
        B   C

between political parties in the early 1900s. No error
    D   E

GO ON TO THE NEXT PAGE

28. Many of the players were professionals who, in prior
    A   B   C

    years, had received gold medals. No error
    D   E

29. A recent conducted poll shows that people are littering
    A   B

    less frequently, a development that reflects a great change
                                    C

    in the public's attitude toward the environment. No error
                            D   E

30. Neither the giant alligator or the tiny lizard is the cause of
                    A   B   C   D

    Joey's nightmares. No error
                       E

31. Marjorie, the newest of the two violinists who
              A

    have recently joined the symphony, has excellent tone
    B   C

    and a marvelous command of her instrument. No error
    D   E

32. The more you read the early works of Michel Tournier,
    A   B

    the more they begin to provoke an emotional reaction.
    C   D

    No error
    E

33. Although they are widely used, standardized test scores
             A

    are not a reliant indicator of a student's academic
    B   C   D

    potential. No error
               E

34. Since 1960, less than three graduates from our school
                A   B

    have won the Rhodes Scholarship. No error
    C   D   E

Directions: The following passage is an early draft of an essay. Some parts of the passage need to be rewritten.

Read the passage and select the best answers for the questions that follow. Some questions are about particular sentences or parts of sentences and ask you to improve sentence structure or word choice. Other questions ask you to consider organization and development. In choosing answers, follow the requirements of standard written English.

Questions 35-39 are based on the following passage.

(1) I used to have an irrational fear of bees. (2) Anytime I heard a buzzing sound, my heart would start to beat faster and faster. (3) Sometimes breathing was hard. (4) I've always loved working in my garden. (5) But once spring came around, all the bees came out. (6) I was terrified of going outside. (7) My garden began to wither away. (8) Finally, I decided to do something about it. (9) I called up my friend Anne. (10) Her uncle happens to be a beekeeper. (11) I wanted to ask if I could meet him. (12) Anne's uncle agreed to take me to his hives the next day. (13) From the second I woke up that day, I was petrified, but luckily, Anne's uncle was very understanding. (14) He suited me up in beekeeping gear so that I couldn't get stung, and then he showed me his bee hives. (15) To my surprise, I found myself fascinated by them. (16) Anne's uncle described how they are organized in castes, how they act as pollinators, and how they make honey. (17) I was so interested by what he said that I went to the library that very night and researched bees for hours. (18) And now—now I can't keep away from bees. (19) Each morning, I have visited Anne's uncle, helping out with the hives, while in the afternoon, I devote my time to my garden surrounded by bees.

35. Which of the following sentences, if added after sentence 3, would best link the first paragraph with the rest of the essay?

(A) It seems that I have had this fear of bees for an eternity.
(B) There were even times that I couldn't move my body, so intense was my fear of bees.
(C) Unfortunately, I couldn't ignore my fear of bees, because I have a garden.
(D) Usually, gardening is a pleasurable experience.
(E) I try not to be afraid of bees, but in my garden it's impossible.

36. Which of the following is the best way to revise and combine sentences 6 and 7 (reproduced below)?

I was terrified of going outside. My garden began to wither away.

(A) Being terrified of going outside, my garden began to wither away.
(B) Though going outside terrified me, my garden began to wither away.
(C) Since going outside did terrify me, it was then my garden began to wither away.
(D) Going outside terrified me, and as a result, my garden began to wither away.
(E) My garden, withering away, as I was terrified of going outside.

37. The phrase "to do something about it" in sentence 8 can best be made more specific by being rewritten as which of the following?

(A) to make my garden grow again
(B) to learn more about bees
(C) to get in touch with a beekeeper
(D) to combat my fear of bees
(E) to reconsider my feelings

38. Which of the following versions of sentence 15 (reproduced below) is most effective?

To my surprise, I found myself fascinated by them.

(A) (As it is now)
(B) To my surprise, I found myself fascinated by it.
(C) To my surprise, they have been very fascinating to me.
(D) To my surprise, I found myself fascinated by the bees.
(E) Fascination was surprisingly found by me in them.

39. In the context of the third paragraph, which of the following is the best version of the underlined portion of sentence 19 (reproduced below)?

Each morning, I have visited Anne's uncle helping out with the hives, while in the afternoon, I devote my time to my garden surrounded by bees.

(A) (as it is now)
(B) I visit Anne's uncle to help out
(C) having visited Anne's uncle and helping out
(D) visiting Anne's uncle to help out
(E) visiting Anne's uncle has helped out

STOP

If you finish before time is called, you may check your work on this section only.
Do not turn to any other section in the test.

SCORING YOUR PRACTICE PSAT

Critical Reading

After you have checked your answers against the answer key, you can calculate your score. For the two Critical Reading sections (Sections 1 and 3), add up the number of correct answers and the number of incorrect answers. Enter these numbers on the worksheet on the next page. Multiply the number of incorrect answers by .25, and subtract this result from the number of correct answers. Then round this to the nearest whole number to get your Critical Reading "raw score." Next, use the conversion table to convert your raw score to a scaled score.

Math

Figuring your Math score is a bit trickier, because some of the questions have 5 answer choices (for these, the incorrect answer deduction is .25), and some are Grid-Ins (which have no deduction for incorrect answers).

First, check your answers to all of the problem-solving questions on Sections 2 and 4. For Section 2 and questions 21–28 of Section 4, put the number of correct answers and the number of incorrect answers into the worksheet on the next page. Multiply the number of incorrect answers by .25, and subtract this total from the number of correct answers. For questions 29–38 of Section 4, the Grid-In questions, simply put in the number of correct answers. Now, add up the totals for both types of math questions to give you your total Math raw score. Then you can use the conversion table to find your scaled score.

Writing Skills

The Writing Skills section should be scored just like the Critical Reading sections. Add up the number of correct answers and the number of incorrect answers from Section 5, and enter these numbers on the worksheet on the next page. Multiply the number of incorrect answers by .25 and subtract this result from the number of correct answers. Then round this to the nearest whole number. This is your Writing raw score. Next, use the conversion table to convert your raw scores to scaled scores.

WORKSHEET FOR CALCULATING YOUR SCORE

Critical Reading

	Correct	Incorrect

A. Sections 1 and 3   _____ − (.25 × _____) =

☐ A

B. Total rounded Critical Reading raw score

☐ B

Math

	Correct	Incorrect

C. Section 2 and Section 4—Problem Solving _____ − (.25 × _____) =

☐ C

D. Section 4—Grid-Ins _____ =

☐ D

E. Total unrounded Math raw score (C + D)

☐ E

F. Total rounded Math raw score

☐ F

Writing Skills

Section 5   _____ − (.25 × _____) =

☐

Total rounded Writing Skills raw score

☐

SCORE CONVERSION TABLE

Math Raw Score	Math Scaled Score	Critical Reading Raw Score	Critical Reading Scaled Score	Writing Skills Raw Score	Writing Skills Scaled Score
0	26	0	25	0	29
1	29	1	27	1	30
2	30	2	29	2	31
3	32	3	30	3	32
4	34	4	32	4	33
5	35	5	33	5	35
6	36	6	34	6	36
7	38	7	36	7	37
8	39	8	37	8	39
9	40	9	38	9	40
10	41	10	39	10	41
11	42	11	40	11	43
12	43	12	41	12	44
13	44	13	42	13	45
14	45	14	43	14	46
15	46	15	44	15	48
16	47	16	45	16	49
17	48	17	46	17	50
18	50	18	47	18	51
19	51	19	48	19	52
20	52	20	49	20	54
21	53	21	50	21	55
22	54	22	51	22	56
23	55	23	52	23	57
24	57	24	53	24	59
25	58	25	54	25	60
26	59	26	54	26	62
27	60	27	55	27	63
28	61	28	56	28	65
29	62	29	57	29	66
30	64	30	58	30	68
31	65	31	59	31	69
32	66	32	60	32	71
33	68	33	61	33	73
34	70	34	62	34	74
35	72	35	62	35	76
36	74	36	63	36	77
37	77	37	64	37	78
38	80	38	66	38	80
		39	67	39	80
		40	68		
		41	69		
		42	71		
		43	72		
		44	74		
		45	76		
		46	78		
		47	80		
		48	80		

Chapter 15
Practice Test 2:
Answers and
Explanations

Section 1

1. **B**   Since Roberta's first book was award-winning but her second is unlike it, we could fill in the blank with a word that means not award-winning. Only (B) comes close.

2. **E**   If we do the second blank first, the trigger in contrast tells us the blank will be opposite from our clue, *excessive violence*. So, *not violent* would be a good word to write down for the blank, and we can eliminate (B) and (D). Our clue for the first blank is *serious physical danger*, because that's what the animals we're comparing here are responding to. So a good word for the first blank would be *danger*. Out of (A), (C), and (E), the only one that fits is (E). Remember, don't waste your time checking the first word in (B) or (D) because we've already eliminated them!

3. **B**   We don't have very specific clues for the individual blanks, so we can work on relationship between the blanks. The word *since* tells us there is a cause/effect relationship between the first and second blanks, which will be a relationship of similarity. (We also know that the words will probably be negative because of the clue *unfortunately*, but we may not even need that information.) Only (B) has a relationship of similarity.

4. **D**   We know that other structures were destroyed during the earthquake, so *survival* might be a good word for the first blank. That lets us eliminate (A), (B), and (E). Remember, even if we see our exact word in the answer choices, we still need to finish the process because it could be paired with a word that doesn't fit in the other blank. If more rigid buildings were destroyed and the girders had a surprising quality, it's probably *flexibility*, the opposite of *rigidity*. That allows us to eliminate (C), and only (D) fits.

5. **E**   The clue *intact* and the time trigger prior tell us to fill in the blank with an opposite word, such as *destroyed*. Only (E) means the same thing as *destroyed*. Remember, if you don't know what a word in the answer choices means, leave it! It could be correct.

6. **E**   The clue *jeered* tells us that the first viewers didn't like the play, so we could write down something like *terrible* for the first blank. That gets rid of (B), (C), and (D). The trigger word *although* tells us the sentence is going to change directions, and the clue *classics of world theater* also tells us that the second blank is going to be a positive word, so perhaps we could write down *quality* for the second blank. *Impenetrability* doesn't come close, so the correct answer is (E).

7. **C**   The clue *relied more on direct confrontation* tells us that *confrontational* is a good replacement for the blank. (C) is the closest fit.

8. **B**   Let's do the second blank first, since we have better clues for it. *Alleging that they were his own* tells us that a word like *steals* would be a good replacement for the blank. That gets rid of (A) and (C). Now let's look at the first blank. Because he steals ideas, few people would call the company president ethical or creative or anything positive. That eliminates (D) and (E), leaving us with (B).

9. **E** The first passage puts patients first; the second puts the quest for knowledge first. (E) is closest to that idea. (A) is incorrect because only Passage 2 deals with both animal and human lab subjects. (B) is wrong because subjective care is never mentioned. (C) is wrong because we're never told which approach is more practical. (D) is wrong because the conflict is between care and knowledge, not doctors and patients.

10. **B** A distinction between research (biology) and patient care (medicine) would weaken Passage 2's assertion that research is the most important part of medicine. (A) strengthens Passage 2 rather than weakening it. (C) is irrelevant. (D) is out of scope. (E) is irrelevant to the argument.

11. **A** The author draws parallels between ancient and modern medicine to emphasize the importance of patient care in medicine. (B) and (D) are incorrect because the author does not mention a change in priorities or make a value judgment about modern medicine. (C) is never indicated by the passage and is extreme. (E) is not mentioned in the passage, so (A) is the only supported answer.

12. **B** Both passages mention the importance of patients in the practice of medicine. (A) is wrong because scientific discovery is not mentioned in Passage 1. (C) is out of scope. (D) is only the opinion of Passage 2. (E) is wrong because Passage 2 does not indicate the primacy of patient care.

13. **B** Here we have to infer something about the northwestern corner of Botswana. The passage tells us in lines 5–6 that "the northwest corner was said to hold abundant game up until 1973." The author wouldn't have added that "until 1973" tag unless something had changed in 1973! This makes (B) the best choice. (A) is too extreme ("All of its wildlife will be destroyed"). (C) is also too extreme ("no effect") and wrong to boot. (D) argues that the world "must" do something, which is almost never right. (E) says the basin "was drained" when the passage says only that it "may be drained" (lines 8–9).

14. **D** Why does the author of the first passage believe that we should study the Serengeti? The Serengeti is, according to the third paragraph, important because of the "light it might shed on man's survival." (A), (B), and (E) are not supported by the passage, and (C) is the opposite of information stated in the passage. (D) is a nice paraphrase of the passage, making it the correct answer.

15. **C** This question is asking for the purpose of a quote. The quote shows how the animals' survival is linked to man's survival. (C) is the answer closest to this. (A), (B), (D), and (E) are not mentioned in the passage.

16. **C** Vocab-in-Context. The clue *produces* tells us we can replace *yields* with something like *products*, making (C) the best answer.

17. **A** Go back to lines 31–37 and read for context. The canaries are used to help save human lives, as are the wild monkeys used to create the Salk vaccine. (B) is reversing information stated in the passage. (C) and (D) are not supported by the passage, and (E) is extreme.

18. **C**   Here we have a Lead Word question. We should find where the passage mentions John Owen and read before that. The author mentions that the wildebeest had appeared to be overgrazing and that they had been counted in 1958; therefore, there had been some prior study of them. That's what (C) says. (A) and (B) are extreme. (D) and (E) are unsupported by the passage.

19. **B**   Line reference question. Go back to lines 61–64, read above and below, and think why the author discusses the three studies. The studies show that the wildebeest were not overgrazing, as their population was increasing. This is what (B) says. (A), (C), (D), and (E) are not supported by the passage.

20. **A**   The "principal regulating mechanism" was the way in which the wildebeest population was naturally controlled through starvation, birth, and death. (B) is not supported by the passage, and (C), (D), and (E) are not even mentioned in the passage.

21. **D**   What did the Research Institute conclude? According to the last paragraph, the Serengeti consists of a system of interdependent relationships. (D) is an excellent paraphrase of this. (A), (C), and (E) are not supported by the passage. (B), while it is a logical conclusion to make with outside information, is not mentioned in the passage.

22. **E**   Passage 2 shows how the animals in the Serengeti have maintained their survival, supporting the claim made in (E). (A), (B), (C), and (D) are not affected by the information presented in Passage 2.

23. **B**   The author of Passage 1 says that the Serengeti is an exception among many areas in that conditions have thus far favored animals over human development. (A) is the opposite of this claim. (C), (D), and (E) are not supported by the passage. (B) is the best answer.

24. **A**   Both authors recognize the system of interdependencies present in the Serengeti. (B), (C), (D), and (E) are not supported by both passages. (A) is.

Section 2

1. **A**   We can see that the perimeter of this rectangle is made up of 14 segments—four sides each on top and bottom, and three each on the left and right sides. Each of these segments has length 2, so the whole perimeter will be 14 times 2, or 28.

2. **B**   Let's try plugging in a number for z to solve this problem. What if we try making $z = 2$? (Remember that we have to obey the rule in the question, which says that z must be an even integer.) If $z = 2$, then (A) becomes 6, (B) becomes 5, (C) becomes 4, (D) becomes 2, and (E) becomes 4. Since the question asks which of the following must be an odd integer, we can eliminate any of the choices that are not odd integers. This means we get to eliminate (A), (C), (D), and (E). This leaves us only with (B), which must be our answer.

3. **E** If 16 feet of the tree are below ground, then the other 80 feet of the tree must be above ground. Thus, the fraction of the tree that is above ground is $\frac{80}{96}$. Now we can divide on the calculator to get .883 or 83.3%.

4. **C** To solve a direct variation problem, set up a proportion. If 24 cookies are sold on the 4th of the month, finding the number sold on the 20th sets up as $\frac{\text{Day 4}}{24 \text{ cookies}} = \frac{\text{Day 20}}{x \text{ cookies}}$; cross-multiplying the proportion gives 120 cookies.

5. **B** This question has the words "in terms of" and variables in the answer choices in it, so we know this is a good Plugging In problem. Let's try plugging in a nice easy number for n. If we make $n = 2$, then we can solve so that x must be equal to $\frac{1}{2}$. The question then asks for the value of n. According to the numbers we picked, $n = 2$. So let's write that number down and circle it—that's our target. Now whichever answer choice equals 2 (remembering that $x = \frac{1}{2}$) will be our answer. (A) is equal to $\frac{\frac{1}{2}}{40}$, which does not equal 2. (B) is equal to $4 \times \frac{1}{2}$, which *does* equal 2. Let's check the other choices to be sure; (C) equals 20, (D) equals 50, and (E) equals 100, so (B) is correct.

6. **E** Admittedly, this is a trick question, designed more to test our ability to read and pay attention than much about functions. The "minus 4" given here is outside the notation $f(x)$, indicating that the function $4x^2 + 3x + 8$ should simply have 4 subtracted from it, leaving $4x^2 + 3x + 4$. (This is very different from asking what $f(x - 4)$ would equal, which is an easy mistake to make if we're not reading carefully.)

7. **D** This is a great Plugging In the Answers problem, but let's do some Ballparking first to narrow down the answer choices we have to work with. Since there are 80 students on the trip and there were more boys than girls, the number of girls has to be less than 40. Cool—that eliminates (A), (B), and (C)! Now we can start with either of the remaining answer choices and PITA. Let's start with (D): If there are 33 girls, we can add 14 for a total of 47 boys. Does 33 + 47 equal 80? Yes, so (D) is the correct answer.

8. **E** This question is testing whether we understand how to calculate the volume of a cube. Remember that the volume of any object is equal to the base times the height times the depth. Since each of these is the same on a cube, we can just take any one side and cube it (or multiply it by itself, and then by itself again) to get the volume. But first we need to figure out the length of the sides. Since the area of a square face is 36, and the area of a square is equal to one side squared, we know that each side must measure 6. Therefore, the volume of the cube will be 6 × 6 × 6, or 216.

9. **B** Because this problem gives us actual amounts (no ratios, variables, etc.) in the answer choices, and it's structured to tempt us to write an equation, it's a great Plugging In the Answers problem. Let's start with (C) and say that z equals 32. Then w would equal four times that, or 128. Add those

numbers to the 125 items already in the chart (33 cupcakes + 68 cookies + 24 doughnuts), and we get 285. The problem said our total was 260, so (C) is too large—which means we can also eliminate (D) and (E). Moving on to (B), we get z equals 27, so w equals 108. Add 27 and 108 to the 125 items already in the chart, and we get 260—bingo!

10.   A   For this problem, you'll have to remember the meaning of "median," which is the middle number in any group of numbers when they have been put in order. In this case, you'll notice that the median of each group of numbers is 6. So the question is: Which group has an average that is less than 6? Of course, one way to solve this is to find the average of each group using your calculator. With a little test-taking logic, though, we can narrow down the choices. Choices (C) and (D) have numbers that are evenly spaced around the middle number (6), so you can probably tell at a glance that their averages will both be 6. Choices (B) and (E) have numbers to the right of 6 that are farther from 6 than the numbers on the left, so their averages will be greater than 6. Verify your work by finding the average of the numbers in choice (A)—it's the only one with an average less than 6.

11.   D   This is another great question for PITA—Plugging In the Answers. Let's start with (C). If a customer buys 7 shirts, then the total bill will be:

shirt 1	4.50
shirt 2	4.50
shirt 3	4.50
shirt 4 (50% off)	4.50
shirt 5	4.50
shirt 6	4.50
shirt 7	4.50
Total:	$29.25

This is a bit smaller than the $31.50 that we know the customer spent, so (C), (B), and (A) can be eliminated and we should try a larger number. How about (D)? For 8 shirts, the total would be:

shirt 1	4.50
shirt 2	4.50
shirt 3	4.50
shirt 4 (50% off)	4.50
shirt 5	4.50
shirt 6	4.50
shirt 7	4.50
Total:	31.50

Our total is $31.50, so (D) is correct.

12.	**B**	Let's factor the top and bottom of the expression to try to find something to cancel out. Starting with the top: $x^2 - x - 12 = (x - 4)(x + 3)$. Next, we factor the bottom: $2x^2 - 10x + 8 = 2(x^2 - 5x + 4) = 2(x - 4)(x - 1)$. So, the equation is now $\dfrac{(x-4)(x+3)}{2(x-4)(x-1)} = \dfrac{5}{2}$. The $(x - 4)$ cancels out of the top and bottom. So, $\dfrac{(x+3)}{2(x-1)} = \dfrac{5}{2}$. Multiply both sides by 2, to get $\dfrac{(x+3)}{(x-1)} = 5$. Multiply both sides by $(x - 1)$ to get $x + 3 = 5x - 5$. Subtract x from both sides and add 5 to both sides to get $8 = 4x$. Divide by 4 to get $x = 2$.

13.	**B**	This could be done with Plugging In because there are variables in the answer choices, but translating English to Math is also a great way to go—do whatever works better for you. Let's try translating: *Is at most* means *the greatest value x could be*, which in math terms means ≤. So $x \le$ something. Already, we can get rid of (D) and (E). *10 less* means we have to subtract 10. (A) and (B) look promising because they both have –10 in them. *The amount by which z is greater than y* means $z - y$, and twice that is $2(z - y)$. The –10 should be outside the parentheses, so the only answer that completely matches is (B).

14	**C**	Instead of figuring out all the factors of each of the answer choices and looking for consecutive multiples of three, let's just take consecutive multiples of three and multiply them until we get in the ballpark of the answer choices. 3 and 6 have a product of 18, which is way too small, so let's move up a bit. 12 and 15 have a product of 180, so that's closer, but still too small. 15 and 18 have a product of 270, which is answer choice (C).

15	**D**	If the line segment is defined by points (6, –3) and (6, 9), we know that the x-coordinate (6) doesn't change. The line, therefore, goes from –3 to 9 vertically through 6 on the x-axis. This is a distance of 12 units, so halfway will be 6 units from each end. This places the midpoint at 3 on the vertical line. So, the final coordinates of the midpoint will be (6, 3). (We could also have made a quick sketch to help us visualize the problem.)

16	**B**	If the ratio of a to b is 4 : 7 and the ratio of c to d is 2 : 5 then we can simply plug in the numbers 4 for a, 7 for b, 2 for c, and 5 for d. This makes the ratio of bc to ad equal to (7)(2) to (4)(5), which is a ratio of 14 : 20. This reduces to 7 : 10, which is answer choice (B).

17	**C**	Notice the word *must* in the question? Let's plug in so that we can work with real numbers, and because the word *must* is in the problem, we can expect to plug in more than once. Because we want to use numbers that are easy to work with, let's use 78, 80, and 82 for the first three tests and 88 and 92 for the last two. That makes I true, II true, and III false. Since the question asks for what must be true, and we've seen an example in which III is false, we can eliminate any answer choice that contains III. Good-bye, (D) and (E)!

18   **D**   First, let's do some Ballparking. Since the square has a side of length 10, the area of the square is 100. The shaded region is pretty small in comparison—maybe about 10 or 12. Only (D) comes close to that approximation; (A), (B), and (E) are negative! (Remember, π is about 3.)

If we want to check our Ballparking with math, we would again start with 100 as the area of the square. Now let's remove the area of the circle to get the size of the remaining area (which includes the shaded region, and the identically shaped area just below it). Since these are each semicircles, together they will make one complete circle, with a radius of 5. (We know the radius is 5 because it's half of one side of the square.) This means that the area of the circle will be 25π. So once we remove the area of the circle, what is left is $100 - 25\pi$. Now the shaded region is only half of this, so we need to divide by two, and the area of the shaded region will be $\frac{100 - 25\pi}{2}$.

19. **D**   We know from the *must* in this problem that we should be prepared to plug in more than once. The value of x has to be divisible by both 3 and 4, because $\frac{x}{4}$ and $\frac{x}{3}$ are both integers. So we can try 12 for x; 12 gives us an odd integer for $\frac{x}{4}$ and an even integer for $\frac{x}{3}$. Now we can go down to the Roman numerals.

Roman numeral I is true, because 3 − 4 is odd. In fact, since the problem tells us directly that $\frac{x}{4}$ is odd and $\frac{x}{3}$ is even, and an odd number minus an even number will always be odd, we can eliminate any answer choice that doesn't have I in it—good-bye, (B).

Roman numeral II isn't true this time, because 12 isn't odd. So we can eliminate any remaining answer choices that have II in them, and (C) and (E) go away.

Now we just have to figure out if III *must* be true. It's true with the first number we plugged in, because $\left(\frac{12}{3}\right)^2 = 16$, which is even. In fact, since we know from the problem that $\frac{x}{3}$ is always even, the square of $\frac{x}{3}$ will always be even, so III is correct. That leaves us with only answer choice (D).

20. **C**   Let's start by finding the area of the triangle. We know that the triangle has a base of 9 and a height of 8, so its area will be $\frac{1}{2} \times 9 \times 8$, or 36. Now, we know that the triangle and the circle have equal areas, so the circle must also have area 36. To solve for the radius of the circle, remember the formula for the area of a circle, which is $a = \pi r^2$. We know the area is 36, so we know that $36 = \pi r^2$.

To solve for the radius r we first need to divide each side by π, which gives us $\frac{36}{\pi} = r^2$.

Now we take the square root of each side:

$$\sqrt{\frac{36}{\pi}} = r, \text{ so}$$

$$\frac{6}{\sqrt{\pi}} = r$$

This is answer choice (C).

Section 3

25. **B** The clue *quiet* and triggers *though* and *surprisingly* tell us that we need to fill in the blank with an opposite word from *quiet,* such as *talkative.* Answer choice (B) comes closest.

26. **E** The trigger *although* and clue *a few critics* indicate that Isabel needed something more than a few critics' support, so *broad* would be a good replacement for the blank. Only (E) fits that definition.

27. **A** The clue *differences* tells us that *different* would be a good word for the first blank, allowing us to eliminate (C) and (D). We need something opposite for the second blank, since they put their differences *behind them,* so *same* is a good word to write down for the second blank. That eliminates (B) and (E), so only (A) is left.

28. **B** Since the divers *could see no more than a few feet in front of their faces,* the water was *opaque* or even *not see-through.* (B) comes closest to our word.

29. **C** The clues are *checked every reference* and *always used the correct form,* so *careful* or *thorough* are good words for the blank. That allows us to eliminate all answer choices except (C).

30. **A** The quote emphasizes what a strong impression meeting Susan B. Anthony had on the author, and is supported by the author's ability to recollect the event in detail. (B), (C), and (E) are not even mentioned in the passage, and (D) is not supported.

31. **C** The pale blue ribbons would *stand out* against the gray clothes, making (C) the best answer.

32. **E** *Predilection* can be replaced with a word such as *tendency,* based on the context of the passage. The closest answer choice is (E).

33. **E** The theory says that both scientists and criminals are driven to achieve in their own fields by the prospect of attracting mates, which is best described by answer choice (E). (A) and (D) are not supported by the passage, and (B) and (C) state the theory incompletely. Furthermore, (B) is too strong by suggesting that finding a mate is the *main* goal of scientific discoveries.

34.   C   This Reasoning question asks what role the parenthetical statement plays in the story. This means we have to read a few lines back and a few lines ahead to get a sense of the context. When we do this, we find that people are worried about the sudden screaming, but don't have the courage to be the first to bring it up. The parenthetical statement offers a scientific-sounding excuse for their inaction—otherwise known as a *rationalization*—and that makes (C) correct. (A) suggests that the narrator believes that everyone should think in the third person, which goes against common sense. (B) makes it sound as if the author actually believes the parenthetical statement is important advice, when the opposite is true: the quoted thoughts are actually being mocked here. (D) pulls a psychiatric diagnosis pretty much out of nowhere, and (E) is wrong because the passage did not say anything about the people being surprised.

35.   E   This question asks with which of five statements the author would agree. Of course, you can't read the author's mind; the only thing you have to go by is the passage. So this boils down to a Main Idea question. In this case, we have a tale of a city that is haunted by a mysterious screaming that everyone is afraid to talk about. Endless disembodied screaming is not very realistic, even if you live in New York, so the screaming is probably symbolic. What does it stand for? You can probably think of all sorts of terrible things that everyone knows about, but few people talk about. (One famous example would be Nazi Germany, where millions of people were carted off in trains and killed, but the people who remained went about their lives as if there were nothing wrong or even strange about this.) The screaming could stand for many things, but they're all bad. That makes the answer (E): The story is about some sort of evil that everyone is well aware of, but won't talk about, and how the fear of speaking out allows the evil to go on. (A) and (B) are the opposite of the lesson the author is trying to teach. (C) is not supported in the passage; the screaming goes on day and night and the author does not indicate that it drives people more crazy at night. (D) might sound like something the author would think, but "never" is too strong of a word.

36.   C   This question is a Vocab-in-Context question. It asks about the moment that the foreign visitor arrives in the city and hears the screaming for the first time. He gives a ------- of horror: a squeal? a jump? Something like that. (C) looks good. (B) doesn't mean squeal or jump and (D) doesn't fit, because he certainly wasn't pleased. (A) is too calm to be the stranger's reaction: a sympathetic stare of horror? And (E) is based on a misreading: The stranger is startled by the endless scream, not producing it.

37.   E   This looks like a Reasoning question, and it is, but since the narrator explains exactly what the line is intended to mean, in effect it's more of a Go-Fetch question. The line being asked about reads, "The packaging of words with varied intentions is like writing a letter to someone in a foreign land and addressing it to oneself; it never reaches its destination." That is, the message doesn't get through. And that's what (E) says. (A) and (C) say exactly the opposite of the author's intended meaning. (B) is too literal; the stranger doesn't really need a translation, because he speaks the same language as the head of the welcoming committee. (D) can be tempting, because there is a foreign visitor in town, but the author doesn't mention dignitaries and is not advocating the "packing of words with varied intentions" either.

38. **A** This is a Go-Fetch question, and lines 68–69 answer this question for us: "He dismissed the thought. The Rest Home was full, and the fees were high. He enjoyed the comforts of civilization." If the Rest Home is full, and fees are high, we can infer that the specialist is making a lot of money. This is confirmed by the next sentence: the "comforts of civilization" are material luxuries—a nice house, a nice car, fine food, that sort of thing. (In line 76 we learn that he drives a Jaguar.) So (A) is clearly the answer, so long as we know that "replete with" means "full of." (B) is too strong, since line 73 indicates that panic is only a possibility. (C) would benefit the specialist, so that's no reason to dismiss the thought. (D) doesn't have any support in the passage, while (E) attributes to him a xenophobia, or fear of foreigners, which also has no support in the text.

39. **B** This is another general Reasoning question that asks us to sum up the purpose of the whole passage. We've read enough of the passage to know that this is a story in which one night a city is suddenly filled with the sound of an endless, disembodied screaming. This is surreal enough that we can probably conclude that the screaming is symbolic. What does it symbolize? Whatever it stands for, knowing that the screaming is a metaphor for something means that we can eliminate (D), which is too literal and which also wrongly calls the story a "trivialization." We can also eliminate (C) and (E), since the story may *contain* many metaphors and symbols, but is not itself a metaphor for or symbol of anything. (A) is not completely right; while job security is mentioned (the assistant fears he will be fired), it's not the main theme. This leaves us with (B), which seems right: An allegory is a story based around an extended metaphor, as this one is.

40. **A** If we go back and read the lines immediately following the idea that slang is nationwide, we find what Pei means by this: "There are some who think that only poorer and less educated people use slang. This is not necessarily true. A little bit of slang, in fact, is used by practically everybody." That is, slang is used by everyone, both educated people and less educated people. Now we need to find a choice that is a close paraphrase of this idea, which is choice (A). Choice (E) is tempting, but the notion of jargon is not addressed until the fourth paragraph, so it can't be the correct answer to a question about the first paragraph.

41. **B** To solve this Vocab-in-Context question, read the sentence, and figure out what the meaning of the word should be from the context. In this case, we'd probably put in a phrase like *has a lot*. The choice that comes closest to this in meaning is (B).

42. **E** This question not only gives us the lead words Dizzy Dean and Shakespeare, but also tells us where the answer will be found: in the third paragraph. Let's go back to that part of the passage and see what it says. The first line states that, "In a many good cases, slang words and uses can be traced to one individual." Shakespeare and Dizzy Dean are given as examples, so our answer should be a paraphrase of this line. Thus, (A), (B), and (C) are out. Be careful about (D), which has deceptive wording. Though the passage does say that slang can be traced to one person "in many good cases," the world "usually" is too strong. (E) is best.

43. **A** According to line 32, the word *cant* was the "language of the underworld." This has to be our answer; now we need to find the choice that best paraphrases *underworld*, which is choice (A).

44. **C** We can use the lead words *François Villon* to find the place in the passage where the answer to this question will be found. François Villon is mentioned in the fourth paragraph, around lines 32–35. The passage states at that point that he "used in many of his poems a type of Paris underworld cant that cannot be understood today." Evidently, the passage cites him in order to show that some kinds of speech can no longer be understood in modern times. Now let's look for a choice that paraphrases this idea. Choice (C) says exactly this: that some kinds of speech are no longer current usage. None of the other choices have evidence to support them from this part of the passage.

45. **D** Let's go back to the lines in question and read what the author says at that point in the passage. He says that some examples of cant "are generally understood and even used, though are not the best language in the world." So even if the expressions aren't always appropriate, they are almost always understood. Now we need a paraphrase of that. (A), (B), and (C) find no support in the passage. (E) is too broad and a little too negative. (D) is a good paraphrase.

46. **C** Here's another Vocab-in-Context question. If we cover up the word *measure* and use context to put our own word in the blank, we'd probably choose something like *a certain amount*. Choice (C) comes closest to this in meaning.

47. **A** Let's go back to the passage, around the middle of the fifth paragraph, where these lines appear. The passage states, "But it is not only the intellectual professions that have jargons; it is also the manual trades and occupations," and then goes on to cite the example of shipboard terminology. This means that shipboard terminology is cited as an example of how jargon has evolved in manual trades and occupations, as well as in other places. Now let's find a choice that paraphrases this idea, which is what choice (A) does.

48. **B** According to the blurb, this passage is about the history and significance of slang. Already this should make (B) and (C) look like good choices, but let's see why the others can be eliminated. Choices (D) and (E) are too narrow—cant and important individuals are mentioned only in one paragraph each, so they couldn't be the main idea. Likewise, jargon is only discussed in one paragraph, so choice (A) can be eliminated. Now we're down to (B) and (C). This is a tough choice, but (C) is a little too broad—it's very difficult to do a complete history of slang in only a few paragraphs. But to discuss some of the origins and variations is more feasible, and this what the passage tries to do.

Section 4

21.　**E**　First let's convert minutes to seconds by setting up a proportion: $\dfrac{1\,\text{min}}{60\,\text{sec}} = \dfrac{2\,\text{min}}{x\,\text{sec}}$. Cross-multiply to find that 2 minutes is 120 seconds. Next, let's set up another proportion to find the number of files: $\dfrac{4\,\text{files}}{1\,\text{sec}} = \dfrac{z\,\text{files}}{120\,\text{sec}}$. Cross-multiply to find $z = 480$.

22.　**E**　Let's draw triangle *ABC* with equal sides. If it's equilateral, that means all the angles are equal, too. Remember, congruent figures have the same shape and size, so draw triangle *DEF* to look the same as triangle *ABC*. Since all three angles in triangle *ABC* are equal and add up to 180 degrees, they must each be 60 degrees, as are all of the angles in triangle *DEF*.

23.　**E**　Make a ratio box. The sum of 7, 8, and 10 is 25, and $\dfrac{1,200}{25} = 48$, so the multiplier is 48. The largest share is 10, and $10 \times 48 = 480$.

24.　**A**　Plugging in $p = 5$, $q = 2$, $r = 6$, and $s = 3$ turns the expression into $\dfrac{\cancel{2}(5)}{\cancel{2}} - \dfrac{6}{2(3)} = 5 - 1 = 4$, our target number. Now let's plug in the same numbers for the variables in the answer choices, to see which equals 4. (A) equals 4, but we have to go through all of the answer choices to make sure only one of them equals our target. (B) equals $\dfrac{1}{3}$, so we can eliminate it. (C) is going to be negative, so we can eliminate it with Ballparking. (D) equals $\dfrac{1}{2}$, and (E) equals -1, so only (A) is equal to our target.

25.　**C**　Because we have variables in the answer choices, this is a Plugging In problem. The easiest variables to start with are *a* and *b*, because they're being used repeatedly and having so many things done to them. Let's plug in $a = 3$ and $b = 2$. Therefore, $c = 3 \times \dfrac{1}{4} = \dfrac{3}{4}$ (remember, negative exponents mean to take the reciprocal of the number being raised to an exponent) and $d = \dfrac{1}{3} \times 2^4 = \dfrac{16}{3}$. So $cd = \dfrac{3}{4} \times \dfrac{16}{3}$, or 4. Our target is 4, so now we need to go through all the answer choices and eliminate anything that doesn't equal 4. We can ballpark out (A), because it's going to be a fraction less than 1. (B) would also be way too small. (C) works, because $2^2 = 4$, but remember we have to keep going until the end. (D) is going to be way too small, and (E) is $\dfrac{3}{2}$, so only (C) equals our target. Alternatively, you can just say that $c = \dfrac{a}{b^2}$ and $d = \dfrac{b^4}{a}$, so $cd = \dfrac{a}{b^2} \times \dfrac{b^4}{a}$. Cross-cancel and you're left with b^2.

26.   **A**   Let's plug in our own numbers, starting with x. If $x = 2$, then $a = 9(2^2) + 4 = 40$ and $b = 3(2) + 2 = 8$. The question asks for the value of a, so 40 is our target. (A) equals 40, so we can keep it and work through the rest of the answer choices. We can ballpark (B) out because it's going to be 4 less than (A). (C) equals 64, so it's too large. (D) equals 360 and (E) is even larger, so (A) is the only answer that works.

27.   **B**   From the information provided we know that $\frac{1}{3}$ of the 15 integers are even. That means $\frac{2}{3}$ of the 15 integers are odd. To find a probability we need the relationship of number of things that meet the requirement to the total number of things. Therefore, Roman numeral I can be determined because the probability of selecting an odd number is $\frac{2}{3}$. Roman numeral II cannot be determined; we have no idea how many numbers in the group are not the mode. Roman numeral III cannot be determined because we don't know what the greatest and least numbers in the group are.

28.   **B**   First, let's draw in $\overline{BC}$ and $\overline{AC}$. A line tangent to a circle is perpendicular to the radius at the point of contact. So, $\overline{AB}$ is perpendicular to $\overline{AC}$, and ABC is a right triangle. If you don't recognize it as a 5-12-13 triangle, you could have used the Pythagorean theorem to find the third side: $AC^2 + 12^2 = 13^2$. So, $AC = 5$. That means the radius of the circle is 5. Plug that into $\text{Area} = \pi r^2 = \pi(5)^2 = 25\pi$.

29.   **139**   We don't actually have to know the individual values of x and y to solve this problem. We know that we have two parallel lines in this diagram, so we know that the angle opposite the angle measuring 41 degrees must also measure 41 degrees.

Therefore we have an angle of 41 degrees plus the angle marked x and y on the same line —which tells us that their sum must be 180. So we know that $41 + x + y = 180$ and that $x + y$ therefore must equal 139.

30.   **1 or 2**

x is a negative integer but $|x|$ is less than 3. So what values of x could satisfy that inequality? If $x = -1$, then $|x| = 1$ and that would work. If $x = -2$, then $|x| = 2$ and that would work. If $x = -3$ then $|x| = 3$ and that isn't less than 3. Other negative values for x will have the same problem, so the only values of x that satisfy the inequlity are -1 and -2. However, we're looking for the value of $|x|$, and thus the answer is 1 or 2.

31. $\dfrac{4}{3}$ **or 1.33**

   If the sum of 4 and some number (we can call it x) is equal to $4 + x = 4x$. Now we can solve for x:

   $$4 + x = 4x$$

   By subtracting x from each side we get:

   $$4 = 3x$$

   $$\text{so,} \; \dfrac{4}{3} = x$$

   That makes our answer $\dfrac{4}{3}$ or 1.33.

32. **90** We know that the angles in a triangle always add up to 180, so we know that $\dfrac{1}{2}a + \dfrac{1}{2}a + a = 180$. Now we can solve for a. If we add $\dfrac{1}{2}a + \dfrac{1}{2}a + a$, we get $2a$, so we know that $2a = 180$ and that $a = 90$.

33. **6,563** The question is really saying that the first term is $2 + 3^1 = 5$, the second term is $2 + 3^2 = 11$, etc. So, the 8th term is $2 + 3^8$. Let's apply PEMDAS and work with the exponent first: $2 + 3^8 = 2 + 6{,}561$. Then, we can add to get 6,563.

34. **105** The best way to try to find four consecutive integers whose sum is 414 is to start by finding the average: Each number is somewhere in the neighborhood of 103. So let's just start trying these numbers: $103 + 104 + 105 + 106$ equals 418, which is too large. So let's try $102 + 103 + 104 + 105$. That makes 414, so these are our four consecutive integers. The question asks for the greatest of them, so the answer is 105.

35. **9** Remember that an isosceles right triangle (which is the same as half of a square) with a side of x will have a hypotenuse of $x\sqrt{2}$. So to get a diagonal of $3\sqrt{2}$, the sides of the triangle (and therefore of the square) must be equal to 3. If the sides of the square are equal to 3, then its area will be equal to 3 times 3, or 9.

36. **8** Let's try Plugging In on this problem. We need to choose a value for n that is a prime number greater then 3, so let's try using 5. The question then reads: How many divisors of 30 are there? The divisors of 30 are 1 and 30, 2 and 15, 3 and 10, 5 and 6, for a total of 8 divisors. For whichever values of n we try, we'll always get the same answer.

37. $\dfrac{16}{5}$ **or 3.2**

   We know that $x^2 - y^2 = 16$, and since $x^2 - y^2$ can be written as $(x + y)(x - y)$, we know that $(x + y)(x - y) = 16$. The question also tells us that $(x + y) = 5(x - y) = 16$. The question then asks us for $(x - y)$, which we can now solve for: $\dfrac{16}{5}$, or 3.2.

38. $\dfrac{2}{9}$ or .222

Since we don't know how many total envelopes there are to stuff, and therefore the question is asking for fractions of an unknown, this is a great Plugging In problem. Let's say there are 120 envelopes to stuff. (120 is a good number because 120 is divisible by 3, 4, and 6.) If Sally could stuff all the envelopes in 3 hours, she works at a rate of 40 envelopes per hour. Abdul can stuff all the envelopes in 4 hours, so he works at a rate of 30 envelopes per hour. Juanita would take 6 hours to stuff all the envelopes, so she works at a rate of 20 envelopes per hour. Therefore, the group can stuff envelopes at a rate of 90 per hour (40 + 30 + 20), since they do the whole job together. Juanita will stuff 20 of every 90 envelopes, or $\dfrac{2}{9}$. We can grid that in as, or divide on a calculator to get .222.

Section 5

1. **D**   Remember to watch out for misplaced modifiers when there's a phrase followed by a comma at the beginning of the sentence. In this case, *A large predatory snake* modifies *the muscular body,* which is incorrect. Only (B) and (D) put *boa constrictor* in front of the underlined portion, where it belongs, so we can eliminate the other answer choices. (B) doesn't make a complete sentence, though, so (D) is the best answer.

2. **C**   Be very careful of verbs that end in *–ing* on the PSAT. They often indicate awkward constructions that should be avoided. "Having received" in this case is a good example of this type of problem. In addition to being awkward, it's also passive, so you can cross off (A). (B) and (D) are adding in a lot of unnecessary words. Remember, on Improving Sentences questions, you want simple, concise answers when possible. (E) simply splices two sentences together with a comma. (C) is concise and correctly uses a semicolon to separate the two clauses.

3. **B**   The split between the answer choices shows that we need to make a decision between *than* and *as*. The correct idiom is *as…as* (e.g., "dancing is *as* fun *as* singing"), so we can eliminate (A) and (D). (C) changes the pronoun *you,* used in the underlined portion, to *one,* so it can be eliminated. (B) and (D) say the same thing, but (B) says it without adding redundant words, so it is the best choice.

4. **A**   The sentence is correct as written.

5. **B**   (A) and (D) try to splice two sentences together with a comma, so we can eliminate them. (C) has all the events of the sentence happening at the same time. Furthermore, it's passive, as is answer choice (E). (B) is the only answer choice that fixes the problem without adding new ones.

6. **D** As is typical when a sentence starts with a phrase followed by a comma, this sentence has a misplaced modifier. William Faulkner's books weren't famous writers—William Faulkner was. So (A) and (B) are incorrect. (C) and (E) use the word *including* to make it sound like Faulkner was doing something, when in fact he was simply known for certain books. Only (D) is short and direct, so it is the best answer.

7. **E** The sentence is passive in two places: *were implied* and *not promised by him*. Only (E) fixes both errors.

8. **C** *Cleaning* is not parallel to the other verb in the sentence, *to watch*. Only (C) makes the verbs parallel.

9. **C** Here again we have two sentences spliced together with a comma, so the underlined portion needs a conjunction that better connects the two parts of the sentence. Since the second part goes in a different direction than the first part, the conjunction *but* is the best option, and (C) is correct.

10. **E** The underlined portion is missing a verb, and only (C) and (E) correct the problem. However, (C) puts *helicopter* before the modifying phrase, *the Italian artist and inventor*, which creates a misplaced modifier. (E) doesn't create a misplaced modifier, so it's the best choice.

11. **D** *Couldn't hardly* is a double negative, and only (D) and (E) correct the error. (D) is shorter and more direct, so it is the best answer.

12. **C** *Seem…to be* is the correct idiom, so we can eliminate (A), (B), and (E). *Intending to* is another idiom, so (C) is correct.

13. **A** The sentence is correct as written.

14. **D** *Prevented…to* is an incorrect idiom, so we can eliminate (A). The proper idiom is *prevented…from.* The remaining answer choices are split between *have* and *has,* so we need to decide whether a singular or plural verb is necessary. Subjects joined by *neither…nor* follow the same rule as subjects followed by *either…or;* if they're both singular, the subject is singular. So we need a singular verb, and only (D) fits the bill.

15. **B** *Considered* does not require either *as* or *to be* after it, so (A), (C), and (D) can be eliminated. (E) changes the meaning of the sentence, suggesting that Hurston herself was a consideration of some kind, so we can eliminate it. That leaves only (B).

16. **C** *Concerned about* is the correct idiom, so we can eliminate (A), (B), and (E). Choice (D) changes the meaning of the sentence, so (C) is correct.

17. **C** Here we have two sentences spliced together with a comma, so we can eliminate (A) and also (E), which repeats the error. (B) and (D) are incorrect because a semicolon must connect two independent clauses, which leaves only (C).

18.   **C**   The *natural source of sugar* is not something that can be done, as the sentence states. (A), (B), and (E) all have that error. (A), (B), and (E) are also redundant because the sentence already says that this is an age-old practice, making it unnecessary to also say that it has been done for many years. (D) creates a sentence fragment. (C) fixes the error without creating new ones.

19.   **B**   The word *would* does not belong in the "if" part of a sentence; if-clauses should use the word *were*. For example, "If I *were* rich, I would buy an expensive car," or "*Were* I to exercise more often, I could probably lose weight." So we can eliminate (A), (D), and (E). (C) is out because *taking* is not right. We're not talking about something that is happening right now. (B) is the best choice.

20.   **E**   As written, the sentence says that all the *children* are sharing one big *stamp*. This seems unlikely. They really ought to bring *stamps*, plural. That narrows it down to (D) and (E). And then (D) says that the kids are ganging up to write one huge *letter!* That needs to be *letters*, so (E) is the answer.

21.   **E**   The sentence is correct as written.

22.   **A**   The preposition *with* isn't idiomatically correct when paired with *indebted. Indebted to* would be correct.

23.   **D**   The possessive pronoun *its* doesn't agree with the subject, *reference books. Their* would be correct.

24.   **D**   The verb *answering* isn't parallel to the verb *to reply.* The correct form would be *to answer.*

25.   **B**   *Peter Straub* is being compared to *the works of Stephen King,* which creates an improper comparison. *To the works of Peter Straub, those of Peter Straub,* or *to Peter Straub's* would be correct.

26.   **B**   *Scarcely no* is a double negative. *Scarcely any* would be correct.

27.   **B**   The verb *are* is plural and is paired with a singular subject, *understanding. Is* would be correct. Be careful—sometimes a subject can come after the verb.

28.   **E**   The sentence is correct as written.

29.   **A**   The adjective *recent* is being used to modify the verb *conducted,* but an adverb should be used instead. *Recently* would be correct.

30.   **B**   *Or* is not correct when paired with *neither. Nor* would be correct.

31.   **A**   The adjective *newest* should only be used when comparing three or more things, and the sentence says that there are two violinists. *Newer* would be correct.

32.   **E**   The sentence is correct as written.

33.   **C**   *Reliant* is a diction error, as it means dependent. *Reliable* would be correct.

34.   **A**   The comparison *less* should only be used when the things being compared cannot be counted. Since Rhodes scholars can be counted, *fewer* would be correct.

35. **C** The first paragraph needs a sentence that connects the author's narrative about being afraid of bees to the fact that the author has a garden (that happens to be a good attractor of bees). (A) and (B) do not mention the garden. (D) doesn't mention the bees. (E) mentions both, but doesn't flow well into the second paragraph. (C) flows well from the first paragraph to the second.

36. **D** (A) creates a misplaced modifier, as it says the garden is terrified of going outside. (B) creates a change of direction between the two parts of the sentence, which is incorrect because the first sentence is the cause of the second sentence. (C) combines the sentences in a way that shows the causal relationship, but it's awkward. (E) is missing a verb and is constructed awkwardly. Only (D) is combined well.

37. **D** (D) best describes what the author does about the garden withering away, as is described in the rest of the passage.

38. **D** The pronoun *them* is ambiguous; it's not clear what it replaces. (B), (C), and (E) also contain ambiguous pronouns. Only (D) clearly states what the pronoun is replacing: the bees.

39. **B** Because the last part of the paragraph is set in the present, which is made clear in sentence 18, the clearest replacement for the underlined portion should be set in the present tense. Therefore, (B) is the best answer.

Paying For College 101

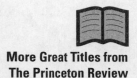

**More Great Titles from
The Princeton Review**
*Paying for College Without
Going Broke
The Best 371 Colleges*

If you're reading this book, you've already made an investment in your education. You may have shelled out some cold hard cash for this book, and you've definitely invested time in reading it. It's probably even safe to say that this is one of the smaller investments you've made in your future so far. You put in the hours and hard work needed to keep up your GPA. You've paid test fees and applications fees, perhaps even travel expenses. You have probably committed time and effort to a host of extracurricular activities to make sure colleges know that you're a well-rounded student.

But after you get in, there's one more issue to think about: How do you pay for college?

Let's be honest, college is not cheap. The average tuition for a private four-year college is about $25,000 a year. The average tuition of a four-year public school is about $6,500 a year. And the cost is rising. Every year the sticker price of college education bumps up about 6 percent.

Like many of us, your family may not have 25 grand sitting around in a shoebox. With such a hefty price tag, you might be wondering: "Is a college education really worth it?" The short answer: Yes! No question about it. A 2007 survey by the College Board showed that people with a college degree earn 60 percent more than people who enter the workforce with only a high school diploma. Despite its steep price tag, a college education ultimately pays for itself.

Still, the cost of college is no joke.

Here's the good news. Even in the wake of the current financial crisis, financial aid is available to almost any student who wants it. There is an estimated $143 billion—that's right, billion!—in financial aid offered to students annually. This comes in the form of federal grants, scholarships, state financed aid, loans, and other programs. Furthermore, the 2009 stimulus package made it easier to qualify for government aid, and lowered the interest rates on government loans.

We know that financial aid can seem like an overwhelmingly complex issue, but the introductory information in this chapter should help you grasp what's available and get you started in your search.

How Much Does College Really Cost?

When most people think about the price of a college education, they think of one thing and one thing alone: tuition. It's time to get that notion out of your head. While tuition is a significant portion of the cost of a college education, you need to think of all the other things that factor into the final price tag.

Let's break it down.

- Tuition and fees
- Room and board
- Books and supplies
- Personal expenses
- Travel expenses

Collectively, these things contribute to your total Cost of Attendance (COA) for one year at a college or university.

Understanding the distinction between tuition and COA is crucial because it will help you understand this simple equation:

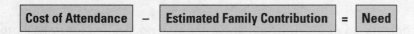

$$\text{Cost of Attendance} - \text{Estimated Family Contribution} = \text{Need}$$

When you begin the financial aid process, you will see this equation again and again. We've already talked about the COA, so let's talk about the Estimated Family Contribution, or EFC. The EFC simply means, "How much you and your family can afford to pay for college." Sounds obvious right?

Here's the catch: What you think you can afford to pay for college, what the government thinks you can afford to pay for college, and what a college or university thinks you can afford to pay for college are, unfortunately, three different things. Keep that in mind as we discuss financing options later on.

The final term in the equation is self-explanatory. Anything that's left after what you and your family have contributed, still needs to be covered. That's where financial aid packages come in.

Check out our Financial Aid Library
PrincetonReview.com/
FinancialAidAdvice.aspx

WHAT'S IN A FINANCIAL AID PACKAGE?

A typical financial aid package contains money—from the school, federal government, or state—in various forms: grants, scholarships, work-study programs, and loans.

Let's look at the non-loan options first. Non-loan options include grants, scholarships, and work-study programs. The crucial thing about them is that they involve monetary assistance that you won't be asked to pay back. They are as close as you'll get to "free money."

Grants

Grants are basically gifts. They are funds given to you by the federal government, state agencies, or individual colleges. They are usually need-based, and you are not required to pay them back.

One of the most important grants is the Pell Grant. Pell Grants are provided by the federal government but administered through individual schools. Under the 2009 stimulus package, the maximum award one can receive through the Pell Grant is $4,800 dollars a year.

You apply for a Pell Grant by filling out the Free Application for Federal Student Aid (FAFSA). Remember that acronym because you'll be seeing it again. Completing the FAFSA is the first step in applying for any federal aid. The FAFSA can be found online at www.fafsa.ed.gov.

There are several other major federal grant programs that hand out grants ranging from $100 to $4,000 dollars annually. Some of these grants are given to students entering a specific field of study and others are need-based, but all of them amount to money that you never have to pay back. Check out the FAFSA website for complete information about qualifying and applying for government grants.

The federal government isn't the only source of grant money. State governments and specific schools also offer grants. Use the Internet, your guidance counselor, and your library to see what non-federal grants you might be eligible for.

Scholarships

Like grants, you never have to pay a scholarship back. But the requirements and terms of a scholarship might vary wildly. Most scholarships are merit- or need-based, but they can be based on almost anything. There are scholarships based on academic performance, athletic achievements, musical or artistic talent, religious affiliation, ethnicity, and so on.

Believe It Or Not!
The Chick and Sophie Major Memorial Duck Calling Contest, held annually by the Chamber of Commerce of Stuggart, Arkansas, gives out a $1,500 scholarship to any high school senior who can master hailing, feeding, comeback, and mating duck calls.

When hunting for scholarships, one great place to start is the Department of Education's free "Scholarship Search," available at https://studentaid2.ed.gov/getmoney/scholarship. This database asks you a handful of questions about your academic history, interests, and future plans. It then uses this data to report on scholarships that you might be interested in pursuing. It's a free service and a great resource.

There is one important caveat about taking scholarship money. Some, but not all, schools think of scholarship money as income and will reduce the amount of aid they offer you accordingly. Know your school's policy on scholarship awards.

Check out the Scholarship Search Page
PrincetonReview.com/scholarships-financial-aid.aspx

Federal Work-Study (FWS)

One of the ways Uncle Sam disperses aid money is by subsidizing part-time jobs, usually on campus, for students who need financial aid. Because your school will administer the money, they get to decide what your work-study job will be. Work-study participants are paid by the hour, and federal law requires that they cannot be paid less than the federal minimum wage.

One of the benefits of a work-study program is that you get a paycheck just like you would at a normal job. The money is intended to go towards school expenses, but there are no controls over exactly how you spend it.

Colleges and universities determine how to administer work-study programs on their own campuses, so you must apply for a FWS at your school's financial aid office.

LOANS

Most likely, your entire COA won't be covered by scholarships, grants, and work-study income. The next step in gathering the necessary funds is securing a loan. Broadly speaking, there are two routes to go: federal loans and private loans. Once upon a time, which route to choose might be open for debate. But these days the choice is clear: *Always* try to secure federal loans first. Almost without exception, federal loans provide unbeatable low fixed-interest rates; they come with generous repayment terms; and, although they have lending limits, these limits are quite generous and will take you a long way toward your goal. We'll talk about the benefits of private loans later, but they really can't measure up to what the government can provide.

Stafford Loans

The Stafford loan is the primary form of federal student loan. There are two kinds of Stafford loans: direct Stafford loans, which are administered by the Department of Education; and Federal Family Education Loans (FFEL), which are administered by a private lender bound by the terms the government sets for Stafford loans (FFEL loans are sometimes referred to as indirect Stafford loans, as well). Both direct and FFEL loans can be subsidized or unsubsidized. Students with demonstrated financial need may qualify for subsidized loans. This means that the government pays interest accumulated during the time the student is in school. Students with unsubsidized Stafford loans are responsible for the interest accumulated while in school. You can qualify for a subsidized Stafford loan, an unsubsidized Stafford loan, or a mixture of the two.

Stafford loans are available to all full-time students and most part-time students. Though the terms of the loan are based on demonstrated financial need, lack of need is not considered grounds for rejection. No payment is expected while the student is attending school. The interest rate on your Stafford loan will depend on when your first disbursement is. The chart below shows the fixed rates set by the government.

First disbursement made on or after	Interest rate on unpaid balance
July 1, 2008 to July 1, 2009	6.0 percent
July 1, 2009 to July 1, 2010	5.6 percent
July 1, 2010 to July 1, 2011	4.5 percent
July 1, 2011 to July 1, 2012	3.4 percent

Finally, depending on the amount owed and the payment plan agreed upon by the borrower and lender, students have between 10 and 25 years to pay off their loan.

As with grants, you must start by completing the Free Application for Federal Student Aid (FAFSA) to apply for a Stafford loan.

PLUS Loans

Another important federal loan is the PLUS loan. This loan is designed to help parents and guardians put dependent students through college. Like the Stafford loan, a PLUS loan might be a direct loan from the government, administered by your school's financial aid office, or it might be administered by a private lender who is bound to federal guidelines. Unlike the Stafford loan, the PLUS has no fixed limits or fixed interest rates. The annual limit on a PLUS loan is equal to your COA minus any other financial aid you are already receiving. It may be used on top of a Stafford loan. The interest rates on PLUS loans are variable though often comparable to, or even lower than, the interest rates on Stafford loans. Borrowers can choose when they will start paying the loan back: starting either 60 days from the first disbursement or six months after the dependent student has finished school.

To apply for a PLUS loan, your guardians must apply to the financial aid office of your school or with a FFEL private lender.

Perkins Loans

A third and final federal loan you should be aware of is the Perkins loan. Intended to help out students in extreme need, the Perkins loan is a government-subsidized loan that is administered only through college and university financial aid offices. Under the terms of a Perkins loan, you may borrow up to $5,500 a year of undergraduate study, up to $27,500. The Perkins loan has a fixed interest rate of just 5 percent. Payments against the loan don't start until nine months after you graduate. Apply for Perkins loans through your school's financial aid office.

Private Lenders

If this section had been written two years ago, we'd have started off with a discussion of common criticisms of the federal loan system. Then we would have mentioned a few private lenders who were fighting what they believed was the good fight against a government-subsidized monopoly. Whether or not this critique was valid, the sudden collapse of the housing bubble, spurred on in no small part by shoddy lending practices from major banks, has made the argument irrelevant.

We said it before, and we'll say it again: DO NOT get a private loan until you've exhausted all other options.

Before the crisis, many private lenders could offer competitive interest rates and relatively generous qualification standards. Now, for the most part, that's no longer the case. Private lenders are growing increasing selective of the borrowers they lend to, and the average interest rate for private loans hovers around 13 percent.

Still, there are some benefits to securing a private loan. First off, many students find that non-loan and federal loan options don't end up covering the entire bill. If that's the case, then private lenders might just save the day. Second, loans from private sources generally offer you greater flexibility with how you use the funds. Third, private loans can be taken out at anytime during your academic career. Unlike most non-loan and government-backed financial options, you can turn to private lenders whenever you need them.

All private lenders are not the same! As the old song says, "You better shop around." Every lender is going to offer you a different package of terms. What you need to do is find the package that best fits your needs and plans. Aside from low interest rates, which are crucially important, there other terms and conditions you will want to look out for.

Low origination fees   Origination fees are fees that lenders charge you for taking out a loan. Usually the fee is simply deducted automatically from your loan checks. Obviously, the lower the origination fee, the better.

Minimal guaranty fees   A guaranty fee is an amount you pay to a third-party who agrees to insure your loan. That way, if the borrower—that is you—can't pay the loan back, the guarantor steps in and pays the difference. Again, if you can minimize or eliminate this fee, all the better.

Interest rate reductions   Some lenders will reduce your interest rates if you're reliable with your payments. Some will even agree to knock a little off the interest rate if you agree to pay your loans through a direct deposit system. When shopping for the best loan, pay careful attention to factors that might help you curb your interest rates.

Flexible payment plans   One of the great things about most federal loans is the fact that you don't have to start paying them off until you leave school. In order to compete, many private lenders have been forced to adopt similarly flexible payment plans. Before saying yes to a private loan, make sure that it comes with a payment timetable you can live with.

WHERE THERE'S A WILL THERE'S A WAY

No matter what the state of the economy, going to college will always make good financial sense. This is especially true today, with the wealth of low-interest federal assistance programs available to you. There are plenty of excellent financing options out there. With a little effort (and a lot of form-filling!) you'll be able to pay your way through school without breaking the bank.

The
Princeton
Review

PSAT

OUR NAME: _____
(Print)
         Last   First   M.I.

GNATURE: _____ DATE: _____ / _____ / _____

OME ADDRESS: _____
(Print)
                Number and Street

E-MAIL: _____

City   State   Zip

HONE NO.: _____ SCHOOL: _____ CLASS OF: _____
(Print)

IMPORTANT: Please fill in these boxes exactly as shown on the back cover of your text book. ▼

SCANTRON F-17982-PRP   P3 2803 628 5 4 3 2 1

© The Princeton Review, Inc.

5. YOUR NAME

First 4 letters of last name				FIRST INIT	MID INIT
Ⓐ	Ⓐ	Ⓐ	Ⓐ	Ⓐ	Ⓐ
Ⓑ	Ⓑ	Ⓑ	Ⓑ	Ⓑ	Ⓑ
Ⓒ	Ⓒ	Ⓒ	Ⓒ	Ⓒ	Ⓒ
Ⓓ	Ⓓ	Ⓓ	Ⓓ	Ⓓ	Ⓓ
Ⓔ	Ⓔ	Ⓔ	Ⓔ	Ⓔ	Ⓔ
Ⓕ	Ⓕ	Ⓕ	Ⓕ	Ⓕ	Ⓕ
Ⓖ	Ⓖ	Ⓖ	Ⓖ	Ⓖ	Ⓖ
Ⓗ	Ⓗ	Ⓗ	Ⓗ	Ⓗ	Ⓗ
Ⓘ	Ⓘ	Ⓘ	Ⓘ	Ⓘ	Ⓘ
Ⓙ	Ⓙ	Ⓙ	Ⓙ	Ⓙ	Ⓙ
Ⓚ	Ⓚ	Ⓚ	Ⓚ	Ⓚ	Ⓚ
Ⓛ	Ⓛ	Ⓛ	Ⓛ	Ⓛ	Ⓛ
Ⓜ	Ⓜ	Ⓜ	Ⓜ	Ⓜ	Ⓜ
Ⓝ	Ⓝ	Ⓝ	Ⓝ	Ⓝ	Ⓝ
Ⓞ	Ⓞ	Ⓞ	Ⓞ	Ⓞ	Ⓞ
Ⓟ	Ⓟ	Ⓟ	Ⓟ	Ⓟ	Ⓟ
Ⓠ	Ⓠ	Ⓠ	Ⓠ	Ⓠ	Ⓠ
Ⓡ	Ⓡ	Ⓡ	Ⓡ	Ⓡ	Ⓡ
Ⓢ	Ⓢ	Ⓢ	Ⓢ	Ⓢ	Ⓢ
Ⓣ	Ⓣ	Ⓣ	Ⓣ	Ⓣ	Ⓣ
Ⓤ	Ⓤ	Ⓤ	Ⓤ	Ⓤ	Ⓤ
Ⓥ	Ⓥ	Ⓥ	Ⓥ	Ⓥ	Ⓥ
Ⓦ	Ⓦ	Ⓦ	Ⓦ	Ⓦ	Ⓦ
Ⓧ	Ⓧ	Ⓧ	Ⓧ	Ⓧ	Ⓧ
Ⓨ	Ⓨ	Ⓨ	Ⓨ	Ⓨ	Ⓨ
Ⓩ	Ⓩ	Ⓩ	Ⓩ	Ⓩ	Ⓩ

TEST FORM

_____

DATE OF BIRTH

MONTH	DAY		YEAR	
◯ JAN				
◯ FEB				
◯ MAR	⓪	⓪	⓪	⓪
◯ APR	①	①	①	①
◯ MAY	②	②	②	②
◯ JUN	③	③	③	③
◯ JUL		④	④	④
◯ AUG		⑤	⑤	⑤
◯ SEP		⑥	⑥	⑥
◯ OCT		⑦	⑦	⑦
◯ NOV		⑧	⑧	⑧
◯ DEC		⑨	⑨	⑨

3. TEST CODE   4. PHONE NUMBER

⓪	⓪	⓪	⓪	⓪	⓪	⓪	⓪	⓪	⓪	⓪
①	①	①	①	①	①	①	①	①	①	①
②	②	②	②	②	②	②	②	②	②	②
③	③	③	③	③	③	③	③	③	③	③
④	④	④	④	④	④	④	④	④	④	④
⑤	⑤	⑤	⑤	⑤	⑤	⑤	⑤	⑤	⑤	⑤
⑥	⑥	⑥	⑥	⑥	⑥	⑥	⑥	⑥	⑥	⑥
⑦	⑦	⑦	⑦	⑦	⑦	⑦	⑦	⑦	⑦	⑦
⑧	⑧	⑧	⑧	⑧	⑧	⑧	⑧	⑧	⑧	⑧
⑨	⑨	⑨	⑨	⑨	⑨	⑨	⑨	⑨	⑨	⑨

7. SEX
◯ MALE
◯ FEMALE

8. OTHER
1 Ⓐ Ⓑ Ⓒ Ⓓ Ⓔ
2 Ⓐ Ⓑ Ⓒ Ⓓ Ⓔ
3 Ⓐ Ⓑ Ⓒ Ⓓ Ⓔ

1 READING

1 Ⓐ Ⓑ Ⓒ Ⓓ Ⓔ   8 Ⓐ Ⓑ Ⓒ Ⓓ Ⓔ   15 Ⓐ Ⓑ Ⓒ Ⓓ Ⓔ   22 Ⓐ Ⓑ Ⓒ Ⓓ Ⓔ
2 Ⓐ Ⓑ Ⓒ Ⓓ Ⓔ   9 Ⓐ Ⓑ Ⓒ Ⓓ Ⓔ   16 Ⓐ Ⓑ Ⓒ Ⓓ Ⓔ   23 Ⓐ Ⓑ Ⓒ Ⓓ Ⓔ
3 Ⓐ Ⓑ Ⓒ Ⓓ Ⓔ   10 Ⓐ Ⓑ Ⓒ Ⓓ Ⓔ   17 Ⓐ Ⓑ Ⓒ Ⓓ Ⓔ   24 Ⓐ Ⓑ Ⓒ Ⓓ Ⓔ
4 Ⓐ Ⓑ Ⓒ Ⓓ Ⓔ   11 Ⓐ Ⓑ Ⓒ Ⓓ Ⓔ   18 Ⓐ Ⓑ Ⓒ Ⓓ Ⓔ
5 Ⓐ Ⓑ Ⓒ Ⓓ Ⓔ   12 Ⓐ Ⓑ Ⓒ Ⓓ Ⓔ   19 Ⓐ Ⓑ Ⓒ Ⓓ Ⓔ
6 Ⓐ Ⓑ Ⓒ Ⓓ Ⓔ   13 Ⓐ Ⓑ Ⓒ Ⓓ Ⓔ   20 Ⓐ Ⓑ Ⓒ Ⓓ Ⓔ
7 Ⓐ Ⓑ Ⓒ Ⓓ Ⓔ   14 Ⓐ Ⓑ Ⓒ Ⓓ Ⓔ   21 Ⓐ Ⓑ Ⓒ Ⓓ Ⓔ

2 MATHEMATICS

1 Ⓐ Ⓑ Ⓒ Ⓓ Ⓔ   8 Ⓐ Ⓑ Ⓒ Ⓓ Ⓔ   15 Ⓐ Ⓑ Ⓒ Ⓓ Ⓔ
2 Ⓐ Ⓑ Ⓒ Ⓓ Ⓔ   9 Ⓐ Ⓑ Ⓒ Ⓓ Ⓔ   16 Ⓐ Ⓑ Ⓒ Ⓓ Ⓔ
3 Ⓐ Ⓑ Ⓒ Ⓓ Ⓔ   10 Ⓐ Ⓑ Ⓒ Ⓓ Ⓔ   17 Ⓐ Ⓑ Ⓒ Ⓓ Ⓔ
4 Ⓐ Ⓑ Ⓒ Ⓓ Ⓔ   11 Ⓐ Ⓑ Ⓒ Ⓓ Ⓔ   18 Ⓐ Ⓑ Ⓒ Ⓓ Ⓔ
5 Ⓐ Ⓑ Ⓒ Ⓓ Ⓔ   12 Ⓐ Ⓑ Ⓒ Ⓓ Ⓔ   19 Ⓐ Ⓑ Ⓒ Ⓓ Ⓔ
6 Ⓐ Ⓑ Ⓒ Ⓓ Ⓔ   13 Ⓐ Ⓑ Ⓒ Ⓓ Ⓔ   20 Ⓐ Ⓑ Ⓒ Ⓓ Ⓔ
7 Ⓐ Ⓑ Ⓒ Ⓓ Ⓔ   14 Ⓐ Ⓑ Ⓒ Ⓓ Ⓔ

3 READING

26 Ⓐ Ⓑ Ⓒ Ⓓ Ⓔ   34 Ⓐ Ⓑ Ⓒ Ⓓ Ⓔ   42 Ⓐ Ⓑ Ⓒ Ⓓ Ⓔ
27 Ⓐ Ⓑ Ⓒ Ⓓ Ⓔ   35 Ⓐ Ⓑ Ⓒ Ⓓ Ⓔ   43 Ⓐ Ⓑ Ⓒ Ⓓ Ⓔ
28 Ⓐ Ⓑ Ⓒ Ⓓ Ⓔ   36 Ⓐ Ⓑ Ⓒ Ⓓ Ⓔ   44 Ⓐ Ⓑ Ⓒ Ⓓ Ⓔ
29 Ⓐ Ⓑ Ⓒ Ⓓ Ⓔ   37 Ⓐ Ⓑ Ⓒ Ⓓ Ⓔ   45 Ⓐ Ⓑ Ⓒ Ⓓ Ⓔ
30 Ⓐ Ⓑ Ⓒ Ⓓ Ⓔ   38 Ⓐ Ⓑ Ⓒ Ⓓ Ⓔ   46 Ⓐ Ⓑ Ⓒ Ⓓ Ⓔ
31 Ⓐ Ⓑ Ⓒ Ⓓ Ⓔ   39 Ⓐ Ⓑ Ⓒ Ⓓ Ⓔ   47 Ⓐ Ⓑ Ⓒ Ⓓ Ⓔ
32 Ⓐ Ⓑ Ⓒ Ⓓ Ⓔ   40 Ⓐ Ⓑ Ⓒ Ⓓ Ⓔ   48 Ⓐ Ⓑ Ⓒ Ⓓ Ⓔ
33 Ⓐ Ⓑ Ⓒ Ⓓ Ⓔ   41 Ⓐ Ⓑ Ⓒ Ⓓ Ⓔ

The Princeton Review
PSAT

MATHEMATICS

21 Ⓐ Ⓑ Ⓒ Ⓓ Ⓔ
22 Ⓐ Ⓑ Ⓒ Ⓓ Ⓔ
23 Ⓐ Ⓑ Ⓒ Ⓓ Ⓔ
24 Ⓐ Ⓑ Ⓒ Ⓓ Ⓔ

25 Ⓐ Ⓑ Ⓒ Ⓓ Ⓔ
26 Ⓐ Ⓑ Ⓒ Ⓓ Ⓔ
27 Ⓐ Ⓑ Ⓒ Ⓓ Ⓔ
28 Ⓐ Ⓑ Ⓒ Ⓓ Ⓔ

ONLY ANSWERS ENTERED IN THE OVALS IN EACH GRID AREA WILL BE SCORED.
YOU WILL NOT RECEIVE CREDIT FOR ANYTHING WRITTEN IN THE BOXES ABOVE THE OVALS.

29 — grid-in answer field (columns with ⊙, and digits ⓪①②③④⑤⑥⑦⑧⑨)

30 — grid-in answer field

31 — grid-in answer field

32 — grid-in answer field

33 — grid-in answer field

34 — grid-in answer field

35 — grid-in answer field

36 — grid-in answer field

37 — grid-in answer field

38 — grid-in answer field

WRITING SKILLS

1 Ⓐ Ⓑ Ⓒ Ⓓ Ⓔ
2 Ⓐ Ⓑ Ⓒ Ⓓ Ⓔ
3 Ⓐ Ⓑ Ⓒ Ⓓ Ⓔ
4 Ⓐ Ⓑ Ⓒ Ⓓ Ⓔ
5 Ⓐ Ⓑ Ⓒ Ⓓ Ⓔ
6 Ⓐ Ⓑ Ⓒ Ⓓ Ⓔ
7 Ⓐ Ⓑ Ⓒ Ⓓ Ⓔ
8 Ⓐ Ⓑ Ⓒ Ⓓ Ⓔ
9 Ⓐ Ⓑ Ⓒ Ⓓ Ⓔ
10 Ⓐ Ⓑ Ⓒ Ⓓ Ⓔ
11 Ⓐ Ⓑ Ⓒ Ⓓ Ⓔ
12 Ⓐ Ⓑ Ⓒ Ⓓ Ⓔ
13 Ⓐ Ⓑ Ⓒ Ⓓ Ⓔ

14 Ⓐ Ⓑ Ⓒ Ⓓ Ⓔ
15 Ⓐ Ⓑ Ⓒ Ⓓ Ⓔ
16 Ⓐ Ⓑ Ⓒ Ⓓ Ⓔ
17 Ⓐ Ⓑ Ⓒ Ⓓ Ⓔ
18 Ⓐ Ⓑ Ⓒ Ⓓ Ⓔ
19 Ⓐ Ⓑ Ⓒ Ⓓ Ⓔ
20 Ⓐ Ⓑ Ⓒ Ⓓ Ⓔ
21 Ⓐ Ⓑ Ⓒ Ⓓ Ⓔ
22 Ⓐ Ⓑ Ⓒ Ⓓ Ⓔ
23 Ⓐ Ⓑ Ⓒ Ⓓ Ⓔ
24 Ⓐ Ⓑ Ⓒ Ⓓ Ⓔ
25 Ⓐ Ⓑ Ⓒ Ⓓ Ⓔ
26 Ⓐ Ⓑ Ⓒ Ⓓ Ⓔ

27 Ⓐ Ⓑ Ⓒ Ⓓ Ⓔ
28 Ⓐ Ⓑ Ⓒ Ⓓ Ⓔ
29 Ⓐ Ⓑ Ⓒ Ⓓ Ⓔ
30 Ⓐ Ⓑ Ⓒ Ⓓ Ⓔ
31 Ⓐ Ⓑ Ⓒ Ⓓ Ⓔ
32 Ⓐ Ⓑ Ⓒ Ⓓ Ⓔ
33 Ⓐ Ⓑ Ⓒ Ⓓ Ⓔ
34 Ⓐ Ⓑ Ⓒ Ⓓ Ⓔ
35 Ⓐ Ⓑ Ⓒ Ⓓ Ⓔ
36 Ⓐ Ⓑ Ⓒ Ⓓ Ⓔ
37 Ⓐ Ⓑ Ⓒ Ⓓ Ⓔ
38 Ⓐ Ⓑ Ⓒ Ⓓ Ⓔ
39 Ⓐ Ⓑ Ⓒ Ⓓ Ⓔ

PSAT

YOUR NAME: _____
(Print)   Last   First   M.I.

SIGNATURE: _____ DATE: ____ / ____ / ____

HOME ADDRESS: _____
(Print)   Number and Street

              E-MAIL: _____
City   State   Zip

PHONE NO.: _____ SCHOOL: _____ CLASS OF: _____
(Print)

IMPORTANT: Please fill in these boxes exactly as shown on the back cover of your text book.

SCANTRON F-17982-PRP   P3 2803 628 5 4 3 2 1
© The Princeton Review, Inc.

5. YOUR NAME

First 4 letters of last name				FIRST INIT	MID INIT
Ⓐ	Ⓐ	Ⓐ	Ⓐ	Ⓐ	Ⓐ
Ⓑ	Ⓑ	Ⓑ	Ⓑ	Ⓑ	Ⓑ
Ⓒ	Ⓒ	Ⓒ	Ⓒ	Ⓒ	Ⓒ
Ⓓ	Ⓓ	Ⓓ	Ⓓ	Ⓓ	Ⓓ
Ⓔ	Ⓔ	Ⓔ	Ⓔ	Ⓔ	Ⓔ
Ⓕ	Ⓕ	Ⓕ	Ⓕ	Ⓕ	Ⓕ
Ⓖ	Ⓖ	Ⓖ	Ⓖ	Ⓖ	Ⓖ
Ⓗ	Ⓗ	Ⓗ	Ⓗ	Ⓗ	Ⓗ
Ⓘ	Ⓘ	Ⓘ	Ⓘ	Ⓘ	Ⓘ
Ⓙ	Ⓙ	Ⓙ	Ⓙ	Ⓙ	Ⓙ
Ⓚ	Ⓚ	Ⓚ	Ⓚ	Ⓚ	Ⓚ
Ⓛ	Ⓛ	Ⓛ	Ⓛ	Ⓛ	Ⓛ
Ⓜ	Ⓜ	Ⓜ	Ⓜ	Ⓜ	Ⓜ
Ⓝ	Ⓝ	Ⓝ	Ⓝ	Ⓝ	Ⓝ
Ⓞ	Ⓞ	Ⓞ	Ⓞ	Ⓞ	Ⓞ
Ⓟ	Ⓟ	Ⓟ	Ⓟ	Ⓟ	Ⓟ
Ⓠ	Ⓠ	Ⓠ	Ⓠ	Ⓠ	Ⓠ
Ⓡ	Ⓡ	Ⓡ	Ⓡ	Ⓡ	Ⓡ
Ⓢ	Ⓢ	Ⓢ	Ⓢ	Ⓢ	Ⓢ
Ⓣ	Ⓣ	Ⓣ	Ⓣ	Ⓣ	Ⓣ
Ⓤ	Ⓤ	Ⓤ	Ⓤ	Ⓤ	Ⓤ
Ⓥ	Ⓥ	Ⓥ	Ⓥ	Ⓥ	Ⓥ
Ⓦ	Ⓦ	Ⓦ	Ⓦ	Ⓦ	Ⓦ
Ⓧ	Ⓧ	Ⓧ	Ⓧ	Ⓧ	Ⓧ
Ⓨ	Ⓨ	Ⓨ	Ⓨ	Ⓨ	Ⓨ
Ⓩ	Ⓩ	Ⓩ	Ⓩ	Ⓩ	Ⓩ

TEST FORM
_____

3. TEST CODE

4. PHONE NUMBER

⓪ ⓪ ⓪ ⓪ ⓪ ⓪ ⓪ ⓪ ⓪ ⓪ ⓪
① ① ① ① ① ① ① ① ① ① ①
② ② ② ② ② ② ② ② ② ② ②
③ ③ ③ ③ ③ ③ ③ ③ ③ ③ ③
④ ④ ④ ④ ④ ④ ④ ④ ④ ④ ④
⑤ ⑤ ⑤ ⑤ ⑤ ⑤ ⑤ ⑤ ⑤ ⑤ ⑤
⑥ ⑥ ⑥ ⑥ ⑥ ⑥ ⑥ ⑥ ⑥ ⑥ ⑥
⑦ ⑦ ⑦ ⑦ ⑦ ⑦ ⑦ ⑦ ⑦ ⑦ ⑦
⑧ ⑧ ⑧ ⑧ ⑧ ⑧ ⑧ ⑧ ⑧ ⑧ ⑧
⑨ ⑨ ⑨ ⑨ ⑨ ⑨ ⑨ ⑨ ⑨ ⑨ ⑨

DATE OF BIRTH

MONTH	DAY		YEAR	
○ JAN				
○ FEB				
○ MAR	⓪	⓪	⓪	⓪
○ APR	①	①	①	①
○ MAY	②	②	②	②
○ JUN	③	③	③	③
○ JUL		④	④	④
○ AUG		⑤	⑤	⑤
○ SEP		⑥	⑥	⑥
○ OCT		⑦	⑦	⑦
○ NOV		⑧	⑧	⑧
○ DEC		⑨	⑨	⑨

7. SEX
○ MALE
○ FEMALE

8. OTHER
1 Ⓐ Ⓑ Ⓒ Ⓓ Ⓔ
2 Ⓐ Ⓑ Ⓒ Ⓓ Ⓔ
3 Ⓐ Ⓑ Ⓒ Ⓓ Ⓔ

1 READING

1 Ⓐ Ⓑ Ⓒ Ⓓ Ⓔ
2 Ⓐ Ⓑ Ⓒ Ⓓ Ⓔ
3 Ⓐ Ⓑ Ⓒ Ⓓ Ⓔ
4 Ⓐ Ⓑ Ⓒ Ⓓ Ⓔ
5 Ⓐ Ⓑ Ⓒ Ⓓ Ⓔ
6 Ⓐ Ⓑ Ⓒ Ⓓ Ⓔ
7 Ⓐ Ⓑ Ⓒ Ⓓ Ⓔ

8 Ⓐ Ⓑ Ⓒ Ⓓ Ⓔ
9 Ⓐ Ⓑ Ⓒ Ⓓ Ⓔ
10 Ⓐ Ⓑ Ⓒ Ⓓ Ⓔ
11 Ⓐ Ⓑ Ⓒ Ⓓ Ⓔ
12 Ⓐ Ⓑ Ⓒ Ⓓ Ⓔ
13 Ⓐ Ⓑ Ⓒ Ⓓ Ⓔ
14 Ⓐ Ⓑ Ⓒ Ⓓ Ⓔ

15 Ⓐ Ⓑ Ⓒ Ⓓ Ⓔ
16 Ⓐ Ⓑ Ⓒ Ⓓ Ⓔ
17 Ⓐ Ⓑ Ⓒ Ⓓ Ⓔ
18 Ⓐ Ⓑ Ⓒ Ⓓ Ⓔ
19 Ⓐ Ⓑ Ⓒ Ⓓ Ⓔ
20 Ⓐ Ⓑ Ⓒ Ⓓ Ⓔ
21 Ⓐ Ⓑ Ⓒ Ⓓ Ⓔ

22 Ⓐ Ⓑ Ⓒ Ⓓ Ⓔ
23 Ⓐ Ⓑ Ⓒ Ⓓ Ⓔ
24 Ⓐ Ⓑ Ⓒ Ⓓ Ⓔ

2 MATHEMATICS

1 Ⓐ Ⓑ Ⓒ Ⓓ Ⓔ
2 Ⓐ Ⓑ Ⓒ Ⓓ Ⓔ
3 Ⓐ Ⓑ Ⓒ Ⓓ Ⓔ
4 Ⓐ Ⓑ Ⓒ Ⓓ Ⓔ
5 Ⓐ Ⓑ Ⓒ Ⓓ Ⓔ
6 Ⓐ Ⓑ Ⓒ Ⓓ Ⓔ
7 Ⓐ Ⓑ Ⓒ Ⓓ Ⓔ

8 Ⓐ Ⓑ Ⓒ Ⓓ Ⓔ
9 Ⓐ Ⓑ Ⓒ Ⓓ Ⓔ
10 Ⓐ Ⓑ Ⓒ Ⓓ Ⓔ
11 Ⓐ Ⓑ Ⓒ Ⓓ Ⓔ
12 Ⓐ Ⓑ Ⓒ Ⓓ Ⓔ
13 Ⓐ Ⓑ Ⓒ Ⓓ Ⓔ
14 Ⓐ Ⓑ Ⓒ Ⓓ Ⓔ

15 Ⓐ Ⓑ Ⓒ Ⓓ Ⓔ
16 Ⓐ Ⓑ Ⓒ Ⓓ Ⓔ
17 Ⓐ Ⓑ Ⓒ Ⓓ Ⓔ
18 Ⓐ Ⓑ Ⓒ Ⓓ Ⓔ
19 Ⓐ Ⓑ Ⓒ Ⓓ Ⓔ
20 Ⓐ Ⓑ Ⓒ Ⓓ Ⓔ

3 READING

26 Ⓐ Ⓑ Ⓒ Ⓓ Ⓔ
27 Ⓐ Ⓑ Ⓒ Ⓓ Ⓔ
28 Ⓐ Ⓑ Ⓒ Ⓓ Ⓔ
29 Ⓐ Ⓑ Ⓒ Ⓓ Ⓔ
30 Ⓐ Ⓑ Ⓒ Ⓓ Ⓔ
31 Ⓐ Ⓑ Ⓒ Ⓓ Ⓔ
32 Ⓐ Ⓑ Ⓒ Ⓓ Ⓔ
33 Ⓐ Ⓑ Ⓒ Ⓓ Ⓔ

34 Ⓐ Ⓑ Ⓒ Ⓓ Ⓔ
35 Ⓐ Ⓑ Ⓒ Ⓓ Ⓔ
36 Ⓐ Ⓑ Ⓒ Ⓓ Ⓔ
37 Ⓐ Ⓑ Ⓒ Ⓓ Ⓔ
38 Ⓐ Ⓑ Ⓒ Ⓓ Ⓔ
39 Ⓐ Ⓑ Ⓒ Ⓓ Ⓔ
40 Ⓐ Ⓑ Ⓒ Ⓓ Ⓔ
41 Ⓐ Ⓑ Ⓒ Ⓓ Ⓔ

42 Ⓐ Ⓑ Ⓒ Ⓓ Ⓔ
43 Ⓐ Ⓑ Ⓒ Ⓓ Ⓔ
44 Ⓐ Ⓑ Ⓒ Ⓓ Ⓔ
45 Ⓐ Ⓑ Ⓒ Ⓓ Ⓔ
46 Ⓐ Ⓑ Ⓒ Ⓓ Ⓔ
47 Ⓐ Ⓑ Ⓒ Ⓓ Ⓔ
48 Ⓐ Ⓑ Ⓒ Ⓓ Ⓔ

Use a No. 2 pencil only. Be sure each mark is dark and completely fills the intended oval. Completely erase any errors or stray marks.

4 MATHEMATICS

21 Ⓐ Ⓑ Ⓒ Ⓓ Ⓔ
22 Ⓐ Ⓑ Ⓒ Ⓓ Ⓔ
23 Ⓐ Ⓑ Ⓒ Ⓓ Ⓔ
24 Ⓐ Ⓑ Ⓒ Ⓓ Ⓔ

25 Ⓐ Ⓑ Ⓒ Ⓓ Ⓔ
26 Ⓐ Ⓑ Ⓒ Ⓓ Ⓔ
27 Ⓐ Ⓑ Ⓒ Ⓓ Ⓔ
28 Ⓐ Ⓑ Ⓒ Ⓓ Ⓔ

**ONLY ANSWERS ENTERED IN THE OVALS IN EACH GRID AREA WILL BE SCORED.
YOU WILL NOT RECEIVE CREDIT FOR ANYTHING WRITTEN IN THE BOXES ABOVE THE OVALS.**

29 30 31 32 33

34 35 36 37 38

(Grid-in answer areas with numeric bubbles 0–9 for questions 29–38)

5 WRITING SKILLS

1 Ⓐ Ⓑ Ⓒ Ⓓ Ⓔ
2 Ⓐ Ⓑ Ⓒ Ⓓ Ⓔ
3 Ⓐ Ⓑ Ⓒ Ⓓ Ⓔ
4 Ⓐ Ⓑ Ⓒ Ⓓ Ⓔ
5 Ⓐ Ⓑ Ⓒ Ⓓ Ⓔ
6 Ⓐ Ⓑ Ⓒ Ⓓ Ⓔ
7 Ⓐ Ⓑ Ⓒ Ⓓ Ⓔ
8 Ⓐ Ⓑ Ⓒ Ⓓ Ⓔ
9 Ⓐ Ⓑ Ⓒ Ⓓ Ⓔ
10 Ⓐ Ⓑ Ⓒ Ⓓ Ⓔ
11 Ⓐ Ⓑ Ⓒ Ⓓ Ⓔ
12 Ⓐ Ⓑ Ⓒ Ⓓ Ⓔ
13 Ⓐ Ⓑ Ⓒ Ⓓ Ⓔ

14 Ⓐ Ⓑ Ⓒ Ⓓ Ⓔ
15 Ⓐ Ⓑ Ⓒ Ⓓ Ⓔ
16 Ⓐ Ⓑ Ⓒ Ⓓ Ⓔ
17 Ⓐ Ⓑ Ⓒ Ⓓ Ⓔ
18 Ⓐ Ⓑ Ⓒ Ⓓ Ⓔ
19 Ⓐ Ⓑ Ⓒ Ⓓ Ⓔ
20 Ⓐ Ⓑ Ⓒ Ⓓ Ⓔ
21 Ⓐ Ⓑ Ⓒ Ⓓ Ⓔ
22 Ⓐ Ⓑ Ⓒ Ⓓ Ⓔ
23 Ⓐ Ⓑ Ⓒ Ⓓ Ⓔ
24 Ⓐ Ⓑ Ⓒ Ⓓ Ⓔ
25 Ⓐ Ⓑ Ⓒ Ⓓ Ⓔ
26 Ⓐ Ⓑ Ⓒ Ⓓ Ⓔ

27 Ⓐ Ⓑ Ⓒ Ⓓ Ⓔ
28 Ⓐ Ⓑ Ⓒ Ⓓ Ⓔ
29 Ⓐ Ⓑ Ⓒ Ⓓ Ⓔ
30 Ⓐ Ⓑ Ⓒ Ⓓ Ⓔ
31 Ⓐ Ⓑ Ⓒ Ⓓ Ⓔ
32 Ⓐ Ⓑ Ⓒ Ⓓ Ⓔ
33 Ⓐ Ⓑ Ⓒ Ⓓ Ⓔ
34 Ⓐ Ⓑ Ⓒ Ⓓ Ⓔ
35 Ⓐ Ⓑ Ⓒ Ⓓ Ⓔ
36 Ⓐ Ⓑ Ⓒ Ⓓ Ⓔ
37 Ⓐ Ⓑ Ⓒ Ⓓ Ⓔ
38 Ⓐ Ⓑ Ⓒ Ⓓ Ⓔ
39 Ⓐ Ⓑ Ⓒ Ⓓ Ⓔ

Our Books Help You Navigate the College Admissions Process

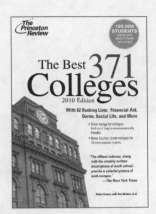

Find the Right School

Best 371 Colleges, 2010 Edition
978-0-375-42938-5 • $22.99/C$27.99

Complete Book of Colleges, 2010 Edition
978-0-375-42940-8 • $26.99/C$33.99

College Navigator
978-0-375-76583-4 • $12.95/C$16.00

America's Best Value Colleges, 2008 Edition
978-0-375-76601-5 • $18.95/C$24.95

Guide to College Visits
978-0-375-76600-8 • $20.00/C$25.00

Get In

Cracking the SAT, 2010 Edition
978-0-375-42922-4 • $21.99/C$26.99

Cracking the SAT with DVD, 2010 Edition
978-0-375-42923-1 • $34.99/C$42.99

Math Workout for the SAT
978-0-375-76433-2 • $16.00/C$23.00

Reading and Writing Workout for the SAT
978-0-375-76431-8 • $16.00/C$23.00

11 Practice Tests for the SAT and PSAT, 2010 Edition
978-0-375-42934-7 • $22.99/C$27.99

Cracking the ACT, 2009 Edition
978-0-375-42899-9 • $19.95/C$22.95

Cracking the ACT with DVD, 2009 Edition
978-0-375-42900-2 • $31.95/C$35.95

Crash Course for the ACT, 3rd Edition
978-0-375-76587-2 • $9.95/C$12.95

Fund It

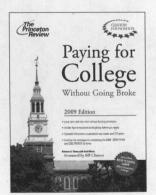

Paying for College Without Going Broke, 2009 Edition
978-0-375-42883-8 • $20.00/C$23.00

Available online and in bookstores everywhere.
PrincetonReview.com

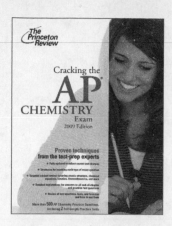

AP Exams

Cracking the AP Biology Exam, 2009 Edition
978-0-375-42884-5 • $18.00/C$21.00

Cracking the AP Calculus AB & BC Exams, 2009 Edition
978-0-375-42885-2 • $19.00/C$22.00

Cracking the AP Chemistry Exam, 2009 Edition
978-0-375-42886-9 • $18.00/C$22.00

Cracking the AP Computer Science A & AB Exams, 2006–2007 Edition
978-0-375-76528-5 • $19.00/C$27.00

Cracking the AP Economics Macro & Micro Exams, 2009 Edition
978-0-375-42887-6 • $18.00/C$21.00

Cracking the AP English Language & Composition Exam, 2009 Edition
978-0-375-42888-3 • $18.00/C$21.00

Cracking the AP English Literature & Composition Exam, 2009 Edition
978-0-375-42889-0 • $18.00/C$21.00

Cracking the AP Environmental Science Exam, 2009 Edition
978-0-375-42890-6 • $18.00/C$21.00

Cracking the AP European History Exam, 2009 Edition
978-0-375-42891-3 • $18.00/C$21.00

Cracking the AP Physics B Exam, 2009 Edition
978-0-375-42892-0 • $18.00/C$21.00

Cracking the AP Physics C Exam, 2009 Edition
978-0-375-42893-7 • $18.00/C$21.00

Cracking the AP Psychology Exam, 2009 Edition
978-0-375-42894-4 • $18.00/C$21.00

Cracking the AP Spanish Exam, with Audio CD, 2009 Edition
978-0-375-42848-7 • $24.95/$27.95

Cracking the AP Statistics Exam, 2009 Edition
978-0-375-42895-1 • $19.00/C$22.00

Cracking the AP U.S. Government and Politics Exam, 2009 Edition
978-0-375-42896-8 • $18.00/C$21.00

Cracking the AP U.S. History Exam, 2009 Edition
978-0-375-42897-5 • $18.00/C$21.00

Cracking the AP World History Exam, 2009 Edition
978-0-375-42898-2 • $18.00/C$21.00

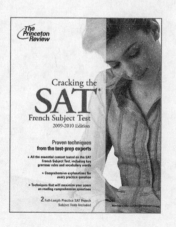

SAT Subject Tests

Cracking the SAT Biology E/M Subject Test, 2009–2010 Edition
978-0-375-42905-7 • $19.00/C$22.00

Cracking the SAT Chemistry Subject Test, 2009–2010 Edition
978-0-375-42906-4 • $19.00/C$22.00

Cracking the SAT French Subject Test, 2009–2010 Edition
978-0-375-42907-1 • $19.00/C$22.00

Cracking the SAT U.S. & World History Subject Tests, 2009–2010 Edition
978-0-375-42908-8 • $19.00/C$22.00

Cracking the SAT Literature Subject Test, 2009–2010 Edition
978-0-375-42909-5 • $19.00/C$22.00

Cracking the SAT Math 1 & 2 Subject Tests, 2009–2010 Edition
978-0-375-42910-1 • $19.00/C$22.00

Cracking the SAT Physics Subject Test, 2009–2010 Edition
978-0-375-42911-8 • $19.00/C$22.00

Cracking the SAT Spanish Subject Test, 2009–2010 Edition
978-0-375-42912-5 • $19.00/C$22.00